Ma, I've Reached for the Moon an I'm Hittin the Stars

Alice Walker, Pulitzer Prize-winning author of *The Color Purple*, on publication of *Ma, He Sold Me for a Few Cigarettes* in the US (Seven Stories Press, September 2012)

'*Ma, He Sold Me for a Few Cigarettes*, by Martha Long, is without question the most harrowing tale I have ever read. Even Charles Dickens, whom we appreciate for being the voice of so many abused children, is left in the dust. Why? Because Dickens was writing about abused children, while Martha Long was herself abused, horribly, unbelievably, by her mother's 'man' and by her own mother. Managing to stay alive, only just, by her own wits, in a world determined to erase her life and to make her believe, in her very soul, that she is nothing. It is a hair-raising read.

'That it is a bestseller in Ireland and England gives me hope. Martha Long is not being abandoned again. Still, it is so difficult a read one might ask: Why should we bother? We must bother because it begins to show us the deeper, perhaps most elemental source of our world's despair: the chronic, horrific, sustained abuse of children. Especially those children who, unwittingly, inherit the brutalities of colonialism, whether in Ireland, where this story is set, or the rest of the globe. I was amazed to feel some of the English, Irish, Scottish ancestors of both enslaved Africans and indentured Europeans (in the Americas) showing up in the characters of the Dubliners Martha Long depicts. There they are, in a Dublin slum in the 1950s, yes (Martha Long's childhood city), but recognisable as the same twisted beings who made life hell on earth for millions of people over the course of numerous centuries. And who, some of them, unfortunately, still walk among us.

'As I read this book I thought: This is exactly why they've kept women ignorant for so long; why they haven't wanted us to learn to read and write. "They" (you can fill this in) knew we would tell our stories from our point of view and that all the terrible things done to us against our will would be exposed, and that we would free ourselves from controlling pretensions, half-truths and lies.

'The destruction of our common humanity through the manipulation of imposed poverty, misogyny, alcoholism and drug abuse is a major source of our misery, worldwide, and has been for a long time. Reading this startling testament to one child's valiant attempts to live until the age of sixteen (four years to go!) is a worthy reminder that we can do better as adults if we turn to embrace the children who are suffering, anywhere on earth, who are coming toward us, their numbers increasing daily, for help.'

Ma, I've Reached for the Moon an I'm Hittin the Stars

MARTHA LONG

MAINSTREAM
PUBLISHING

EDINBURGH AND LONDON

First published in Great Britain in 2012 by

MAINSTREAM PUBLISHING COMPANY

(EDINBURGH) LTD

7 Albany Street

Edinburgh EH1 3UG

ISBN 9781780575742

A catalogue record for this book is available
from the British Library

Printed in Great Britain by
CPI Group (UK) Ltd, Croydon, CR0 4YY

1 3 5 7 9 10 8 6 4 2

Who is that woman staring back at me?
Only yesterday she was a young girl staring into the future!
Now she knows yesterday is gone and tomorrow may never come.
I am grateful this day belongs to me. I can make happy memories.

ACKNOWLEDGEMENTS

'Tis better to have loved and lost,
Than never to have loved at all.

To my readers, who have faithfully followed me through every footstep back along this journey, I say a quiet and humble thank you.

The first step I took with *Ma, He Sold Me for a Few Cigarettes* was the loneliest journey I have ever taken.

Even then, when the little 'Martha' came back to life, I wasn't sure how you would take it. She, I, could never be sure what kind of world we would be stepping into. This was my life; I had exposed myself. I was now left naked, shivering with the terror: I had let it go for publication! Oh, sweet Jesus! What will happen? Would you ridicule me or my children? Would the people I know turn away from me? Never mind me, have I destroyed their lives?

Well, I did find out! I cried when the response came pouring in. Unbelievable! My God, you cared. Not just that, but you understood, you accepted me warts and all. What a world we live in. You gave me courage to write the next step, you cheered me on. 'Go on! Keep going,' you said. So I looked back at you, I checked what you were saying, then started into a run!

Oh, the snots, the tears, the laughing, but I wasn't alone. I felt you all leaning over my shoulder, whispering, 'Here, wipe them snots, dry your tears, you are not alone. We're all here now behind you. Not just that, but we've all felt the same pain hurting, because some of us have gone through what you have. So, go on! Hurry! You're the one doing the writing. Let's all see it, then we can remember and talk about it. For some of us, it's our story too.'

What a wonderful world! And you and me, we all make it happen!

To Bill Campbell, my publisher: without him, I wouldn't be writing and you wouldn't be talking. To Peter McKenzie, the great man behind Bill the genius. To my poor, long-suffering editor, Ailsa Bathgate! The woman one day should be awarded the MBE for surviving under fire and prevailing to bring you these works! All done in the line of duty as an editor. I am an impossible cow to work with. I cherish, protect and hold these works clutched very covetously to my skinny chest. 'Get yer hands off! Ye're not changing one word a this!' was the constant roar through *Ma, He Sold Me*. Now we have a truce. She knows me and I know her.

So, it's all quiet on the Western front as we settle down to bring you these steps I have taken in my journey, now nearly reaching their final end.

My love to you all.

Martha.

AUTHOR'S NOTE

Here I am again, down but not out. Let's take this journey. It marks my first tentative steps back into the land of the living after trying to take an almighty plunge on the fast express out of this world. There I was, holding a glass of orange juice laced with half a bottle of vodka, snots, tears and a few regrets. On the table, a couple of bottles of something lined up that was sure to give you rigor mortis and get you planted pronto! Bloody hell! It is hard to kill a bad thing.

When I woke in the land of the living, there was nothing for it but to dust myself down and give up suicide as a bad job. After, of course, I got loose from the loony bin! (The authorities are very interfering in this country! 'Tut, tut,' they said. 'Lock her up!')

Anyway, in this book I am now on the march again, heading straight for France, looking to meet the one and only great love of my life. The bold priest and medical doctor Father Ralph Fitzgerald. The man who broke my bloody heart when I was only a young one of eighteen years. Now he has written to me after all these long years. Anyway, you know all this, those of you who read the last book, and the previous ones!

So here we go! Forget death, I'm now a woman on a mission, taking the fastest route out of Dublin.

I

We drove up the incline, then slowed down to cruise in behind a line of taxis, all waiting to spit out their cargo of early-morning passengers. One moved off, leaving three businessmen standing on the footpath wearing coats of different designs but the same navy-blue colour. You could see the pristine pinstripe trousers, with the razor-sharp crease down the front, and you knew they were wearing a very expensive business suit under their top coats. They picked up their matching slim brown-leather briefcases – well, nearly the same! The design crest was maybe different. Then lifted their overnight black-leather bags and swung them over their shoulders, then looked up, facing into the Departures, and took off, ready to do a day's business in London, France, Belgium or even Zurich.

We eased forward, then finally we were along the footpath, and the taxi glided to a stop. I opened my bag, looking at the meter as it finally stopped rolling. Now I could see how much the taxi was going to cost me.

'There you are,' I said, handing him the notes.

'Thanks very much. You just wait now and I'll get your suitcase from the boot,' he said, opening the door and rushing around to the back of the car.

I took the small note he gave me in change and shoved it into the back of the purse. I won't be needing that once I get to France. I will then have to start using my French francs.

I put the bag over my shoulder and stepped out onto the footpath, immediately feeling the cold, frosty air bite into my face, making me catch my breath. I pulled up my fur collar and held it around my neck as I took up the handle of the big suitcase, saying, 'Thank you very much.'

'Yes, and thanks again,' he said. 'Have a nice journey, and a Happy New Year to you.'

'Yeah, a very Happy New Year to you too,' I smiled, waving as he got back into his taxi and I headed off into Departures.

I pushed in through the doors and immediately the warm air hit me. It wasn't that warm, though. Not with the draught blowing in behind me as the doors were getting pushed in and out with people constantly on the move.

The place was nearly empty. A policeman with a well-fed belly on him stood staring out into the cold early morning. He looked like he wasn't in any hurry to move himself, trouble or no trouble. There was no life in him, with him standing there looking like a statue. Then he shifted, trying to wake himself up. I watched as he jammed the eyes shut tight, letting a noise rip from his tonsils as he took in a huge yawn. Then he opened the eyes wide, hoping to see better as he smacked his lips, getting a taste of his mouth. Finally he was nearly ready as he scratched himself, cocking the leg to pull out the trousers caught up inside his arse.

I made for the stairs, seeing the sign saying Departures, then looked around for the Aer Lingus desk. There were only two people, both businessmen, in the queue. I got in line behind them, opening my bag to pull out my ticket and passport. I dropped the passport just as a man came up behind me, and he bent down, beating me to it as he picked it up.

'Thank you,' I said, looking into the face of a smiling businessman wearing the coat and suit with the leather overnight bag on his shoulder and holding his briefcase. Jaysus, another one, I thought. A high financial flyer saying, 'You may speak to God, but make an appointment to speak to me!'

'Pleasure,' he beamed, then straightened himself as he stood in behind me, waiting his turn at the desk.

'Thank you, Miss Long. Have a nice flight,' the Aer Lingus woman said in her best posh accent, wearing her green hat with the wings brooch, the suit and the scarf fitted around the neck. She had her hair swept up and sitting on the back of her neck, with the hat looking crooked on the side of her head.

Jaysus, they must clone them, they all look the same, I thought.

Like milk bottles on an assembly line at a milk factory. Even the businessmen. No, we don't go in much for variety, not like the Continentals, I thought.

'Thank you,' I said, walking off leaving her with the suitcase, feeling delighted to get it off my hands.

Right, I have one hour before the plane takes off. I might as well go and get a cup of tea. I headed into a pub serving coffee, wondering do they do tea, then sat myself down at a table nearest to the door, where I could see all the comings and goings.

'A pot of tea for one, please,' I said, looking up into the face of a fella who looks like he never gets any rest. He'd washed and shaved, but you could see the red shaving marks scattered around the white-grey, scurvy-looking skin. That's probably from a blunt blade, I thought, feeling sorry for him. Jaysus, they mustn't pay well here, that poor fella is in threadbare order, I thought, looking at the arse out of his uniform trousers. Jaysus, he could fit himself and two more into them trousers. My eyes peeled down to the shoes. Ah, Jaysus, that's criminal, look at the state a them! They're so worn down at the sides the poor unfortunate is having to walk bokety, I thought, peeling my eyes back up the length of him, seeing him studying me.

'Can I get ye anythin else?'

'No, thanks, that's lovely,' I said, giving him a big smile. It was wasted – the fucker rambled off mouthing, 'Jaysus! The last a te big spenders.'

Then I heard the announcement. I listened, hearing them mention my flight. 'Will all passengers wishing to travel to Charles De Gaulle, Paris, please make your way to the departure gate immediately. The flight is now ready to board.'

OK, here we go, I thought, standing up and making my way over to the passport man, then headed on as he barely nodded at me, not bothering to check my passport.

'Welcome aboard,' the smiling stewardess beamed, delighted to see a few passengers as we climbed up and made our way down row after row of empty seats. Not bleedin surprised. You could buy a car for the price they charge for the ticket! I thought, wondering where I would sit. At the back. No, the wing. That's the safest! I can hang onta that if the plane crashes. *It won't, Martha, you're on board. You have ninety-nine lives!* Yeah, true, I smiled happily, losing the run of meself there for a minute. I nearly always go everywhere by ship, never on a plane. It's too expensive.

I sat just down from the top, where I could see the goings-on of the stewardesses. There was nothing else to look at.

'Hello, we meet again,' said the tall businessman who'd picked up my passport, as he stopped in the empty seats just across from me. Then he reached up, landing his briefcase inside the luggage rack, and took off his coat, folding it, and put that sitting next to the case. Then he sat down at the aisle seat and looked across, saying, 'Are you heading to Paris?'

'I am,' I said, giving him a half-smile. He looked a bit gamey. On the mooch for an opportunity – maybe squeeze me in between his meetings or hold me for his dinner hour.

I looked down the plane, seeing there were five of us on board altogether, plus two air hostesses. They pulled up the steps, then the lights blinked and the engines started up. Then we eased away, heading for the runway. Suddenly the speed increased and we were tearing down, then it lifted, soaring into the air, and we were away. I sighed, taking me ease back in the seat as I looked out, seeing Dublin vanishing into little dots as we whipped away, flying above the clouds.

'This is Captain Robert Martin, your flight captain for the journey. We should be arriving at Charles De Gaulle, Paris, in approximately an hour and a half. Please remember to set your watches one hour forward, French time. Weather conditions are unstable over Paris, with strong winds and torrential rain, so please be prepared for some turbulence.' Then the microphone was switched off.

I looked over to see Mister Gamey giving me a look with a grin on his face.

'Turbulence!' he said. 'That means hang on to your hat, we're in for a bumpy landing,' he laughed, then raised his eyes to Heaven, saying, 'French weather – we're lucky it's not a blizzard!'

'Yeah, at least we will be able to land, not having to circle around or even divert,' I said, giving him a generous smile, deciding maybe he's not too bad after all.

'Are you going to Paris? Going into the city?' he asked, standing up and mooching over to sit next to me. I shoved in, wanting to have my own space, then letting my arm drop on the armrest, grabbing territorial rights, giving him the message, *Don't crowd me!*

'Do you mind if I sit here?' he said, already shifting in the seat, making himself comfortable.

'No, feel free,' I sighed, turning my head to the window. Yeah, I was right first time. He's on the mooch for a woman. He obviously wants me for dessert, after his big French dinner along the tourist strip somewhere. Probably along the Rue St Denis. Or if I'm lucky, dinner on board one of the cruising restaurants down the Seine.

'Is it business or pleasure?' he said, smiling at me.

I stood up, ignoring him, and took off my coat, then handed it to him, with his hands already waiting. 'Would you mind?' I asked.

'Delighted,' he said, giving the fur a quick feel as he turned it inside out, deciding I was worth a few bob. 'Would you like a lift into the city? I can give you a lift in my car. I have one waiting at the airport,' he said, not wasting time on trying to chat me up.

'It's not really necessary, there's good transport to the city,' I said, smiling at him.

'Where are you heading? What district will you be staying in?'

I shook my head. 'My final destination is not Paris. I am heading to the Gare du Nord, or Lyon, have to check which. From there, then I have to travel down nearly the length and breadth of France. It's at the foot of the Alps.'

'Where?'

'Bordering with Spain and the Pyrenees, not close!' I said, looking back out the window.

'Pity,' he mused, staring ahead, letting his voice drop and the smile slip, showing his disappointment.

'Yeah, it is, isn't it?' I said, giving a grin, delighted to see the bloody chancer get a let-down.

'Yeah, maybe another time,' he said, looking hopeful, trying to give himself a lift.

'Yeah, maybe,' I said. 'So, what are you up to?' I asked, feeling more at ease now we got that one out of the way.

'Oh, I work for a state body, a well-known organisation,' he said, saying the name and grinning at me. 'I try to convince foreign investors to set up business in Ireland,' he said, looking at me and smiling.

'So, are you successful?'

'Moderately. It's a long drawn-out process, working out package incentives. You know, offering them capital inducements. It's all to try and bring employment into the country. So, that's the way it is,' he said.

Then he said, looking at me more hopeful, 'What time is your train? Maybe we can have time for a quickie!'

'WHAT?' I said, dropping my mouth, ready to box him in the choppers.

'Oh, my God, sorry! No, no, that's not what I meant at all!' he said, burying his head in his hands, then looking up at me, saying, 'I meant lunch! I was thinking we could have a quick lunch together, somewhere close to the Gare de Lyon.'

'I know what you meant,' I said. 'You and your quickie. You must think you are bloody down along the Rue Pigalle already!'

'What! You know about that place?' he said.

'Of course! I am not a virgin tourist to Paris, you know.'

'Oh, I do like your turn of phrase,' he said.

'Yeah, not intended as a double entendre!' I said, letting him see the smile in my eyes but keeping my face straight.

'Listen, how about giving me your phone number at home? Maybe we can get together and have a meal out some night?' he said, moving in closer, getting more hopeful again.

'Sure, will you be bringing the wife? You forgot to take the wedding ring off,' I said, pointing at the gold band on his finger.

'No point in telling you I'm a widower, is there?' he laughed, looking at me.

I shook my head, smiling at him.

'Or it was willed to me by the granny?'

'No! Bring the wife! I'll bring myself, and you can entertain the pair of us. How's that?'

'Jesus, no, she would kill me,' he said, thinking I was serious.

'Oh, well then, pity, because I am bisexual! In fact, I prefer women to men,' I said, keeping my face very serious.

'Nooo!' he breathed, letting his eyes bulge out of his head.

'Oh, yes! Nothing like three in a bed,' I said, sounding like a Reverend Mother giving a lecture.

'Tell us,' he said, letting the eyes spin and the head fly while he got pictures and millions of sudden questions to ask.

'Excuse me,' I said, smiling as I stood up, not giving him a chance to ask his questions.

'Oh, sorry,' he said, looking confused as I waltzed off to the toilet, giving him time to work it out.

I came out and headed back to my seat, seeing his was now empty. I looked over, seeing him sitting back in his own seat, pretending to look out the window, ignoring me. I sat down, making myself comfortable, and grinned over, seeing him with the nose pressed to the window, finding the clouds suddenly very interesting. Ha, that put a stop to his gallop, I laughed, looking out the window.

'This is your captain speaking. We are now coming in to land. Please fasten your seatbelt. I must warn you we may experience some stiff turbulence. Winds have increased and the torrential rain has now deepened.'

I put on my belt and looked out, seeing nothing but black clouds. After a while, nothing happened. We didn't land and I had the idea I had seen some of them black clouds before.

'This is your captain speaking. We are awaiting clearance from the air-traffic control. Please remain in your seats and keep your safety belts fastened.'

Fuck, I knew it, I thought, looking out at the same black cloud I had seen at least five times before. 'Do you think we might run out of petrol?' I said, half-joking but really meaning it.

He looked, wanting to pull his head away, but I kept my eyes fixed on him. 'Oh, I don't know. I know nothing about these things,' he said, whipping his head back to the window, looking like I had frightened the life out of him.

I tore me head to the window, snorting out a laugh. Jaysus, Martha, I think you went a bit too far with that one. You should have gone easy on him.

'This is your captain speaking. We are now coming in to land.'

Suddenly the plane bounced, fell, lifted and rattled. I watched the air stewardesses. They sat with their belts fastened, keeping their heads down. Uh oh, if they're nervous, then this might be more than a few bumps, I thought, suddenly thinking we wouldn't be the first plane to crash.

'Hope you made a good confession,' I said, looking over to your man, seeing him hanging on with both hands pressed to the armrests.

He looked over, blowing out his cheeks, saying, 'That might not have been a bad idea,' then he shut his eyes as suddenly we dipped and the engine gave a whirring sound.

Ah, Mammy! It's diving out of control! I hope that pilot can see where he's going. Maybe his window wipers might have seized up! Shut the fuck up, Martha. It runs on autopilot! Oh, Jaysus, the very thing that can go wrong! Oh, dear God, don't let us crash. You know you can't, it's me! Remember? I'm only unlucky in love. I always come up smelling of roses for everything else. I'll be content with that, God, so you can keep the love. Now! Just let this plane land in one piece!

Suddenly the plane lifted again and the engine sounded more normal as it died down to a hum.

'This is your captain speaking. We are going to abort our landing at Charles De Gaulle, and we will now be landing at Orly airport. Remain seated and please keep your seatbelts fastened.'

There was a groan from the other passengers. This was supposed to be business class. Get going early and get there on time. Bloody hell! I hope I don't miss my train connection. Anyway, nothing I can do now. So sit back and just take it easy.

'Ladies and gentlemen, this is your captain. Please fasten your safety belts. We are now preparing to land at Orly airport. We hope you enjoyed your flight with us and may choose to travel with Aer Lingus again. We are the safest airline, with a long track record to prove it,' he chirped, making it sound like an American country and western singer about to burst into song.

We all looked out, seeing the runway coming into view. I held my breath as the plane dipped then looked like it was nose-diving as it aimed for the ground. We landed with a bump, then hopped and we were back rushing along the ground. I looked out, holding me breath. Oh! We're coming in too fast. Jaysus! I wonder if the brakes are still working. You can't tell, what with all that rain after getting at them.

I let me breath go as the plane eased off, finally coming to a standstill as I listened to the silence. Then people were on their feet, rushing to grab their stuff out of the luggage racks. I stood up, seeing your man turn his back, burying himself in the luggage, getting his hands on his coat and briefcase. When he turned around, I was waiting.

'Please would you mind getting my coat down? Ta, you're very good. Pity, but I'm not lovely and tall like you,' I said, letting my lips purse and giving a sniff like it was all very sad.

He snapped his eyes then flew them up and grabbed my coat, landing it on top of me, covering my head.

'Oh, you are good,' I purred. 'Such a gentleman. Listen,' I whispered, 'why don't you give me your office phone number, then we can discuss terms on the telephone. I do a cut rate for wives! . . . Fuck, such rudeness!' I snorted after getting pushed outa the way while he was already flying down the steps, looking like someone had set fire to his arse. I grinned and passed the stewardesses, smiling, saying, 'Thank you for the wonderful service. I do indeed, yes, most indeed will be sure to travel with Aer Lingus when I next travel.'

'Oh, thank you,' they gushed, with me knowing full well they probably thought I was tuppence ha'penny short of a shilling. Come to think of it, no! With the fur coat they would just say 'Eccentric'. You're only mad when you are a pauper. But it works – you can get away with murder! Nobody takes you seriously. Then you can wrong-foot them. Catch them on the hop! Walk off with the goodies! Nah, they didn't see that coming. They were too busy thinking what an eejit you are.

'Oh, happy days,' I sang, muttering to myself coming through passport control. They waved me on. Oh, the curse on them! The good-for-nothing shiftless wonders. Now I've no stamp in me passport to show where I travelled. Lazy fuckers!

I leapt into the station with the hounds of hell lapping at my feet. 'Jaysus!' I said, shaking my head, seeing stars of raindrops flying in all directions. I stopped to get my bearings and take a breath. 'Here at last,' I gasped, taking in the noise, the sounds, the smell and the rush of people in all directions. Then I heard another boom of thunder at my back as I looked out, seeing the coal-black morning as the rain and wind lashed, with lighting streaking across the glass doors, then hearing the roar of thunder.

God, it's great to be in out of that, I thought, seeing the water dripping off my fur coat. Bloody hell, I look like a drowned brown rat. Never mind, I will have more than enough time to dry off in the train. It is going to be a very long journey.

OK, tickets? I looked around, seeing the queue of people standing waiting to buy their train tickets. Right, on you go, Martha, keep moving.

'*Bonjour, monsieur, express Paris à this,*' I said, giving him the destination I had written down.

'*Oui, madame!*' he said, nodding and handing me a ticket, after writing down how much. 'Platform 11,' he said in English.

'*Merci, monsieur. Au revoir!*'

I stood up as the train moved off and took off my wet coat, shaking the hell out of it, sending drops of water spraying around me, catching my face. Then I laid it out on the seat in front, hoping nobody would want to sit there. The train looked empty enough, with only a few people scattered, sitting by themselves or in pairs. Then I sat back and looked out the window, seeing Paris flying past and now we were heading into the country. The train fled Paris so fast it looked like we had the devil on our tail. Good, at least the trains here are fast and on time. So I should arrive tonight around ten o'clock, then make me way to where he lives using the *omnibus*, the local trains.

God knows what time I will arrive there, but it won't be the first time in my life I have been stranded in the late hours of the night, stuck in the middle of nowhere. But I don't mind. I don't care how long it takes, or how far I have to travel, I would go to the ends of the earth knowing Ralph is there. Only thing is, he doesn't know I am coming.

My heart started to hammer in my chest at the thought I will be seeing him so very soon. Jesus, after all this time, all these years. I was only eighteen the last time I ever saw or heard from him. Now here I am, a fully grown woman with a grown-up child of my own and a whole lifetime behind me. Now at last we will finally meet again.

2

God, when I think back on the first time I ever met him, I was only sixteen – so young, so desperate. I had nothing and nobody. Nowhere to lay down my head and not a penny in my pocket. In a way, I knew no better. I had no expectation that someone would help me. I only wanted to help myself. I knew there was nothing for nothing; you had to earn it. I didn't miss anybody, and nobody missed me.

Somehow my life had been simpler then. I needed to get above and beyond who and what I was. A nobody. The bastard of an unmarried mother, a fallen woman – we were outcasts in a Catholic, God-fearing little island that should have been called the 'Isle of the Squinting Windows'. Everybody knew everyone, and everyone looked down on everybody else. God help you if you stepped out of line. Everybody had their place, and there's a place for everyone. Mine was at the bottom of the heap. I was the scum nobody wanted. I grew up with it. I had been well taught by the world around me. Even among the poorest of the poor I was at the bottom of the heap. Scabby head, filthy dirty, barefoot, lice-ridden, no knickers. Don't come near us, we don't want to catch your disease. Men can do what they like with you; you can be sold for a few Woodbines.

But when I was sixteen, I was free and away. Yet I still lacked the resources. I was too young to earn enough to survive in lodgings – not enough pay. I wasn't qualified for a job, except what the nuns trained me for. A skivvy. Fuck that! I had ideas of my own. I just needed to get a way in. But how? I had ended up on the streets because I wouldn't take their guff. To hell with the middle classes when they got you as a skivvy. You gave them your labour but they thought they bought you as a slave. No, I had an innate sense of my own worth. I knew I was as good as them. But they didn't accept that. Ireland, the land of peasants. They didn't know how to treat the lesser off with respect. Because it was accepted that if you were poor, then you were dirt. You couldn't do much about it because you were dependent on them. So it was a vicious circle.

But I had put all that pain and misery it caused me into a dream. I used the energy to burn a fire in my belly to climb up there alongside them and say, 'Fuck you, now tell me you are better!' I even knew by then I would not waste my time with them, one way or the other. I would be simply proving to myself I had achieved my dream. I could say, 'Look, Ma, I am standing on top of the world! See! We are not at the bottom of the heap any more. Now we are someone, Ma. We get respect!'

Yeah, that is what it was all about for me back then. Respect. I had dignity. I was a human being. I wanted to be treated as one.

When I met Ralph, he showed me such respect, such dignity, at a time when I was at my lowest. I was on the streets, a tramp. He even gave me more. He looked at me like I was special, someone who could not just be liked but someone who could be loved. He made me feel lovely. Like I was wanted, I was somebody, I was special. Ralph, the man who had taken me, a lonely young waif wandering in a cold, uncaring, dark world, who had never felt the warmth of a mother's arms, or rarely glimpsed the human side of kindness. It was he who picked me up and carried me, showing me the wonders and magic of life. To me, he was a god. The only man who had ever sent me soaring to the heavens with his gentle love for me, giving me a glimpse of a hidden magic. It was the wonderful world of life and love and just being alive, and how precious we are, just to be born.

Yes, he was the only man I had ever felt safe with and I very quickly became addicted to it. I couldn't get enough of him. He was the father and mother I never had. He was the cure for the kids at school and on the street, and the neighbours and the strangers who never thought much of me. They had shunned me, but he had made up for all that. He had enough love for me to fill up all the empty places they had left.

But everything comes at a price. I had to pay very heavily for that bit of happiness. I often wondered since, was it worth it? The awful memory of that last time I ever saw him still remained vividly clear in my mind. The bittersweet memory of that awful day when he let me down and walked away, thinking he had put me standing on my feet. He had tenderly nurtured the child, then fell in love with the young woman I suddenly became. A young girl who was forbidden to him. Then it all ended. He had walked away because he thought he truly loved me. But it broke my heart, leaving me only a shadow. I very quickly took a wrong turning, ending up in a nightmare that cost me dearly. But nightmares were familiar to me and nothing kills us if we don't let it.

From then on, I was left to fly through life on a broken wing. I had to adapt, because the pain never healed. I was left to wander through my days, searching the faces of strangers, looking for another him. But I never did find him again. No, nobody ever came close to filling up the hole he left in my heart. A huge gaping hole that pained me for years. It only settled into a wound that got covered up by a big thick scab. Then it eased and I was able to forget and carry on. Now I thought I had found him in Sergei when I looked into his deeply penetrating, bright-green eyes. I thought he was hidden in the spiritual Sergei, the monk. But, no, I never did find Ralph. The only man I have ever loved.

It had all happened so very long ago but now he is back in Europe, right here in France. Home after years spent thousands of miles away, working as a missionary doctor. Yes, my incredibly handsome, majestic Ralph. The caring doctor, the loving man, the priest forbidden to me. But he doesn't say if he is still a priest.

I opened my bag, took out the letter and read it again, then I held it gripped in my hand, not wanting to let it go. This is part of him, something of himself poured into this letter. It happened when he held it in his two very own hands. He breathed over it as he was writing it. Then he let it rest against him, making contact with his body. He had been thinking about me when he wrote it, and now, yes, this letter is my way back to him.

Jesus, I'm still stunned, it's knocked me clean off my feet. I can't think or feel about anything else but him. All my senses are filled up with him. He's in my head and in my heart, and I can even sense him in my skin. Oh, but it does frighten me, that does. What will I do if something goes wrong?

God almighty, here I am sitting on this train, and with every passing minute now it's taking me closer to him. I can feel my heart thudding away in my chest, sensing him closer as the train thunders on through the dark night. But how will I take it if he doesn't really want to know me? What if he has changed? Of course he's changed. He could be someone with only a vague memory of me. A person moved on so far now he is well beyond what was once important to him then. I could be looking up into the face of someone who barely remembers me. Time could have changed him from the man he was to someone who is a stranger. Then what, Martha? I don't know. I can't look that far or even think that way.

I have written to Sergei. I told him I need time to think, we both need to adjust. Especially him. It's a huge step for him to leave a monastery after so many years, then try to adjust to life in the world without the back-up of a big organisation behind him. He will have to earn his own living. No, asking him to wait was the best decision I've made. One way or the other, even without Ralph, it would have been madness to jump into a decision to just get married out of the blue. No, I will be all right. Whatever happens, I am on my feet. My troubles are behind me. I had fallen as low as I could get, hitting rock bottom when I nearly succeeded in taking my own life. Now I am definitely growing stronger every day.

Right, I thought, lifting my head and looking out the window. It's pitch dark. I can see nothing out there now. Surely we must be well down into France by now. I wonder what time it is? I thought, looking around to see if someone had the time. No, forget it, that's more trouble than it's worth. I can't speak the language and I'm not in the mood for stretching myself into getting understood. I better save my strength for when I need it.

I folded the letter and put it carefully back in my bag, then leaned across to see if my coat was drying out. Lovely, it's nearly dry. Gawd, the heat is grand on this train. Not like the bloody Irish ones, they would freeze the arse off you. But this is the height of luxury, I thought, looking around at all the velvet-looking soft seats, and how clean and shiny and well taken care of everything looked. Right, I think I will close my eyes and have a bit of rest. That should help to pass the time, I thought, stretching out and leaning my head against the padded backrest.

Oh, that's feels better, I thought, as I stretched out my legs and lit up a smoke. I could feel my face red and hot from the lovely feed and the heat in the place. Here at last, I thought, looking around, seeing the owner of the inn talking to some aul codgers. They were sitting over in the corner, eating and downing the local wine. I lifted my empty glass, deciding I will have another one. I need it to get me moving. Now that I am right here, just down the road from Ralph, I have lost me nerve completely. No, this was definitely a very bad idea. I can't just go turning up on his doorstep in the middle of the night, without word or warning. Bleedin hell! It had seemed so straightforward when I was back home in Ireland. Oh, yeah, great plan that was, Martha. Just hop on a plane. Stagger into Paris. Find my way to the Gare de Lyon. Take a train so far down into France that Spain is only a few minutes across the water, with the Pyrenees mountains on my left. You can't go any further without leppin into the sea or taking on the mountains. Jaysus, Ralph, you sure know how to hide yourself. But it has to be the most beautiful place I have ever set foot in. From what I can see of it anyway, in the bleedin pitch black.

Oh, my God, what a job I had getting here! Holy Jesus, the Parisians may speak a bit of English. But you have no chance in the provinces. I found that out when I pressed the address under their noses. *'Excuse me, monsieur, ou à vu le maison?'* I spluttered, then gave up. 'Where is this place?' I croaked, pointing at the address. Well, the confusion. *'Non!'* they moaned, slowly drawing out the no bit, with the head shaking. But they were good. I ended up with everyone who passed being stopped to get dragged in on the discussion. Many heads make light work. Now here I am, and not just that. I got taken to this place. It's a lovely little inn and they even have accommodation overhead. Lovely, I'm all set. Now all I need is another drink, then I can think better.

'*Madame!*' I croaked, losing all me puff after that hundred-mile walk.

'*Oui, madame?*' a grey-haired woman said, moving over slowly, taking me in, looking at me very suspiciously. Because clearly they don't get many strangers around here, not this time of the year, anyway.

'Eh,' I said, trying to think how I would ask.

She stood patiently, polishing her glass, wearing a long black frock with a long apron and very strong-looking sensible laced-up boots.

'*Une blanc vin!*' I said, hoping that made sense.

She took up the glass, then walked off at her ease, shouting and arguing with the two aul fellas. They were all going on about something that sounded very serious. It could even be that someone had been murdered in their bed, judging by the long mournful faces and the shaking of the heads, not to mention the long sighs and sobbing as they stared mournfully down into their glasses, looking very sorrowful altogether.

After I drank the wine, I could feel myself beginning to shake as I stood up and fastened my fur coat. Then I lifted my chin, straightening myself and taking in a deep breath. Well, here goes. Time to go and see Ralph.

'*Merci, madame. Bonne nuit!*' I said, turning to look at her standing by the table with the men.

'*Bonne nuit, madame,*' she said. The others just muttered, and nodded their heads at me. Then I stepped out into the cold dark night, feeling the wind hit me as it blew in from the sea. I could hear the roar of it but not see it with the buildings in front. But it's there, all right.

I walked on, leaving the lights behind me as I headed out into the countryside. I could see the odd house here and there but they were hidden behind big trees. Then suddenly there was a break in the very high old stone wall with trees hanging over it. Then I saw it! The entrance with big black gates. I stopped dead in my tracks, staring up at them. This is it!

I looked in, seeing the long drive up to Ralph Fitzgerald's French home. Will I go in? It's very late, there might be dogs roaming around the place. I could get eaten alive. Suppose this is his French order? There could be all priests living here. Jaysus, I hadn't thought of that. Of course he would be living in a big college or the order house. They don't live in a church parish house. Fuck! I never thought beyond just getting here. Well, go on anyway! Who cares? You can only make a big eejit of yourself. It won't be the first time, I laughed, feeling myself beginning to get a bit hysterical. In for a penny, in for a pound, Martha. You have nothing to lose but your dignity! Right! I snorted, taking in a long deep breath, holding it, then let my shoulders go and grabbed up me suitcase, fixing my coat.

I walked in through the gates, making my way up the very long dark drive. The trees whistled and moaned in the dark, and I could feel myself rattling, with me legs turning to jelly the closer I got to making for the house. Then I caught sight of it. A very big old house staring back through the trees. It was very French-looking, like a big old-fashioned fancy loaf of bread with a fancy-looking roof. You couldn't see all of it from the front. It went on further to the back. I could see lights on here and there in some of the windows. Then it hit me. My nerves went completely as the life drained out of me, taking all my strength, leaving me weak as a kitten. I sat down on the suitcase, looking up at how forbidden it all looked. No, whoever lives here likes their privacy. It's not the sort of place you can just call in without an appointment. Or certainly not if you don't even know them.

Oh, holy divine lamb of Jesus, Martha. You are like a fuckin refugee coming out of nowhere! This is the worst, daftest thing you have ever come up with yet! Ralph can have a terrible temper if he's crossed. All he has to do is lift the finger, open his mouth and cut the ground from under you if you overstep the mark. Exactly like what you're doing right now. He might not even want to see me! Maybe he was only being polite when he wrote to me. Oh, my nerves are gone. I can't bear it. I am just about to make a thundering right aul eejit of myself.

Fuck this. Quick! Turn around, get moving straight back the way you came, Martha, just in case you are seen from one of the windows. I turned, nearly running back down the drive. You bloody moron, Martha. Suppose he is married? He could even have children! What would his wife say? Oh, I feel sick.

Right, get going, move faster. Pity there's no bleedin taxis to be had in this godforsaken place. I'm in the middle of the arsehole of nowhere! OK, make back for that little inn, or *pension* or whatever it's called. Stay the night there, then high tail it out of here first thing in the morning. Forget Ralph! Well, for now anyway!

I put my case up on the bed, taking out my night- and wash-things, feeling I had done the right thing. But my heart was breaking with the let-down. I longed to see him. I couldn't bear to be so close to him, here in this place just a couple of miles away from his house, yet so far away. I left the things sitting on the chair and sat on the side of the bed, thinking about it. What happened? Well, it sounded fine when I sat in my own kitchen at home. Go there, I told myself. Tell him you never stopped loving him. Say you are thinking of getting married. But it is him you have always wanted. So what did you want from him? For him to leave the order and stop being a priest . . . If he is still one! Be together, start a family. Be happy!

Grand, so you got here, Martha, now what happened? The bleedin reality, that's what happened! Imagine! What was I prepared to do? Turn up banging on his door in the pitch-black night and what? 'Hello! It's me. I've come to stay!'

I started to laugh, but I could feel myself shaking with the shock of loss and pain, and knowing it was all only a dream. I think I had convinced myself it would work out. Without me even realising, I had pinned so much hope on this meeting. On the surface I thought I was just steeling myself with determination to face him.

Jesus! I feel shattered. That journey has been never-ending. Yet, I feel too restless to sleep. But this was a good plan. Getting in here was one of my better ideas. Yeah, this place is good to get some rest and think.

An idea was forming in my head. I have come too far to give up now. Yeah, so do something, Martha! But first see if you can get a drop of tea out of that aul biddy, the owner of this place, then think!

I pulled out my tobacco and rolled a cigarette, lighting it up, then put my head down on the pillow, leaving my feet dangling over the side. I wasn't too sure yet whether I was prepared to call it a night. I think I will go out for a walk. Get rid of the cobwebs smothering my brain. The lovely country fresh air will do me good. Maybe help me to think. I jumped up, putting on my fur coat, grabbed my bag and rattled out the door. Jaysus! I am really tired, but I'm too worked up to relax, never even mind sleep. Wonder if the aul biddy will give me a key? I will that need to get back in.

3

I took off on the trot again, heading in the direction of Ralph's house. Right, it's not so bad this time, and I have somewhere to stay, I'm not dependent on him. Right! I'll just take a better look. It might give me some clue as to what's going on. Maybe I might see sight of a wife, or maybe a child's swing or toys thrown around. I'll just take a look anyway. That can't do any harm.

On the other hand, why not just ring him? Yeah! But what would I say? *Hello, Ralph, how are you? Listen, I'm just down the road in the village, and I thought it might be a good idea to drop in and see how you are! Good idea?* I roared laughing, thinking, Jaysus, Martha, you are going from bad to worse. Particularly if Eleanor told him I was in the loony bin having a nervous breakdown! The whole bleedin madness of what I was putting myself through suddenly hit me, and I started roaring laughing. Ah, well, never mind. It won't kill you, Martha. What have I got to lose? Fuck all! We owe each other nothing. I have weathered too many storms to let this get the better of me. Right, play it by ear, I thought, as I turned in the gate again, heading back up the drive.

Suddenly a figure appeared from around the side of the house. Fuck! Who is that? I took off, flying to hide behind a tree, not wanting to meet whoever that was, because then I will have burnt my bridges.

I watched as an elderly woman marched past, about ten feet away from me, carrying a basket under her arm. She looked like she was in a hurry to make her way somewhere. I watched her go, wondering if maybe she was a mother-in-law or something. Who knows? I thought, heading out of the trees and making for the front door. Then I stopped, as something else hit me. He may even be still a priest! Jesus, Martha! Do you ever grow up?

I thought about that, deciding, Yeah, Martha, you do. But you just do everything different from everybody else, that's all. Most people would write or phone. No, not me! This is too important. Talking face to face is better. Fuck! Here we go again!

I walked up the steps and looked for the doorbell, then decided to use the big black knocker. The hollow sound blasting around the dark, cold night air, along with the dead sound thudding inside the house, made it feel like something out of a Boris Karloff film. One of them old early Dracula films, shown in the 1930s.

I waited, taking in deep breaths, feeling me heart flying, and my body shivering with the nerves. I started to breathe faster and deeper, hoping it would help. But now I could feel myself going dizzy, I'm making myself worse, with everything turning black. Jaysus, now I won't be able to see him.

I heard footsteps, then the door swung open. I stood staring up into the face of a very distinguished gentleman looking to be in his very early forties, but I knew different. He is in his late forties, or even early fifties, because I am now in my thirties. His hair was beginning to turn grey, with silver starting to grow at the temples and a sprinkling running through his silky brown hair. It made him look even more incredibly handsome, giving him the distinguished look of a well-bred, imposing aristocrat.

My breath caught and I heard myself giving a little gasp. Then I stared up at him, remembering to take a blink, trying to clear my vision to take him in. It's Ralph! My heart stopped.

He stood with his hand on the door, keeping his back held ramrod straight. I watched as he looked at me with a cold indifferent look in his striking green eyes. I could see how they studied me and there was an aloofness in his closed-down face that said, *I know who I am. I belong to the ruling classes.*

I now knew instantly why I had been attracted to Sergei. To his strangely familiar looks, especially his strikingly green eyes. Yes, they had reminded me of Ralph. But it was a painful memory, filling me up with bittersweet memories of him. I saw now that Sergei was only a poor substitute. I thought he was the nearest I could ever get to Ralph.

I stared up now at Ralph, with no words coming to me. I could feel my heart sinking. It was the coldness of him, like he didn't suffer fools gladly, and I felt like a fool. He looked like he could easily put you down with just a simple look of contempt. I didn't want to see that. I wanted to run, say something, anything. Even, 'I've got the wrong house!' Then just turn around and walk away. He doesn't seem to have recognised me yet. He just stared at me, waiting, saying something in French. It sounded like, 'May I help you? Do you want something?' But I can't understand French.

Then I heard myself saying in a whisper, 'Hello, Ralph! I've come a long way to see you.'

'What?' he said, with his face turning white as his head bent, leaning in to get a closer look at me.

I could feel the colour draining out of myself. I shook me head, saying, 'Yes, Ralph! It's me, Martha. I got your letter. Are you going to invite me in? I'm sorry it's so late, but I've moved into the local *pension* for the night. Just down the road.' I pointed, starting to babble.

'Good heavens! My God! Is it really you, Martha? How can this be?' he roared, going into shock and half-laughing. 'Are you alone?' he said, looking around to see if anyone else was here.

'No, just me, Ralph. I brought myself.'

'Oh, my goodness. For heaven's sake, do come in. Oh! How did you get here?' he said, slamming the heavy door shut and moving over to stand close to me, still trying to work out what just happened.

I let me face move in a half-smile and just looked at him, feeling afraid to make even another move.

'Come on, come with me,' he whispered gently. 'Let us go inside to the warmth,' he said, putting his hand lightly on my arm, then taking me down a hall and into a huge sitting room. I walked in slowly, as he moved ahead to stand, holding the door wide open. Then he turned and shut it while I took in the high ceiling and two big sofas facing each other. They sat beside a big, open roaring log fire.

'Are you hungry? Goodness! You must be freezing!'

'No,' I shook my head, looking at him. I could see he was nervous and his face was still white. Then I noticed his hands shaking. Even though you wouldn't notice if you didn't know him. He is very good at keeping his feelings under control. It's the way he was brought up. Good manners are everything.

'Oh, I am sure you are hungry,' he said, trying to smile and ease the tension. Then he looked at the door, making to leave the room. 'I shall just get us something in the kitchen. I have not as yet eaten and I am sure Madame Bouclé, my housekeeper, has prepared something for supper. Do please just let me check,' he said, sounding very formal as he headed out the door.

Jaysus! This is not looking good, I shivered, feeling I'm standing on terrible ceremony. Then he turned back, saying, 'Oh, I am sorry! Please allow me take your coat,' he said, rushing back to help me off with the fur coat. 'You look pale and wan and terribly thin, Martha,' he murmured, whispering to himself as he took my coat, then letting his eyes run over me with a sad look on his face. Then he rushed off out with the coat, looking like he was glad of the opportunity to get away for a few minutes.

I sighed with the nerves, wishing I could feel more at ease with myself as I looked around the room then back at the sofa, wondering if I should sit down. I think I may have done the wrong thing, I'm feeling a bit out of my depth. Ralph is just being a gentleman, he's too well mannered to come out and say I'm not welcome. Decorum is everything with him. There are certain ways to behave and good manners dictate that. One of them is not to show your guest up. Uninvited or not. Fuck! That's me. This is my worst nightmare. Being somewhere I'm not wanted. Ah, well, I'll just play it by ear. I'm certainly not going to show my hand unless I know I'm on firm ground. So just pretend you hopped over to see him for a visit.

'Martha! Do come and eat,' he said, rushing in the door and heading towards me. I stood up as he put his hand lightly on my back, saying, 'You look exhausted. When did you arrive?' he said, leading me out the door and down a passage, then into another room that looked like a big old-fashioned kitchen. The table was set with white napkins rolled in silver rings and left beside a big white plate, with knives and forks laid out. A light-brown, brick-coloured casserole dish sat on a wooden board in the middle of the table, with wooden bowls of salad and stuff in glass dishes. The table was heaped with food. I took in the sight of foreign-looking fruit, and a lump of cheese with a cutting knife sat on a board, with a basket of fresh bread cut up in chunks. The smell was gorgeous and I waited to see where he wanted me to sit.

'Come on, don't be shy,' he said, grinning at me and pulling me down to sit next to him while he sat at the top of the table. It was a very long, old wooden table, with scars deeply etched into the thick heavy wood that came from years of wear and tear and standing up to a lot of hard knocks. This table would easily seat about ten people, I thought. The chairs were high-backed with old calf-leather backrests.

I sat down next to him, watching as he picked up the ladle then handed it to me, saying, 'Do help yourself, it's chicken and vegetables in a cream sauce. You do like chicken?' he said, grinning at me.

'Yes,' I nodded, giving a little smile. 'Thank you, Ralph, I love chicken.'

'Good, give me your plate, and I will serve you,' he said, seeing me get distracted.

'What?' I said, whipping me head to him as I stared around at the lovely, warm old kitchen.

'Shall I serve?' he said, pointing at the steaming casserole.

'Yes, of course, thank you,' I said, handing him back the ladle.

'Would you like some wine?' he said, getting up and walking over to a big old cupboard and taking out a bottle of red wine.

I hesitated, saying, 'Eh, sorry?'

He saw that and said, 'Red or white?' then leaned in again to bring out another bottle.

'White, please,' I grinned, delighted he had some. I don't like red, it gives me a headache, I thought. Then I picked up the ladle and decided to do the serving. 'Is this enough, Ralph?' I said, putting down his plate, letting him see the one piece of chicken with a few vegetables and some sauce. I didn't want to make a show of myself by overfilling the plate. I know it's considered bad manners in his world.

'Yes, thank you,' he said, concentrating on pouring the wine.

I helped myself, taking the same amount of chicken, then reached over and passed the bread basket to him, taking out one piece for myself. 'Thank you,' he said, indicating with his head I should leave it in front of him. 'Yours,' he said, landing down a huge glass filled with wine.

I took a sip, feeling the heat and strength of it go right through my veins, warming me. Then I took in a quiet sigh, hoping we could both thaw out. The strain was difficult, with the pair of us not knowing what to make of the other.

'Eat,' he said, picking up his knife and fork, and pointing at my plate. 'Go on, before it gets cold,' he said, breaking a piece of bread and starting on his chicken. 'So, when did you arrive?' he said, lifting his head and looking straight at me. I could see his eyes were guarded; he was being almost formal, like he was entertaining a guest, but one who was not particularly close.

'Early today,' I said, lying through me teeth. I didn't want him to know I arrived and high tailed it up here in my haste to see him, thinking, I only stopped to get a bit of Dutch courage in the local inn.

'Oh,' he said, figuring out I was in no hurry to see him. 'So, is your living accommodation comfortable?'

'Yes, it suits the purpose,' I said, feeling my heart sink even lower. No such luck is he going to invite me to stay here with him.

'How long do you intend staying?' he said, looking like it really was no concern of his.

I could feel myself beginning to get annoyed. Fuck him, I thought, lifting the glass and taking a big mouthful. I need it, it's the only bit of comfort I'm going to get here, I thought, hating this pussyfooting around but knowing he is himself and I am me. We both take a different approach to life.

He is governed by his sense of duty, of what is acceptable behaviour and belief in doing the right thing. Whereas I am liable to take a gamble. I like to face things head on. But not in this instance am I going to be able to act as I usually would. No, he's too shut down. This is not going to work out. If anything, he has become even more deeply entrenched in his ways. He doesn't act on his own wishes, feelings or what he wants. Even now, I could tell by his reaction that he still has feelings for me. I could see that by how nervous he was, just like myself. But I know he won't act on it, because it is not the right thing to do. Fuck this! In other words, I would be an indulgence. Not a real necessity for him. So, let's just wait and see. But my gut feeling tells me I am right.

'Would you like some more?' he said, seeing me leave my knife and fork down after watching me mop up the sauce with bits of bread and nibble away with sips of wine, leaving a very shiny, nice white plate. That's not the bleedin done thing either! You're supposed to leave something sitting on the plate. Show you're not a glutton! Well, they can keep that rule! But I do have my boundaries. I shook my head, saying, 'No, thanks, Ralph, that meal was delicious. I think I've eaten enough, thank you.'

'Hmm! Good to see you have a healthy appetite,' he said, grinning at me as he stretched across the table. 'Cheese?' he asked, holding up the cheeseboard and landing it down in front of himself.

I shook me head, then thought, Why not? 'Yes, please, seeing as I seem to be making good inroads into the wine. I need something to soak it up,' I said, feeling myself getting very sleepy.

4

'I think we ought to be getting you into a bed soon,' he said, watching me give a big yawn under my hand.

'No, if it's OK with you, I don't mind staying on a bit longer. Is that OK?' I said, looking straight into his face, seeing his eyes light up.

'I have no problem, Martha. I would quite enjoy that,' he said, giving me a huge grin, then letting his eyes soften, showing me he meant it.

I felt myself melting inside, thinking, I still can't believe I am sitting here with Ralph, the man I have never stopped loving. God knows it wasn't for the want of trying. I have gone through hating him, aching for him, crying at the loss of him, then burying him. Banishing him to the deep, dark recesses of my mind. But he has never gone away. Now here I am, sitting right next to him, sharing a meal. No, it doesn't feel real. I am all wound up and shut down, locked tight inside myself, just like him. Maybe he will open up yet, then we could talk, I felt myself hoping. Dear God, I do indeed have a lot to lose, it was slowly dawning on me. If I walk away without getting through to him, there will be no turning back.

'Have you had enough to eat?' he said, looking at me like he wanted to move.

'Oh, yes, thank you, Ralph, that was delicious. Did you enjoy it?' I said.

'Yes, it was quite good. Madame Bouclé is a very competent cook,' he said, standing up and throwing down his napkin.

I stood up and started to gather up all the plates. 'No, you sit. I shall attend to these. No need to wash up. Madame would not take kindly. We can leave them sitting in the sink. I tend to just leave them steeping. Why don't you sit by the fire and I will join you shortly,' he said, jamming all the plates into the sink, then clearing away the rest of the stuff.

'OK, if you are sure,' I said, looking at him, seeing him occupied, then headed myself out the door, making back for the sitting room.

I sat down on the sofa feeling a little bit more at ease in myself but not much. Then I lifted my bag off the floor and opened it, pulling out my tobacco. It's just as well I have the key, I thought. Now I can go back when it suits me and let myself in quietly. But it's a pity, though, I wasn't able to come here first. I would love nothing better than to be able to stay here with Ralph. Still, it's just as well I got that place. It's very handy, as now I'm under no compliment to him. I have somewhere to go, and it's showing him I'm independent and not completely throwing myself at his mercy.

Right, I sighed, thinking Ralph is more formidable now than I ever thought possible. He's keeping himself very much to himself. We don't have that easy way with each other like we did when we were both young. Jaysus! Middle age is a bitch! I thought, thinking we get more cautious and take fewer risks. It takes the fun out of life. Well, I still haven't lost too much of it. Otherwise I would not be bloody here!

'Ah, here you are,' he said, swinging open the door and walking slowly in, taking in the sight of me sitting back comfortably, then he drew his head to the fire, thinking. 'Hmm, perhaps more logs,' he said, making for the basket next to the fire and pulling out a big log. He humped it on the fire and it immediately started spitting and blowing out smoke, sending a lovely smell of pine wafting around the room.

'That takes care of that,' he said, rubbing his hands and looking at me, giving me a big grin. 'Have you not given up that dreadful weed?' he roared, pointing at my roll-up cigarette.

'No, have you?'

'Yes!' he said, bowing his head at me, then lifting it before making out of the room again. I watched him go, wondering when he was going to sit down and relax. I wanted to be at ease with him. I wonder if he's going to offer any more wine? Jaysus, it must be me fourth glass today. I still don't really feel the effects of it. Normally I would have enough after even only half a glass. Wonder where

I'm putting it? Anyway, I want another bloody drink. It's my nerves, they're getting the better of me!

'Wine?' he asked, flying in the door carrying two glasses and a new full bottle.

I felt myself lifting straight away. Oh, happy days! I could hear meself humming suddenly, listening to it inside me head, as I grinned up at him. 'Ta, you always were a gentleman,' I laughed, taking the glass before he even offered it.

'My, we are enjoying the vino!' he said, showing me his still very white teeth, with the dimples in his lovely creamy skin.

He hasn't changed a bit, I thought. Just got even better looking, I sighed, feeling the longing in me as I held out the glass, looking up at him while he filled it. I looked at the size of it, then heard myself saying, 'Right, you better be prepared to carry me back to that guesthouse! Because it looks like I am going on a binge. Believe it or not, I would not normally dream of wanting this much wine. But you foreigners, French frogs,' I said, grinning at him, 'you drink it like water.'

'Tut, tut, don't let the locals hear you call them that,' he laughed. Then he clinked my glass, saying, 'Cheers, Martha, to your good health! Though I still say it is almost impossibly difficult for me to believe you are here,' he said, shaking his head and looking into my face as he let himself drop into the sofa opposite me.

'Yeah,' I muttered. 'I must have slept-walked here, because if I really thought about it, quite frankly, Ralph, I would not have done it,' I said, only half-lying through me teeth this time. Because a part of me told me I was bleedin nuts!

'What would you not have done?' he asked, staring into my eyes with a knowing look. He knows me well, and I just stared back, studying him, seeing what I could read. A smile played around his lips, knowing what I was thinking. If I give him a direct answer, he will give me an even quicker one. It will not be to my liking.

'Do you mind if I take off these boots?' I said, stretching my legs and letting the long, woollen, oatmeal-coloured frock cling to my legs. It showed off what was left of my chest and the rest of my still-skinny body. It was lovely and warm, with a big roll-top neck. I wore it with a wide black-leather belt fastened around my waist, showing my figure off to its best advantage.

I saw him following the length of me, with his lovely green eyes taking me in, then letting a smile play on his lips. Then he looked at me, murmuring with his eyes flashing, 'You have become a very attractive woman, Martha. Then, you always were,' he said quietly, taking a sip of his wine then standing up and reaching into a box sitting on a big press behind him.

'I have a confession to make,' he said, taking out a cigar. 'I smoke these occasionally,' he continued, opening a drawer and picking up something to cut the end off. Then he dropped it back in the drawer and reached over to pick up a box of matches sitting on the mantelpiece.

He said nothing as he leaned himself against the mantelpiece and sucked on the cigar, taking a huge drag into his lungs, then watching as he blew the puff of smoke into the air, sending out a delicious scent.

I stared at him, with his ankles crossed, admiring his long legs with the lovely dark-brown, soft wool trousers and the turned-up end that looked tailored. He was wearing a dark-wine cashmere sweater with a crisp white-linen shirt underneath, open at the neck. I looked down at his shoes. They were black Italian leather, slip-on. He looked casual yet very elegant. I knew those clothes were expensive. No, Ralph never wanted for much. He always had good taste, even if it was only a priest's black suit. It was always quality.

I looked down at my own boots. They were wine-coloured, with kid-glove leather. They went great with the wool frock. But they were bloody expensive, too. Not the sort of money I could afford. No, they were a Christmas present from my friend Blondie, who I'd met in the mad house, to go with the fur coat she gave me. Jaysus! She spends money too, like it's going out of fashion. Oh, well, she's keeping me well dressed. I must say I'm a credit to her.

'So, what about the boots, Ralph? Can I take them off?' I said, crossing my legs and grabbing hold of one to pull it off.

'Would you like me to help you?' he said, lifting his chin then dropping his eyes, taking in the bit of leg I was showing.

'Well, if you insist,' I said. 'I am pretty ragged at the minute. I have been travelling for what feels like years now,' I laughed, then gave a big sigh, holding out my leg for him.

He looked around, searching for the ashtray, then spotted it sitting on a table behind my sofa and leaned across, leaving the cigar smouldering in it. Then he dropped on his knees and lifted my foot, pulling off the boot. Then he held his hand under my foot and lowered it to the floor. 'Give me your leg,' he said, lifting the other boot.

'Certainly, sir!' I said, lifting my leg and landing it on his thigh. 'Oh, I do like a knight in shining armour,' I sighed, feeling his hand on my thigh as he pulled off the boot. Then he flung it behind the sofa, sending the other one flying after it, and stood up. I laughed, thinking, he always did that. Sent things flying to land on chairs whenever he took something off. Then it hit me! 'Mind my boots!' I warned, looking from them to glare up at him, saying, 'They were bloody expensive, you know!'

'Hmm! I can see that,' he said, then muttered, 'So is the fur. Did you come into an inheritance?'

'No, Ralph. I enjoy collecting friends' cast-offs! They don't call me "Second-hand Rose" for nothing,' I laughed, seeing his face break into a big smile as he shook his head, saying, 'You are funny.'

'Yes, well, needs must and all that,' I sighed, looking around me. 'Now, where is my bag, Ralph? I need a cigarette.'

'Beside you,' he grinned, throwing his head at the bag sitting right beside me on the floor.

'Oh, right!' I sighed, leaning down and pulling it up.

'So,' he said, sipping his wine. 'How are you feeling now? Is your health recovered?'

'Yes, I am very much on the mend,' I said slowly.

'What happened to you, Martha?' he said quietly.

'What do you mean?'

'Well, I believe you married, you have a child. I know only what you read in the letter I sent you. Tell me, how have you been?'

'Yes, well, I married the bold Ulick in a shotgun wedding. The child was a shotgun birth. She arrived two months later. Then we had a shotgun divorce! Or at least separation. He divorced me a few years later. Happy days! It was a match made in hell. As you predicted, we were totally unsuited. I reared her alone, educated her, provided her with a good home, bought with my own sweat. She left home. I had lost my health. Recovered it somewhat, after months in hospital. Then undid all the good surgeon's hard work. I plunged to the ground, hitting it hard. Tried to top myself, recovered again, now I am on the loose. Over twenty-one, fancy-free, and I have turned up here to visit my old friend Ralph. Your good self! My first excursion into the brave new world I intend making for myself, thank you. So, that is it! My life since I last saw you, fitted into a matchbox!

'Now, what about yourself? What have you been up to?' I said, seeing him smile at me, shaking his head, saying quietly, 'I always said you would become a wonderful woman, and you have.'

I stared at him, seeing him looking at me with the most gentle look in his eyes, looking like he wanted to cry. I felt myself suddenly filling up inside. Like I wanted to burst into tears. My heart was breaking for the want of him. Yet he still keeps his distance. I recognise the signs of him holding himself back. He won't let go.

'Tell me,' I said, half-croaking then clearing my voice and taking a big sip of the wine. I looked, seeing I had drank half of it. Jaysus! And I am still not drunk! Happy! Oh, very happy days. I would hate to get drunk! Can't bear all that spinning around in me head.

Then I looked up at him, seeing him staring at me. 'What are you doing here, Ralph? Are you still a priest?' I said, shocking myself with that question, then holding my breath, waiting for his answer. He nodded slowly, looking at me, watching my reaction. My heart sank. Ah, fuck!

'So, what are you doing? I mean, why are you here? Is this a presbytery?'

'No,' he said quietly, shaking his head. 'I have been abroad for many years, working as a missionary doctor for my order. I did tell you that in my letter. This house was left to me by a relative. I decided to come back and spend time here. So, it is as you see me now,' he said, waving his arm around the room, then taking a sip of his drink.

'But are you working as a priest here, Ralph?' I said, feeling confused, wondering what was going on.

'No,' he said, slowly shaking his head.

'So, does the order own this house now? Because you have a vow of poverty. Anything you own, they get.'

'True,' he said, slowly lowering his head in a nod. 'But, no, they do not own this house. I do.'

'But how?'

'That rule applies only if I am a priest, and I am presently taking time away from the order. Call it a sabbatical, if you will. But my time is my own. I am not sure if I wish to remain in what I was doing. I need to re-evaluate my life. I may need, perhaps, a change of direction.'

I listened, forgetting to take a breath as it caught in the back of my throat, nearly choking me. I started coughing, then he was over gently tapping my back, saying, 'Breathe slowly.'

I did, after taking in gulps of air, trying to get a rhythm, then he put the glass to my lips, saying, 'Take a drink, Martha! Sip slowly,' he said, holding the glass to my lips as he watched me drink, keeping his other hand held gently on my back.

I gasped, taking in a long sigh, and turned my head away still gasping. 'Thank you. Bloody hell, my breath just caught,' I spluttered, looking at him, seeing him watching me carefully, making sure I was OK.

Then he stood up, saying, 'Would you like some tea or coffee?'

'Yes, tea, please. I would like that! Yeah, great,' I groaned, hearing my voice croak, with the eyes burning out of me head and tears streaming down my face. Ah, fuck, now my mascara is running, I sobbed to meself, thinking, I have left everything behind in that bleedin guesthouse!

I stood up, saying, 'Where is the bathroom, please, Ralph?' Wanting to get out of the room, feeling in a hurry to get a look at meself. For sure, I'm not going to win any beauty contest, not with the red nose dripping, the black eyes and the red face. Ah, fuck! Why do I always manage to make a holy show of meself?

'Come with me,' he said, putting his hand on my arm and leading me out the door. I leaned into him, seeing as it was a squash getting out the door together, because I was holding on to his jumper without realising it.

'Are you all right?' he said, stopping to look at me as he lifted my face, staring into me.

'No!' I squawked, pulling away from him. 'I'm looking miserable! So stop staring at me, it's making me worse,' I said, half-laughing, nearly crying. Then seeing his face break out into a huge grin, showing his dimples, with the white teeth and the spark of mischief in his all-knowing, lovely green eyes.

'Nonsense!' he purred. 'Let me see you,' he said, pulling me towards him and holding my chin in his hand, leaning into my face to examine me. Then he whispered, 'Martha, you have a magnetic charm. It comes through even with streaming mascara,' he laughed, throwing his head back, thinking that was hilarious. I felt like telling him to fuck off, only I knew he meant well. But I still felt a fool. He was just drawing attention to it.

I stared at myself in the mirror, seeing a watery pair of red eyes staring back at me and two black streaks making a line down my flushed cheeks. I took some tissues sitting in a box and dipped them under the tap, wiping away the mascara, then blew my nose, making it more red. Ah, well, at least my face looks clean now. The eyes I can do nothing about. It's the bloody exhaustion. But I don't care about that. I don't really feel it any more. I would stick pins in me eyes just to keep them open so I could stay talking all night to Ralph! Gawd, how did I ever get on without him? I didn't! Not really, Martha. You were like the clown, hiding the tears behind the laughter, my dear. Yes, you did, I told myself, looking in the mirror.

Right, I sighed, thinking, I am going to have to continue that way. The man is not for turning! I can sense it. On the surface, it looks like he's having a late mid-life crisis. Nearly hitting the fifty-mark. But he has been a bachelor too long. Besides, the old public schools pumped too much of the old ethos of 'Loyalty, Fidelity and, above all, Discipline!' Ralph will not give up 'Old Mother Church' too easily. Not even medicine could hold him from that. Well, one good thing, at least he's not married!

I opened the door, following the direction of noise. It sounds like he's in the kitchen. Right! In we go, then it hit me. Great! This is good. I'm now making inroads. Jaysus, just a few hours ago I was afraid to even breathe, never mind move in the place.

'Hello there! Feeling better?'

I nodded.

'Good! You are just in time,' he said, handing me a mug of tea. 'Do help yourself to milk and sugar, Martha,' he said, pointing at the tray with a very civilised silver jug and matching sugar dish, with a silver spoon sitting on the side.

'Very nice,' I said, eyeing the silver, then lifting up the spoon and dropping a teaspoonful of sugar into the mug. 'Did you also inherit the silver?' I said, throwing my head at the tray.

'Yes, everything came with the house,' he said. 'It belonged to my uncle. I became his heir when he died leaving no children, not even a wife. In fact, he hardly used the place,' Ralph said, swinging around to look at the lovely old-fashioned kitchen.

I looked down at the long black Aga-type cooker that was taking up nearly one end of the big room. It was sitting itself snugly inside a huge old brick arch. Oh, I would love to have that, I thought, feeling the lovely heat it sends out. 'So, where did he live then?' I asked.

'Oh, he had other residences. London, Switzerland! He liked to move about. I also inherited his housekeeper, Madame Bouclé. She came as an old retainer. She has been with him for years. She lived here when he was abroad. Now she has moved into the village. She lives with her maiden sister. So I have the place to myself,' he said happily, giving me a big grin.

'So,' I said, grinning back at him. 'You are not letting the Church get their paws, then, on this little pile?'

'No! Absolutely not!' he said, shaking his head. 'The will came with a codicil. It stipulates I must make use of the house for myself or it will pass to another member of the family, if there is a danger of it being lost to the Church. In other words, the family hold this house in trust. They act on my behalf as trustees to all of my estate.'

'Are you serious?' I said.

'Oh, yes, of course!' Then his face broke out into a slow smile as something hit him. 'You know!' he said, staring straight into my face, looking at me with amusement dancing in his eyes. 'I do think the old rake was fiendishly clever. He never approved of my decision to leave medicine for the Church. I believe he spoke to my mother about it – she was his sister. Of course, there was nothing she could do to influence me. She would never have even dared try. I was a grown man. Quite capable of knowing what I wanted to do with my life. But in this instance it came at the right time. I think when I heard about the house it quite made up my mind for me. I had been thinking about doing something for some time anyway. So, here we are!' he said, putting his arm around me and leading me over to a chair.

'Wait, I need a cigarette,' I said, leaving down the mug and making off for the sitting room to get my bag with the smokes.

'Well then, let us take our drinks back inside,' he said, taking up the two mugs and following me.

'So, Ralph, are you thinking of leaving the priesthood?' I said, seeing him lying back, with his feet hanging over the side of the sofa, sipping on his coffee. He looked at me, then took in a deep slow breath, looking away and landing his eyes in the distance, thinking about it.

'I have no idea, Martha. I am simply taking time to reflect. I am making no decisions. It will become clear to me in time. I do not intend to force it.'

I said nothing, just bent down and picked up my bag to roll myself another cigarette.

'Martha!'

I looked up, seeing him looking intently at me.

'Why did you come? I know you, you came for a good reason. Otherwise you would simply have written to me or perhaps even telephoned. So talk to me, please!' he said, swinging himself to a sitting position and putting down his mug on the little wine table that sat in the corner next to his sofa.

I watched, seeing him sit up straight, letting a smile play around his mouth as his eyes pinned on me, locking me into his gaze. I could see he was reading me, searching my eyes for the answer. I dropped my head, not wanting to let him see what I was thinking.

'Come on! Do tell me,' he said, springing off the sofa and landing himself beside me. 'Tell me, Martha! Why did you come?' he asked, putting his arm gently around my shoulder and turning me to look at him.

I stared into his eyes, seeing his softness, the strength of him, the power that makes him the man he is.

'Come on, Martha, don't be frightened of me,' he whispered, staring at me more intently.

I stared back, seeing him let a longing show in his eyes. I could feel my breathing start to go faster as I watched his eyes searching my face. He looked like he wanted to get inside me. I could feel the heat coming from the nearness of him as his thigh brushed against mine. He still loves me, I thought.

Suddenly my heart started to hammer in my chest. I was afraid he could hear it. I wanted to throw myself into his arms and let go of all the pent-up emotion I had buried since the last day I ever met him. I wanted to cry until there were no more tears. But I could say nothing. I needed to hold back. I was terribly afraid he would let me down again. I know him well. Like me, his old loves never die. The Church has too much of a hold on him.

I shook my head. 'No! I can't bring myself to say it, Ralph. We both know what it is.'

He stared at me, looking deep into my eyes, reading all there was to know about me. Seeing the new Martha, the woman he has just met, is not really much different from the young girl he once walked away from, breaking her heart. I am still that girl inside. I still love him, only much more deeply, with all the maturity of a woman who has lived a lifetime. He let out his breath slowly and took me in his arms, gently wrapping them around me, and pulled me to him, holding me against his chest. 'You do still love me, Martha, is that true?' he whispered, resting his lips on the side of my head.

'Yes, Ralph, I have never stopped loving you. I will love you until the day I die!' I whispered.

'You have come here to tell me this, have you not, my Martha?'

'Yes, I needed to see you,' I said. Then I lifted my head and pulled away, looking at him. 'Ralph, do you still love me?'

He closed his eyes and dropped his head, nodding. Then he lifted it, looking at me, and said, 'Yes! Very much, Martha. More deeply than I ever dared believe. You have always been with me. In my thoughts, in my prayers. Always, Martha, always have I carried you with me. You have never left my heart,' he said, putting his hand on my face and stroking me.

We stayed quiet, while I put my head back on his chest, feeling his arms around me as he fell back on the cushions, taking me with him.

'Martha, what is it you want from me?' he asked, whispering with his lips on my cheek.

'You know full well what I am here for, what I want to ask you!'

'Yes, but you must tell me. We need to be clear what the other is asking, I do not want to second-guess you, Martha. We are both mature adults now. What is it you are asking of me, Martha?'

I took in a sigh, saying nothing. Not feeling ready to be rejected.

'OK, I will say it for you,' he said, taking in a deep sigh. 'You want us to be married, is that it, my love?'

I nodded, saying, 'Yes! I want to have a family of my own. Start again. Sarah is reared. But I have been alone too long. I need a family, Ralph. I want to have children with you, wake up with you beside me. Share all my thoughts and all my dreams with you. I want you to be the other half of me. I want us to make decisions together. I have always needed you, Ralph, but I had to go it alone without you. Because I could never find another to replace you. That's why I stayed alone, and do you know? I knew from the moment you left me for the last time that would happen. I knew! You don't really know me, Ralph. You never saw far enough inside me to see I could only love one man, and that was you, Ralph Fitzgerald. The first and last man I ever really loved. The first person who ever showed me love. The only person who ever had a powerful influence over me for the good. It was only matched by one other man, and his influence was also very powerful. But it was for pure evil. But that is centuries ago.

'Ralph, I am a free woman. That's what allows me to come here now and meet you face to face. I am not running from you any more, Ralph. I must face up to my need for you. For better for worse, resolve it once and for all. I didn't want to discuss this with you now, not all in one go. Because I don't want to pressure you. I realised that this evening. I had hoped it would come from you. You would slowly arrive yourself at the decision. See for yourself. I know you love me, we love each other deeply. But I hoped over the next week we might grow close together. Be at ease with each other. But now it's out in the open. I'm not sure it's for the good, Ralph,' I said. 'Maybe it's all too soon. I don't know what I was thinking,' I said, seeing him staring at me, listening very intently. I could see his eyes were looking very worried. There is also a sadness in them. Like he doesn't want to pain me. Yet he will, we will both hurt each other all over again. Jesus, I know it! I thought, feeling the numbing pain already running through me, making me want to shiver.

'Martha, I need time,' he said, looking at me. 'So do you,' he sighed, pulling me down to lie on his chest. 'Come, you are shivering,' he said, wrapping himself around me. 'Martha, please, I feel I must say this to you. Do not rush. We make only bad decisions when we are rash. Take life more slowly, you still need time to recover,' he said, pressing his head down, leaning it on me and whispering gently as he smothered me in his arms.

I said nothing, just thought about it. Knowing he was right. But I can't continue as I am. I, too, must make decisions.

'Ralph, can I ask you something?' I said, lifting my head and pushing myself away from him.

'What is it, Martha?' he said when he saw me hesitating, with me wondering how I could ask him. 'Come on! Ask!' he said, giving me a little shake by grabbing my waist.

'Can I stay here tonight?' I suddenly said, not wanting to go back to the *pension*.

He thought about it, then grinned, saying, 'Yes,' looking at me as he lowered his head, not taking his eyes off me, making it look also like a warning. Meaning I have to behave myself!

'Don't worry, your virtue is safe with me, Ralph!' I said, laughing and burying my head in his chest again.

'What a disappointment,' he muttered. 'I was hoping for more!'

'Are you serious?' I said.

'No, Martha, sorry, I should not jest. It is not fair to us. We both need to be very circumspect, my Martha. Because, you see, technically I am still a priest. I have not yet decided what I am going to do,' he said, letting his voice fade away as he thought about what he just said.

'Well, Ralph, how much time do you think you will need?' I said, sitting up to grab a smoke.

'I don't know, Martha. Really I don't!' he said, gazing at me with a tragic look in his beautiful green eyes.

I wanted to grab him and smother myself inside him. I kept looking at him, seeing him so close yet so far. I just can't get beyond that bleeding grip the Church has on him. But one thing I do know. He must give himself freely to me or there would be nothing there at all. It has to be his commitment to me, as I will willingly give my commitment to him. So, it's keep me hands off him, back off and let him breathe.

I lifted my head, looking into his face, seeing him turn away from his thoughts and pin his eyes on me. Then I saw his eyes lighten as his gaze dropped from my eyes and stopped on my lips, with his head looking like it was inching forward, moving closer to me. I felt my heart suddenly begin to race as he drew closer. I could feel his arms tighten around me and very gently begin to move around my back.

'Martha, I love you so much,' he said, moving his hands and resting them gently on my face, brushing my hair back. Then he took in a deep sigh and suddenly looked like he had made a decision. But before I knew what was happening, he grabbed me around the waist and shot himself up, swinging me onto my feet.

'Come, Martha. You are exhausted. Let me show you to your room. Do you have something to wear?'

'No, it looks like I will be sleeping in my knickers!' I said, laughing at the idea, seeing his face crease in a big grin.

'Don't tempt me, you little Jezebel!' he grinned, grabbing me around the waist and heading me out the door. 'You may have a pair of my pyjamas,' he said. 'Sorry, but it is the best I can offer you. Unfortunately, I do not have ladies dropping in to spend the night,' he laughed.

'I would hope not,' I snorted, thinking I shouldn't let him see me being jealous. He might think I am pushing my luck.

'Grand! They will do fine,' I said, thinking I will have to go down to the *pension* first thing tomorrow and collect my bag. Collect my bag? I took in a big breath, letting it out quietly, then said, 'Ralph, do you mind if I stay here with you for a couple of days? Not long!' I said, looking up at him.

'Of course, Martha! Would you like me to collect your bags? Where is the place you were supposed to stay?'

'Oh, she gave me a card. Hang on. I'll get it out of my bag,' I said, rushing back in, with him following behind. 'Here we are. Oh, hang on! I better give you the money to pay her. Pity, I didn't even get to use the bloody bed!' I said, moaning at me loss.

'Never mind that, Martha. I will see to it,' he said, looking at the card and putting it in his pocket. 'You sleep on in the morning. You must have some rest. Then perhaps we can take a drive and stop somewhere for a spot of lunch. We will eat dinner at home, unfortunately; Madame would not brook otherwise. One must give fair warning of one's intention not to return for dinner,' he said, looking half-serious.

'Really?' I said, not too impressed with that idea. But not really believing it.

'Oh, yes! Quite the tartar, our Madame Bouclé,' he laughed. 'She obviously has been spoilt, running this house according to her own wishes,' he said, lifting his chin like he intends doing something about it.

'God, she has her work cut out for her, Ralph, daring to try and rule you,' I laughed, reaching up to give him an unexpected hug and land a kiss on his cheek. Then I pulled back quickly before he thought I was going too far. I'm certainly tempted. But, bloody hell, I would soon be repulsed, even if it was in the most gentle way. No, I'm too fragile to take rebuffs or rejections at the minute. Anyway, it has to come from him. He must make the first move. It's not my choice. I know what I want. Yes! I'm here to make a decision for my life ahead. I won't get that made by messing about.

'Come along, it is quite late! Let us get you to bed,' he said, taking my hand and pulling me out the door before stopping to switch off the light.

'Imagine, you own this house, Ralph. Does the Church pay for your upkeep?' I said, stopping on a half-landing to look at him.

He shook his head, saying, 'No, certainly not! I suppose they would if it was necessary. But it is not. I am well provided for. Money is not a consideration,' he said, sounding like he took that for granted.

'So, do you mean you have your own private income, Ralph?'

'Yes, of course! I am not quite within the order now,' he smiled. 'I live privately. But, of course, I am not out of it either,' he laughed, sounding confused now, thinking he's in a no-man's-land of being neither one or the other. 'Oh, well! It is not a difficulty. I am quite happy with how things are working at the present. Now, off to bed with you, Martha. Come along,' he said, wrapping me to him then walking on, taking me with him as his arm held tightly to my waist.

I spread my arm across his back, feeling the firmness of his muscles. Yet the softness and the warmth made me feel safe and comforted as I leaned into him, letting my body rest against him. I felt cherished and protected – something I had very rarely experienced. It made me feel young and very female. I had been independent for much, much too long. I have never turned over my life to anyone. I yearned now for Ralph to take care of me.

'Here we are,' he said, as he threw open a door and showed me into a huge bedroom. I instantly took in the big picture window, with heavy gold drapes hanging down in folds and drawn across to keep out the night. They were crowned with a big matching pelmet edged with hanging tassels. I looked up, seeing a high ceiling with ornate carvings and a big rose in the centre. Then my eyes lit on the king-size bed standing against the wall, to the far right of the door. It was very ornate carved wood and painted in a lovely blue-grey, making it look very elegant and terribly French.

'Jaysus! You could get lost in that bed,' I said, diving at it and plastering meself on top, then spreading myself out. 'Ohh, I have died and gone to heaven,' I moaned, rubbing my hands over the velvet quilt and bouncing to test the springs, feeling its softness under me.

Ralph stood grinning and saying, 'Yes, Martha, it was meant for more than one!'

'Would you like an invitation?' I said, hopping up and forgetting myself.

'Don't tempt me,' he murmured, shaking his head and giving me a slow smile before looking away. Then he looked back at me, saying quietly, looking a bit more serious, 'The bathroom is on the next landing down. Terribly sorry, we do not have en-suite! Any complaints, please take them up with management. I am only the night porter. You will meet Madame Bouclé tomorrow,' he laughed. Then he took himself out the door before I could ask him where his room was.

There seemed to be a lot of rooms on the way up here! Jaysus! All this space for just one person! His mother was the same. A huge house all to herself. But it wasn't too big to her, or him. She grew up in an even bigger house! Bloody hell, I forgot how well off his family were. I knew all right. But somehow I just forgot it. Right, I wonder if he remembered to get me something to wear for bed? Just as the thought hit me, the door was whipped open and he breezed in. My heart leapt at the sudden sight of him again.

'Here we are, Martha,' he said, dropping a lovely pair of soft cotton pyjamas on the bed. 'Now, do you have what you need?'

'Yes, everything for now, thanks, Ralph. I will just have to wait for tomorrow to get my stuff. So no worries, I am perfectly fine, thanks. In fact, I was never better.'

'OK, I wish you goodnight! Sleep well,' he said, grabbing me in a hug and kissing my cheek.

Jaysus! That was very quick, I thought, seeing him vanish out the door and hearing his footsteps disappear down the stairs again. Wonder where he's gone to? Better still, I must take a look tomorrow and see what his room looks like. It would be nice to get a look at his stuff. That tells you volumes about a person! I have never really gotten a look into his personal life. He always lived in a big institutional order house for priests. Hmm. Brilliant, get to see a bit more of the private Ralph. Right, Martha! Off with the clothes and into the bed. Jaysus! What a day, I'm exhausted, I sighed, mooching around and snuggling down into the deep mattress, feeling meself sinking into its softness. The lovely weight of the duvet and the feel of the heavy quilt over me was heaven on earth. I yawned, then closed my eyes, feeling them instantly go heavy, then I was out like a light.

5

I woke up with a golden light radiating in through the heavy curtains. My eyes shot open and a ripple of happiness flowed through my chest and made its way down into my belly, making me tingle all over. I could get the scent of foreignness in the room. It was the French air coming from the wild herbs and the trees and the thick foliage making its way over from the gardens and the surrounding countryside.

The room had a scent of its own, too. It was the polish from the old, highly glossed stout furniture, and the dust coming from the thick heavy drapes and wafting up from the old heavy rugs sitting on the painted, creaking wooden floorboards. I took it all in instantly, without really seeing or looking at anything. I was with Ralph, in his house, alone with him, and had all the time in the world to enjoy it. I only had something like this once before, being alone with him and able to spend time. That was a wonderful day. He had swept me off my feet by suddenly announcing he was taking me for a drive out to the country. Then we stopped for an unforgettable meal in an unforgettable, magical setting. Then it had all ended with a crashing suddenness. I had lost him for ever. Until now.

I stretched in the bed, feeling his deliciously soft pyjamas gently caressing my skin. They felt like silk. Hmm, Ralph sure loves himself, no cheapy stuff from Dunnes Stores for him. Perish the thought! God forbid! Ah, now, come on, Martha! No sarcasm, you love him, and he can afford his lifestyle. It's how the rich live. So be it. Anyway, you're not exactly a pauper yourself, either. Oh, no, indeed not! I have great friends like Blondie to keep me in style. Which reminds me. What did I pack? I thought, trying to get a picture of what I put in the suitcase. Yeah, I think I put in most of the good stuff I got from Blondie. That should be suitable for here. I want to look my best.

Right, I groaned, taking a very long stretch, then yawned, thinking I could maybe go back to sleep. Then it hit me. Not on yer nelly. Out of the bed and get moving. Start the day. I do not want to miss one precious minute with Ralph.

I threw back the bedclothes and swung my legs out of the bed, then sat on the edge, rubbing my eyes and yawning, taking another stretch, then I remembered my suitcase. Ah, Jaysus, I won't be able to get dressed until I get me hands on that. What will I do? I bet I look a holy show. My eyes must look plastered with the two black rings around them from the mascara.

I looked around the room, slowly taking in the lovely old rosewood wardrobe in an alcove by the window. Then I spotted my suitcase sitting next to the dressing table. My heart leapt and I was off the bed in seconds to slam it on the floor and open it up. Ah, Gawd, Ralph is such a wonderful man. He had it sitting here all ready for when I woke up. He must have come in quietly and left it here without waking me. Oh, he is so good! I thought, feeling my heart melt as I whipped open the suitcase. Right! What do I need? First get a bit of order.

I rushed up and whipped around, making a dive to tidy up the bed. Then, satisfied it was as I found it, I stood back to admire my work, seeing it all nicely made up and covered with the heavy quilt. Grand, that's done. Now to make myself look respectable. Respectable? Forget that! Look for something sexy!

I rummaged through the suitcase, taking out half the stuff and landing it on the bed. Bloody hell, it's the middle of winter, I have nothing here to look sexy in, I thought, feeling disappointed as I let my eyes fly over the frocks, skirts and nothing but heavy winter stuff. This lot would do a modern-day nun proud, I snorted with disgust. Yeah, no doubt about it, she would definitely feel safe in this stuff! Ah, fuck! What will I wear? Come on, Martha! Hurry up, think! Or the bleedin day will be gone.

I settled on a cream silk blouse that Blondie threw at me when she was doing her weekly spring clean. I like to keep her in order. That's why I suggest she shouldn't be hoarding all that stuff she never gets around to wearing. 'It's a sin to waste, Blondie!' I do snort at her. She agrees with me and now I'm always in the best of style.

Lovely! OK, what to wear with cream? No! Forget sexy. That's vulgar. What I need is demure. Shy and retiring looking, but gorgeous! Then I got the picture of a Victorian maiden wilting away from all her blushing. No, forget demure. I'm a bit too long in the tooth for that caper. Right! What the fuck then? I ran me hands over the mountain of clothes sitting on the bed. Jaysus! They're all getting creased. Then I spotted the lovely linen charcoal pencil skirt, lined of course, with the slit down the back. It went just below the knees.

Lovely, Brown Thomas best. Nothing but the best for me. That's what Blondie told me when she swooped in with me on her heels and fitted it up to me. Jaysus! I see more of her than her husband does. We're nearly living together. We would be lost without each other. Which reminds me, I better remember everything that happens here. She will want a blow-by-blow account.

'Ahh! Poor Sergei!' she said, when I told her me tale of woe.

'Never mind him!' I said, marvelling at my ruthless streak in letting nothing get in my way while I chased down the man of my dreams, going nearly to the ends of the earth. I would have gone to the Congo if I'd known he was there! But yeah, poor Sergei! Still, any woman with a drop of blood easing its way through her veins would pant after our Sergei. Blondie might be more than happy to get him back for herself. We nearly killed each other over that fella! I only got him because? Well, Jaysus! I can't even remember now. The poor fella is already fading away!

Still, cut out the messing, Martha. Think straight. If Ralph does not want me? Then it's over. I'm going to keep moving. I do want a family. And Sergei? Well, he's a lovely man. As he said, we could make a go of it.

Right! That's sorted. Now back to business. What was I doing? Oh, yeah, the skirt. Now, what colour jumper with that? The dark V-neck cashmere sweater. Right, ahh! Back to sexy. I know what I'll wear. The suspender belt with stockings and the pale-lemon French cami knickers! Yeah, with the silk bodice! Ohh! And the black low-heeled leather shoes. Yes, OK, I will put them all to one side and hang this stuff up in the wardrobe while I'm at it.

Now, that's all sorted, I sighed, standing back to admire my stuff hanging up in the lovely old wardrobe, with the smell of mothballs pouring out, threatening to suffocate me. Jaysus! I will smell like one of them old lavender-and-gin aul biddies with the smell of mothballs pouring off their fur rabbits hanging around their necks! Never mind. You don't want the moths getting a mouthful of your good stuff. But they don't come out this time of the year. I'm still OK!

Oh, bloody hell! Will you ever get a move on? Look at the state of you! I thought, staring at meself looking back in the mirror. I looked like a floozy that's been left stranded, wandering out of her mind for the want of a bit of sense! Right, get moving down to the bathroom. Grab the washbag. Wonder if they've got towels there? I haven't got me own. Ah, yeah, of course there is. Right, hike up the pyjamas and off you go.

I brushed out my hair and bent forward, grabbing it up in a bundle and twirling it around, tying it in knot after knot. Jaysus, the length of it. It's sitting at me knees. Just as well I got a few inches off the bottom. It will help keep it in good condition. Well, I took nearly a foot off. It looks lovely and thick now, but it's not for letting out. That is only for rare occasions, it's too long. I could tie it at the back of my head in knots, then let it hang as a ponytail! Never – this is not the time.

I tied it on the back of my head in a chignon, sliding through an ivory hairgrip to secure it in place, then stood back to admire myself. Lovely, it looks soft in the front and sits high on the back of my head, looking very elegant. Perfect! If this doesn't work, then, Ralph, you are definitely a bleedin eunuch!

I opened my make-up bag, taking out the lipstick, then ran it around my lips and stood back to pout at meself, seeing which is the most demure! Oh, my dear, you look . . .? Sexy? Too skinny? Demure? Too old? Fuck . . . Maybe a bit sophisticated? Yeah, I would get away with that look over here. Particularly with the rouge lipstick. It gives me an air of, eh . . .? I leaned into the mirror to get a closer look. No, not a hooker. This lipstick makes me look like something out of the Parisian gay 1890s. But on the whole? I thought. Smashing, it's the elegant look!

Right, that's the best I can do with what I've got. The good Lord didn't go mad when he made me. I would have preferred the blonde look. Very Nordic with the big baby-blue eyes and the pouting lips

with the mass of golden hair and a figure a man would sell his soul
for. Ah, will you stop. Come on! Your figure's grand and so is the rest
of you! If he doesn't like that, he can go and fuck himself!

God, I nearly forgot. My bit of seduction! Where's me Chanel No.
5? I dived back into my make-up bag and gave myself a liberal splash
around the ears. Don't forget the chest. Right, now a bit around the
wrists and I'm any man's fancy.

Ready! I took in a deep breath and made my way out the door and
down the stairs. I could get the smell of cooking and voices coming
from the kitchen. I opened the door and walked straight into the face
of a well-rounded woman in her sixties with stone-grey hair held up
in a tight bun at the back. She was wearing a long brown skirt with
a matching long wool jumper, and lace-up shoes on her feet. She
stared at me for a split second, then nodded, saying, '*Bonjour, madame!*'

I hesitated, taking her in, then nodded back, saying, '*Bonjour
Madame Bouclé!*'

Then her gaze lingered on me for a few seconds more, before she
turned away looking like she was thinking. I bet she's wondering
what Ralph is up to! Ha, not much, Madame, not much! The radio
was on beside the large French dresser and music blasted out, with
someone playing an accordion. I recognised the song. 'How would
you like to be' were the words in English. I forgot the name of it, but
it was lovely. Very romantic! Ohh! How so very French ze French
arrre! I sang in my head, feeling a rush of delight run through me
at the thought of where I was.

I looked around, seeing no sign of Ralph. Wonder where he is? I
thought, feeling the kitchen a bit empty without him. The Madame
looked back at me from the big trough she was working at, preparing
some little birds left sitting naked and skinny, looking like little
chickens that never made it past the chick stage.

'*Que prendrez-vous?*' she said.

I looked at her thinking, What's she saying? Ahh, I remember. '*Je
prendrai une tasse de café,*' I said, looking at her. Hoping I didn't tell
her she smells rotten.

She picked up a metal jug from the stove, holding a tea towel over
the handle, and poured it into a mug set for breakfast. I sat myself
down, watching the coffee pour in. It looked nice with plenty of

milk through it. Then she went to the tiled shelf beside the stove and lifted off a tea towel, putting some home-made bread on a plate and putting it down on the table beside me. Then she pointed to the jams sitting in a dish on the table.

I smiled up at her. '*Merci*,' I said, seeing her move away.

'*De rien*,' she said quietly.

Then I started in on the bread and stopped to examine it, looking to see how different it was to what I am used to.

'*Brioche!*' she said, pointing at my bread, saying, '*Non?*'

'*Oh, oui, oui! Bon! Merci, Madame!*' I said, shaking me head as I started to plaster it with the butter and jam, digging into it. Then she turned to me, saying something. I stared at her, not understanding one word of her rapid French. I probably wouldn't even know it if it was slow. I just looked blank then said, '*Je ne parle pas bien français.*'

'Auh!' she muttered, deciding she had enough of me, and went back to her dead little chicks.

Good, now I can get on about my business, I thought, digging into the breakfast. I don't suppose there's any chance of asking her where Ralph is. That would only break my head trying to work that one out! No, he must be gone out.

I was just finished what was offered and wondering how I could get myself another coffee when I heard a noise from down the house. A door slammed, sounding like the front door from the heavy thud, then there was silence. I held my breath, waiting. Then I heard the sound of footsteps thudding along on the rugs, then the march of leather shoes on floorboards. I was still holding my breath when the door swung open. I looked up at the vision of Ralph suddenly appearing, looking all windblown and fresh, with his hair falling down over his right brow. He lifted it with his hand and brushed it back through his fingers, then his eye caught mine. I smiled up at him, landing my eyes on him from head to toe. I took in the fawn-coloured cord trousers with the turn-ups, and the striped cotton shirt under a heavy knitted wine sweater. He was wearing brown, handmade leather shoes with laces. You could see your face in the shine. My breath caught, seeing him looking even more brutally handsome now than I ever remembered him. Then he shut the door, making straight for me.

'Good morning, Martha!' he boomed, looking all smiles, teeth and dimples, and flashing green eyes that lit up his face, the room, me and even Madame Bouclé.

'*Bonjour, Monsieur!*' she simpered, going all girly, with her ample body wriggling, batting her eyes and screeching at him in rapid French.

It lit me up, too. I could feel me insides going like the hammers of hell while he stood behind my chair, booming back at her in a wonderfully mellow French tone. It sounded like music to me. I could get a whiff of his aftershave and the animal male nearness of him. Jaysus! I wonder if I'm in heat! I felt even more girly than the Madame Bouclé.

Now, now, Martha! Don't be vulgar. Where's all this coming from? You are not usually so base! Cut them disgusting thoughts outa yer head this minute. I took in a slow deep breath to control my breathing, my heart and the rest of me innards. Ridiculous, Martha. A woman of your age! You have hit the thirties . . . On the other hand, someone once told me, or I heard it somewhere, women reach their sexual peak when they hit the thirty-mark. Right, that's me. I haven't missed the boat. Good! My days of living the life of a professional virgin are over! I thought, as I lifted my head to look up at him.

'Ralph!'

'Yes, Martha?'

'Eh!' I said, trying to think up something. What I wanted was to sit down on his lap somewhere without the jealous prying eyes of the Madame Bouclé staring daggers. I threw me eye, seeing her doing just that now the attention was off her. She sniffed and went back to her onions. She was now examining a long rope of them but keeping her ear cocked in this direction.

'Are you all right, Martha?' he said, leaning down to rest his hands on my shoulders, then whisper, 'It is wonderful to see you. Did you sleep well?' he said, leaning his face into me.

I went tongue-tied and smiled like a halfwit. 'Oh, lovely, thanks,' I finally croaked.

'Have you breakfasted?' he said, then turned to say something to Madame Bouclé. She shrugged and *oui-oui*'ed, probably telling him I ate most of the newly baked bread she was saving for later!

'*Trés bon!*' he said crisply, then bent down to give me a kiss on the cheek. 'Good, Martha, I am glad you have eaten something. Would you like more coffee?' he said, pointing at my empty mug.

'Oh, yes, please,' I cheered, flashing him an instant smile of delight.

He grinned back, rushing over to get the coffee jug and poured out mine, then one for himself, and sat in his place at the top of the table.

'Oh, I forgot my bag,' I said, wondering where did I leave it.

'Stay there, Martha. Did you leave it in the sitting room?'

'Yes, I don't smoke in the bedrooms, or generally around the house. I am a creature of habit. I like to confine it to one room,' I said, listening to myself babble as he disappeared out the door.

Bloody hell, Martha! Just try staying quiet if you can't be intelligent. The man will think I am a right cretin! I took in a deep sigh, trying to calm myself down. Now, just relax, take it easy. It's only Ralph!

OK, I sighed, thinking this is grand. But not exactly the greatest of comfort, sitting here with your woman taking everything in. I don't think she could understand much, but she was taking in the pair of us laughing and me looking very cosy, trying to inch my way closer to Ralph. He didn't seem to notice every grab I made for his hand on the pretext of telling him something. But she certainly did. Her eyeballs were getting plenty of exercise swinging slyly around, trying not to miss out on seeing anything.

'I think I will just pop upstairs for a minute,' I said, grabbing up my bag and making out of the room.

'One moment, Martha!' Ralph said, turning himself around and stretching his legs out for ease of comfort.

Oh, that lap looks so inviting, I thought, feeling the blood rush to me head. 'Yes?' I said, looking at him, trying to make direct eye contact, but I couldn't, I was all in a heap. Worse than a young one out on a first date or a loony let out for the day.

'Would you like to take a ride?' he said, looking at me.

I stared, wanting to say, 'Yes, please,' with a double meaning. That thought made me nervous and I could feel meself letting loose. Suddenly my face broke into a huge grin and I started roaring with the laugh. But then it turned into hysterics. I could even feel my eyes watering with the heat on me from the shock of what I just did. But I couldn't stop laughing the head off meself.

'What? What is it?' he said, half-smiling with his eyebrows raised and his face looking the picture of confusion.

'Eh, nothing. I, eh, sorry!' I babbled, turning to fly out of the room. I was up the stairs and rushing to find my bedroom when I heard him calling me from the bottom.

'Martha, shall we go soon? Is that all right with you?'

I went back down the flights of stairs and looked from the landing. 'Yes, thank you, that would be lovely,' I said, hearing myself sound like a Victorian mistress giving a polite thank-you to one of the servants.

'OK,' he said quietly, wondering what was coming over me.

'I won't be long,' I said. 'I just want to get my coat.'

'Oh! That is down on the coat rack in the hall,' he boomed up.

'Yeah, thanks,' I croaked, wanting to dig myself a hole and bury meself in it.

Fuck, that's it. I've really gone and lost the run of meself. Oh, why could I not act like a grown woman? Jesus, I'm acting like I've lost my marbles. What must he be thinking of me? I nearly cried. Well, asking me would I like to go for a ride! Of course I bloody would! Oh, let it go. Now, decorum is everything with Ralph, so remember that. Act your age, keep quiet, don't speak until he speaks, then think before you open your mouth, that way you won't go wrong. Right, that's the plan. Now! But above all, mind the diction, he hates nothing worse than poor diction and bad manners. All you have to do, Martha, is . . . just be yourself. Normally I can take myself anywhere. I generally do behave when I have to. So just be yourself, then you'll be grand, I told myself as I took in a deep breath, sucking in my cheeks and puffing out my chest. Trying to get oxygen into me brain. It's all that bleedin smoking. It's killing my brain cells! I used to be able to handle myself a hell of a lot better than this! Right, now brush the teeth, comb out the hair, tie it up, and now for a bit of lipstick. Oh, will I change my earrings? No, keep the pearl. They're real, so definitely more classy. Here we go, ready!

I took off and arrived down into the hall, seeing Ralph come back in through the front door wearing a long cashmere coat with a dark, multicoloured men's silk scarf.

'Are you ready?' he said, letting his eyes sweep up and down the length of me. The skirt and sweater showed off my figure, and I was certainly not as thin as I had been up until recently. I managed to put on quite a bit of weight over the summer since I got out of the hospital. It's just as well! Jaysus, I looked like a walking skeleton then.

'Thank you,' I said, as he stood holding out my fur coat.

'Do you have a scarf?' he said, looking at me wrapping the coat to me, then fastening the loops.

'No,' I said, pulling up the collar, feeling the softness warming the back of my neck and head. 'I don't need one,' I said, looking up at him and smiling, feeling snuggled up inside my fur.

'OK, Martha, we may go now. I have brought the car around,' he said, leading me out the door and slamming it shut behind him. He rushed ahead and whipped open the car door, waiting while I drew in my legs, then slammed it shut before walking quickly round to climb into the driver's seat.

I put on my safety belt, seeing him do the same. Then he started the engine and we took off down the avenue and turned right, driving through the village where I was supposed to stay.

'Oh, thank you very much, Ralph, for collecting my suitcase this morning,' I smiled, looking over at him. 'It was a lovely surprise!'

'Yes, you were sleeping like a baby,' he said, looking over at me and grinning.

'You really are very thoughtful,' I said shyly, feeling a rush of heat and emotions running through me at how wonderful he is, and wishing I could be able to let it out.

'Martha, I am delighted such a small thing can bring a wonderful smile to your face,' he said softly, resting his hand for a split second on my knee.

I sighed gently, letting it out slowly, snuggling back into the comfort of my fur and the warm leather seat heating under me.

We drove on with a restful, companionable silence sitting between us. This is definitely going to be my year, I thought. Last year was the end of the dark days for me. God knows it came roaring in with a malignant violence. It nearly cost me my life. But here I am now, enjoying a golden time. No matter what happens from here on, I will never hit rock bottom, down and out like that, again. No, I am just back to my old self. Full of purpose and energy, knowing exactly what it is I am about.

I looked out at the sights and sounds, breathing in the smell of the French countryside. It was very green with lots of trees and lush foliage. The houses were very different and cosy-looking, with not too many all looking the same. It's lovely and clean, nothing like dirty aul Dublin, or the bogs out beyond the city! Jaysus, but it's great for the tourists. Well, the Yanks and the Continentals love us! They think we're quaint!

We drove out of the countryside and into a town, then Ralph slowed down. People were milling around, all looking busy and scattering in different directions. Some were walking and old men carried onions over their shoulders, wearing black berets. Old women moseyed along, carrying baskets of fruit and vegetables under their arms. Lorries carrying bales of hay got stuck in the middle of the road, trying to get past the cars and bikes, and mammies with kids, and old people walking out in front of them. I looked at the line of shops – bread and tobacco shops, and some with hams hung in the windows. They were all separate, specialising in one thing or the other.

'Oh, today is market day,' Ralph muttered, letting his eyes fly around, taking it all in. 'Shall we stop here? Would you like to stretch your legs and take a look around?' he said, looking at me, interested in what I wanted.

'Yeah, yes, that would be great, Ralph, see a bit of the native life,' I said happily.

'OK, we need to find parking,' he muttered to himself, while his eyes peeled along the street, looking to squeeze in somewhere.

We drove to the edge of the town then turned around. 'We don't want to go too great a distance,' he said, as we looked back, not being able to see the town. We were practically out in the country again.

'Here we are,' he said happily, as a truck moved off and Ralph drove straight in, taking up the spot. He switched off the engine then looked around and climbed out, waiting for me to emerge on the other side. Then he locked the car and put out his arm for me to follow. I took his arm, putting my hand through and holding on.

'Let us take a look inside here,' he said, pointing out a big building. We walked into a big marketplace with stalls selling everything from fish to fruit and vegetables. It was like an Aladdin's cave, with some stalls at the far end of the building selling clothes and jewellery, and others selling antiques. I could see stalls with old farm equipment, stools, wardrobes, chairs, even postcards from the last two wars.

'Do you enjoy this sort of thing, Martha?' he said, grinning at me as my head whipped in all directions.

I didn't know what to look at first. I kept stopping and then moving on, while Ralph would wait patiently whenever I stopped.

'Oh, yes, this is manna from heaven for me,' I gasped, thinking I am in my element. Then I hit on a stall selling postcards from the Great War. They were sent home to relatives while the soldiers fought on the front lines.

'Oh, they are written in French,' I said, knowing bloody well they would be, but really meaning I couldn't make head nor tail out of what they said.

'Would you like to buy some, Martha? I can read them to you later, if you wish.'

'Oh, yes, that's a great idea, Ralph. Ask the man how much he wants.'

'Just choose what you want,' he said, moving in close to get a better look. 'Here they are in a bundle. Would you like them?'

'What? The whole bundle?'

'Yes, of course, why not? Best keep them together.'

'OK, ask him how much!'

'Give them to me,' he said, putting out his hand, letting me pick them up.

He handed them to the man, saying something in French, then he opened his wallet, pulling out a big note.

'No, Ralph, how much does he want? I don't need you to pay, thanks,' I said, thinking he will consider me cheap if I leech off him.

'Please,' he said quietly, 'allow me, it is nothing. Really, I would be happy to get them for you. All right?' he said, smiling gently at me.

'OK, you're the boss,' I said, seeing he didn't mind and was quite happy about it.

I put the paper bag into my handbag and trotted off to see what else there was to see. Then Ralph stopped at a stall selling home-made sweets.

'Choose something, Martha!' he said, pointing at the rows and rows of gorgeous-looking sweets and chocolates.

'No, not me, would you like some?'

'Yes, and I think you would too. You are simply being abstemious. You need to put some flesh on those bones,' he said, tapping my arse through the fur coat. Then he pointed to some bonbons and chocolates as he spoke to the stall owner. We waited while the man handed them over in a paper bag, then we went off happily again.

'Here, open your mouth, Martha,' Ralph said, landing a bonbon in my mouth, then popping one in his own and shoving the bag in his coat pocket. I linked my arm through his and he pulled away, taking me to him and wrapping me under his arm, holding me tight around the waist. I felt my heart lurch with the happiness as we walked on, side-stepping people in and out of the crowds.

'Shall we go and eat something?' he said, leaning close in to my face.

'Yes, good idea, Ralph. Madame Bouclé's bread and jam has worn off and I'm feeling starved with the hunger.'

'OK, Martha, let us go,' he said, heading us out of the marketplace.

We drove on, then Ralph pulled into the car park of a country inn.

'Would you like to take something here? Or shall we drive on? Perhaps we could see what they have to offer here. But do have what you wish, Martha. Only I would caution, Madame Bouclé is right now, as we speak, slaving over her hot stove. So be prepared to save some appetite.'

'OK,' I said happily, opening the door and whipping myself out. 'Actually, Ralph, I have an appetite like a camel.'

'A camel?' he said, grinning at me.

'Yes, well, I can stock up on grub, eat enough in one go sometimes to keep me going for a whole month,' I said, starting to babble again.

'Oh, darling, you are funny,' he said, coming around to take me in his arms and land a flash kiss on my lips, barely touching, it ended so fast. But I felt it nonetheless. It sent a ripple of heat and a buzz of electricity flying though my veins. Then he took my hand and walked me with him, side by side.

We went into the dark inn, which had tables in corners and lights around the walls. I could see waiters rushing around wearing black shirts and trousers, with long striped aprons. They carried trays in their hands held high in the air, balanced in the palm of one hand. Oh, yes, this is definitely the French way of life I'm getting to see, I thought, looking around happily, taking it all in.

A man in a black suit and white evening shirt came up, asking something in French. Ralph spoke to him, then the man put out his arm for us to follow. Ralph stood aside then smartly followed behind me as I took off after the waiter. We were shown to a little corner alcove then the menu was pressed into our hands. I had a look, not making sense of any of it. We finally settled on an omelette for Ralph and a fish chowder for me. Then he ordered a bottle of wine.

'Do you have a preference, Martha?'

'Yes, white, please. Otherwise, whatever you are having.'

I stared at the empty plate after polishing off the paté, half a basket of bread, followed by the fish chowder and now a plate of salad. All washed down with half of the bottle of wine.

'Oh, that was simply delicious,' I mewled, thinking it will keep me going until dinner. Then I looked at Ralph to see him watching me with a grin on his face as he sipped his wine.

'Good heavens! Where do you put it?' he laughed, giving my belly a gentle poke.

'I am telling you, Ralph. It's hard to fatten a greyhound.'

'Nonsense, you are more like a little poodle, my precious,' he said, moving over to wrap his arm around me. 'Would you like something more?' he said, holding me and sipping his wine.

'No, your Madame Bouclé warning is still ringing in my ears,' I said, laughing happily.

'This is nice,' he said, lying back in his chair, resting me beside him.

'Yes,' I sighed. 'Life can be a wonderful bowl of cherries.'

'But not always, from all accounts given by the Sister . . . Can't quite remember her name. Oh, yes, Eleanor. She filled me in on only the barest details. What happened to you, my sweet?' he said quietly, moving away to take my hands in his.

I gently pulled my hands away, reaching down for my bag to get my tobacco. Then I lit up a cigarette.

'It was toxic thyroid, Ralph, Graves' disease. I was ill with it for years. It went undiagnosed. Then finally I was so ill they had to come up with something.'

He nodded quietly, staring with great concentration. I went on, quietly telling him the story of how it had all affected me.

'Oh, Martha, if only I had known,' he whispered. 'How you must have suffered! You are so powerful, darling! You have iron running through your veins,' he said, pulling me to him and stroking my hair. 'I was away for so long . . .' he said, not continuing what he wanted to say.

'Did you ever think about me, Ralph?' I whispered, looking up at him while my head rested back on his arm.

He stared at me, bringing his face very close, then let his eyes follow down to my lips.

'Yes, oh yes! It is as I told you. In fact, I asked myself so many times . . .'

'What, Ralph?' I said, seeing him stop what he was saying, then just stare at me, looking at my head resting on his arm.

He moved in, pulling my face close to him. 'I love you,' he breathed, barely above a whisper.

I could taste and feel his warm breath wafting in through my half-open mouth.

'You are so wonderful, darling, so extraordinary, you never cease to amaze me,' he smiled, shaking his head as he slowly searched my face, with his eyes looking so soft. 'Yes,' he whispered. 'I love you so very much,' he nodded, letting his eyes rest on my lips.

I stared back, leaving my mouth half-open, drinking him in, desperately loving him. I wanted to imprint every line, every facial movement of him, to have it all deeply etched in my memory. I wanted this moment, this time, to last for ever.

He suddenly bent in closer, dropping his face to let his lips rest on mine. I could feel the soft moistness and the warmth as a surge of heat and a tingling electricity started to roar up, locking our lips together. It was threatening to explode a raw passion, bursting it into life. But before it could even be born, he gently pulled his head back. Then he lifted his face, looking at me, and I could see it – the softness and the languid look in his eyes as they settled on mine. I knew he was letting me see his raw need and the desire not to stop. He wanted to take that pulsating raw passion all the way to the end. Just like he could see I was letting my deep longing for him show in my open face and my mouth slack with desire.

I sighed, saying, 'How much wine did I drink?'

'Enough for now, darling,' he laughed. 'Or would you have me carry you to the car, then take you home to bed?'

'Eh?' I said, getting the lovely picture of that.

He laughed, seeing me thinking, and said, 'But you will miss the best yet to come.'

'Oh! What's that?' I said, feeling my heart leap with excitement, wondering what could be better than this.

'Madame Bouclé's cordon bleu! She is a marvellous cook!' he laughed, seeing my face drop, knowing what I was thinking.

'Hmm! You are the boss, Ralph. I intend following your lead. So, lead on!' I said, breaking away from him to reach for a last cigarette.

He leaned over to take the bill just handed to him by the waiter who was wearing the dinner suit. I saw him whip out his wallet then stick some notes inside, saying, 'Yes, I think we should finish up the afternoon and perhaps steer the car for home. What would you think, Martha?'

'Yes,' I said, as the waiter suddenly reappeared, holding out my fur coat.

'Ready?' he said, waiting as I fixed my coat, then he took hold of my arm, leading me out the door, heading for the car.

I lay back in the seat, feeling warm and soft and relaxed as I looked over at Ralph. He stared back with a smile in his eyes, saying nothing.

'Thank you, Ralph, I really enjoyed this afternoon,' I whispered, seeing him getting ready to start the engine and drive off.

'Martha, the pleasure for me was in your charming company,' he said slowly, looking like he wanted to give me another kiss. But then he grinned and winked at me before starting the engine and driving off.

I took in a big sigh, wishing I could wrap my arms around him and just melt into him.

6

'More wine, Martha?' Ralph said, holding up the bottle as I smoked my cigarette.

'Yes, please,' I said, pushing over my glass.

'Let us take our drinks inside,' he said, looking back at the table covered in our dirty dishes from the evening meal.

'No, let us get the table cleared and the stuff put away first,' I said, walking back and landing my glass on the table.

'Oh, no, Martha! Please allow me to do that. I want you to rest, you need to build up your strength,' he laughed, looking at me giving him a dirty look.

'Ralph, I am not helpless. My health is well recovering, believe you me. Look at me, for God's sake!' I said, looking down at my silk frock that clung to all my lovely growing curves. Another one of Blondie's presents! Oh, it will be great to see her. Just wait until she hears all about me and Ralph!

'Look at me,' I said. 'Do I look undernourished to you?'

He stood staring at the length and breadth of me, letting his eyes rest on my curves. 'Hmm, you are filling out nicely,' he said, showing his dimples in a smile to break my heart with the longing in me for him. 'But, darling, you are still fragile, believe me. Listen to the voice of wisdom. I speak now as your doctor,' he said, wrapping his arms around my stomach as he came up behind me. 'I am not brooking any disobedience from you, my cherished one. Off with you, put up your feet and let me spoil you! Hmm?' he whispered, breathing into my ear and smelling my hair. 'You have glorious hair,' he said, letting his hands stroke it.

I turned around and wrapped my arms around his neck. 'Do you really love me, Ralph?'

He stared, saying nothing, then pulled me tighter into him. 'Yes, I do. I wish I could love you completely,' he said, letting his face lower, looking like his lips were going to touch mine.

'Do you want to kiss me?'

'Yes, that and a lot more, darling. I want to drown in you!'

'So, what do you mean, you wish you could love me more?'

'I am not free to do that.'

'Oh!' I sighed, letting out a huge sigh of resignation. Not wanting to draw him out. Knowing what the answer would be.

'Now go, please. I will join you shortly, as soon as I have cleared up this mess,' he said.

'OK,' I said, swooping down to pick up my drink and wafting out of the room in a cloud of smoke, puffing like mad to ease my frustration at not being able to draw him out into a real discussion on what he is planning on doing in the future. Then I turned back and said at the door, after thinking of something, 'Well, Ralph Fitzgerald. As my doctor, you are not supposed to be leading poor me, a helpless woman, a patient!' I sniffed, 'astray! I'm having you up before the medical council for disorderly conduct!' I snorted, then turned and sashayed out the door, wriggling my arse.

'What!' he roared. 'You little minx! Get back here and apologise at once!'

'Never!' I boomed, putting me head back in the door, then vanishing out, getting myself moving.

'I warn you, Martha! You know I do not take threats lightly,' he said, laughing as he made out the door after me.

'Oh, bleedin hell!' I laughed, looking for something to throw at him.

He came tearing in the door, saying, 'Martha! Where are you? Stand your ground and face me. I intend taking you to task for this outrageous impertinence!'

I flew out from behind the door, dumping my shoes behind me, and shot through the hall, making a breakneck dive for the stairs.

Immediately he was thundering up behind my heels. I screamed with the laugh, hauling meself up the stairs.

'Come back, you are only making it worse for yourself,' he warned.

'Don't be silly, you are too bloody old now, to catch a spring chicken like me,' I panted, thinking how I called him an old man once when he did the very same thing – chase me for all he was worth – back that awful, wonderful day all those years ago in the forest! My heart thumped and I felt eighteen again. All the feelings of joy and youth were coursing through my veins. Never again after that had I felt such joy.

'Oh, Ralph! You will never catch up with me,' I screamed, hauling myself onto the landing, making for the bathroom.

I was just in the door, sending it flying behind me, when he thudded into it, getting it slammed against him.

'Oh, rot!' he moaned, hesitating for a split second while I wondered if he was all right. Then the door flew open, sending me flying backwards to land on my arse! I tried to scramble to my feet, but he was too quick. He hauled me to my feet and grabbed me, carrying me kicking and screaming out the door.

'Come along! Take your punishment like a man,' he said, turning me across his arm, giving me a little tap, then pinning me against the landing wall with his body pushed up tight against me. Then he wrapped me in his arms and kissed me hard on the mouth, holding me tight and stroking my body. Then he pushed himself away and grinned up at me, panting like mad. My body was on fire with the electricity flying through me. I could see him shaking and his face was pale, with his eyes glittering for the want of me!

'Now, my sweet, cherished, divine woman. Tell that to the medical council!' he ordered. Then he hesitated, with his head going for the door, then looked at me again and decided to keep going straight out the door and down the stairs.

I stayed where I was, still in shock from what just happened. It was the unexpected, the suddenness of it all! I marvelled, feeling me chest heave up and down, while my heart went like the clappers, with me still trying to catch my breath.

Later on, I lay on the sofa listening to Ralph talk about his work in the Congo.

'Oh, the mission was hundreds of miles deep into the jungle. It took hours to get to the nearest civilisation,' he said. 'Goodness, I remember some chaps and I had to take a trip across tracks which had dried out in muddy hard concrete hills, and we were travelling in a dreadfully uncomfortable Land Rover that had no suspension. We were bounced like rubber balls all over the place. My head kept hitting the ceiling. And our driver was a lunatic! Quite bloody mad. He insisted on taking every turn and hill at full throttle. Making us roar like gibbering fools as we clutched on to our seats,' he laughed, roaring like a maniac. 'I wanted to knock his bloody block off,' Ralph said, still getting the picture as his jaw tightened and he took in a deep slow breath, obviously not forgiving or forgetting.

Gawd, he can be quite fierce, I thought, seeing that side of him. But he is too much of a gentleman to ever lose control. I love him for his kindness and his strength, and his dedication and commitment to something he sets his heart on. I love him for so many things. I loved him once as a father, a mother a brother. Then it changed as I grew. I wanted all of him for myself. Body and soul.

I watched him sip his wine as he sat looking very thoughtful, lost in his memories. 'We did indeed have to do a lot of travelling from one medical mission to another. Some were so remote it took days of travel through some very hostile terrain just to reach them.'

'What did you do, Ralph, in the mission hospitals?'

'Oh, ask more what we did not do. We had a hospital set up for leprosy.'

'Lepers?' I screeched.

'Yes, of course. You will find it in Africa,' he said, looking at me, astonished by my ignorance.

'How many of you were there, Ralph?'

'Oh, I was the only missionary priest doctor. There were quite a few native medically trained staff. Nurses mostly, and, of course, we had people from abroad. Our German doctor, Helmut, he was very competent. Quite a likeable chap. We got on very well. We also had two Irish nurses. One from Northern Ireland and the other from south of the border. Eileen! She was a ticket! I enjoyed her immensely,' he laughed. 'The mothers and children loved her. She was awfully good with them. Quite the polyglot, too, she was. She could speak six of the native dialects. We would bellow for her when someone came in from the bush with a strange dialect.'

I listened, watching his face change and light up with the mention of 'Eileen', the bleedin polyglot!

'The nearest priest was actually two hundred miles away, driving through treacherous terrain. I would drive there perhaps one a year, just to check up on him, see how things were going. We also had an order of nuns, two of them in fact, both doctors with whom I also helped out.

'Geraldine was an astonishing woman,' he said. 'She ran a very fine hospital. Mostly we dealt with tropical diseases. It was dreadful when a plague broke out. Then it would spread like wildfire. We would expect to work and travel for weeks on end, feeling lucky to grab a bit of shut-eye, two hours over a period of days on the trot,' he said, sighing.

'So, what brought you home, Ralph?'

'Oh, the workload, the climate – it wears you down and eventually you become burnt-out! Most of the overseas workers stay no more than a few years. Then one must simply take a break. I stayed sixteen years, then . . . No more! I upped sticks and came home. One becomes less than useless when the challenge is no longer there. So, here we are, my darling. Now we have turned full circle. You are here with me, and I am once again reunited with you. How wonderful and glorious that is,' he said, coming over and pulling me to my feet. 'I wonder how it is I ever managed without you. Goodness, I thought I was delirious when you turned up at my door,' he said, throwing his head back and roaring laughing. 'I must say, you are improving with each day,' he said, holding my shoulders back to look at me. Then he sighed and pulled me in to him. 'Come, let us go to the kitchen and get something to drink. What would you like? Tea coffee wine, hot chocolate, or . . . Your wish is my command. I just want you with me for company,' he said, taking my hand and dragging me off behind him.

'What do you mean, Ralph, when you say, "managed without me"?'

'What?' he said, staring into the fridge, looking to see where the milk was.

'It's at the side, bottom shelf,' I said, making a grab for it.

'Oh,' he said, now just hearing what I asked him. 'I mean, darling, you have grown on me so quickly. I find it lonely when you are not by my side. Oh, I know you are in the house, but it is as if something is missing. Like I feel hollow, empty in the silence without your presence close to me.'

'Really?' I said, wondering if that was important. Would it make him come to a decision about us? But I dare not bring that up. If he had something to tell me, there is no better man to do it. So I kept quiet, saying nothing.

'Yes, darling, really!' he laughed, suddenly lunging for me and lifting me off my feet, swinging me around, holding on close to me.

I screamed, feeling myself going around with him, terrified I would fly out of his arms. Jesus, I just had a feeling of déjà vu!

'What was it?' he said, putting me back on my feet and holding me until I got steadied.

'Being thrown at the ceiling and flying through the air, then feeling pain,' I half-laughed. 'Getting fractured pictures of it and sensations of fear and terror and the suddenness of it.'

'So, it appears you were thrown but not caught,' he said, looking at me very carefully.

I stayed still, holding on to that vague memory. 'Yes, Jesus, I must have been only a baby. Because I know I can remember back as far as being around fifteen months old!'

'Good God! You can remember that far back?' he said, half-smiling at me, looking amazed.

'Yes, I was standing in a cot and my mother appeared. I was barely walking at the time. She came to claim me back from a home for adoptive babies. I was up for adoption.'

'How do you know all this?'

'Well, she used to go on about the fact I was nearly adopted from a home in Dublin. I knew the place she was talking about. It was run by nuns. And I remember her taking me home. In fact, I remember her wheeling me there in a go-car with my legs sticking out between the cloth over the bar in the middle. I remember she used to put up the footrest when I was sleeping! Oh, I remember every incident of that particular time. The room, the cots, the nurse at the desk in the middle of the room. I remember my mother was wearing red lipstick. She put out her arms when I woke up suddenly, seeing her standing at the end of the cot. Yes, she was smiling at me,' I said, wondering where I was getting all this from. It was all suddenly coming back to me.

'Just because you swung me around, Ralph!' I said, looking at him, seeing him staring at me, listening very intently. I shook my head in amazement. Not able to get over the fact I could remember that from all those many years ago.

'Yes,' he said slowly and quietly, putting his arms around me and stroking my hair. 'It would appear you are getting flashbacks, darling. That one was triggered indeed by me,' he said, sounding very worried. 'Come, darling. Would you like me to make you some delicious hot chocolate? I'm awfully good at making that stuff,' he whispered to me, leading me to the table and sitting me down.

'Yes, that sounds great,' I said, feeling myself begin to lift out of that time, that memory. 'It wasn't unpleasant, you know, Ralph. That particular time, with my mother. I don't think so anyway! It was, in fact, a happy memory. Because I think I was pining for her. I know I wouldn't let go of her skirt after she picked me up and then set me standing on the floor beside her. I know I was terribly anxious then, all right. But it worked out. I remember she asked the nurse for clothes for me. She said she was taking me home. The nurse told her she would have to check with the nun in charge. I remember watching her disappear down a little passage. I understood my mother was anxious, too. I could feel it.'

Ralph sighed, then appeared over beside me with a mug of hot chocolate and a coffee for himself. 'Yes, darling, it would seem your past may now be coming to the fore. All the bad memories that have lain hidden are coming back at you. In a way, darling, it is a good thing. It proves you are growing stronger. This is clearly related to your difficulty when you hit rock bottom, as you said. Now your emotions are trying to heal. This could continue for many years to come. It depends on how much damage has been done to you,' he said, suddenly sniffing.

I looked up to see him turn away and rush to the trough, looking out into the lawns.

'What's wrong, Ralph?'

'Nothing, darling, just give me a minute, please, to collect myself,' he said, holding on to the big old stone sink.

He's upset by what I just told him, I thought, feeling upset myself now. I had done that. Spoilt everything by talking about the untalkable! I had never done that before. Never even thought about it, never mind talked about it.

'I'm sorry,' I muttered, getting up to walk out and find me cigarettes.

'No! Stop! Where are you going?' he said. 'Darling, please! I'm sorry! I'm not deliberately being insensitive.'

'What?' I said, looking over at him rushing to come to me. 'No, no, I'm just going to look for my tobacco, Ralph, but I'm sorry I upset you, talking about rubbish. It's long dead, for God's sake. I'm really sorry. I don't know what came over me.'

'No, please, darling,' he said, grabbing me to him. 'I wanted to spare you my tears,' he whispered. 'I am an old-fashioned gentleman. They do not show tears in public. I am sorry, darling. The apology is all mine. It is like a sharp knife cutting through me, to see how brutally you have been abused,' he said, kissing the top of my head and trying to suffocate me inside his arms.

God, if only you knew, Ralph, if only you knew. They were actually the good years! I thought, getting pictures of dark images of the Jackser times, as blurred images and feelings started flying at me, bringing a feeling of walking through endless nights of cold and hunger and exhaustion. I shook my head, trying to blink them away and replace them with happier pictures. I am here now with Ralph, I am wrapped in his arms. I am very content and happy. I have no worries.

'I need a cigarette, Ralph,' I whispered, taking a big sigh and opening my eyes, seeing him smiling at me.

'Darling, you are so precious to me. I love you very much,' he said, giving me a tight hug then releasing me.

'I love you too, Ralph. You are the only man I have ever loved,' I said, reaching up and planting a kiss on his lips. Then I walked out to collect my cigarettes, wondering where I left them. I haven't smoked for ages, I just forgot about them. Jaysus, things are looking up, I might just be able to give them up yet! I thought, seeing Ralph come into the sitting room, then walk across to switch on a music centre sitting buried beside a big press in the corner. A song came wafting into the room sounding lonely and haunting. It was the memorable voice of Edith Piaf.

'Ah, one of my favourite singers,' I said. 'The great Edith Piaf, "the Little Sparrow" as she was known by all of France.'

'Yes, she was much loved,' he said nodding. 'Unfortunately, her battered body was diseased and wasting from—'

I interrupted, saying, 'Too much hard living, too many lovers breaking her heart, and too much neglect as a child.'

He bowed his head, agreeing with me solemnly. 'Indeed, quite right,' he muttered.

'Still, she went out with a bang,' I said, thinking, if I was on my last legs, I would like to be doing the ton down a long, lonely motorway. Then with full throttle let rip and go out with a bang. My last thought would probably be, Jaysus! That was lovely! Or, the other extreme, die in me sleep! But both fast. I don't want to know about it. No lingering for me.

We listened to the music softly filling the room as she sang, '*Non, je ne regrette rien!*'

'Do you have any regrets so far, Ralph?' I said, looking over at him stretched out on his favourite sofa.

'I'm not sure,' he said. 'Would I do things differently? I have thought that if I were not a priest then I would surely not have met you. So I do not regret that, if it was for only that reason,' he said, giving me a gorgeous smile, lighting up his face, then staring at me knowingly, looking up and down the length of me with longing in his eyes.

My heart turned over, missing a beat. I wanted to run to him and throw myself on top of him, getting lost and smothered inside him, but I stayed rooted in my place. Then he lowered his head, examining his fingernails and thinking.

'Oh, you were going to ask me something as I came in. What was that?' he said, looking up at me with his head cocked.

'I was? Don't remember! Oh, yes, I do! Listen, Ralph,' I said, taking in a deep breath.

'Uh-oh! This sounds ominous!' he muttered, giving a little laugh.

'Well, you did ask what I was going to say. I wanted to ask you a question!'

'Yes, do go on,' he said, curious to hear what I wanted to know.

'Did you ever fall for anyone while you were working abroad? I mean, this Irish nurse, what's her name?'

'Eileen,' he said, grinning. 'Ah-ha! I knew perhaps that may come up. I did note your reaction, darling. The little green god was at work in you.'

'Well!' I snorted. 'It doesn't matter to me now. I mean, whatever

happened, happened! So I am sure it's not happening now. Because
I'm here! But I am still curious. It tells me more about you than
about her. I want to know about you, Ralph!'

'Oh, do you mean I should start making a clean breast of all my
foibles and—'

'Yes! No! I just want to know, did you and your woman get close?
Were you fond of her?'

'Of course I was. We were colleagues! Working together.'

'Oh, so you were involved with her on an emotional level?'

'No, Martha, not emotional, of course not. I do not mix my personal
life with my professional life. It would have made life very difficult
for everyone.'

'So you made a decision, then, to keep your paws off her, is that it?'

'No, of course not. I was not in the slightest attracted to the girl. She
was terribly good fun to be around. An extremely competent nurse,
very dedicated. But, no, no romance, darling. Sorry to disappoint you!'

'Oh, what about the nun then?'

'Oh, darling, you should take to the law, you would be awfully good
at it,' he laughed, roaring his head off with the laughing.

'Well?' I said. 'You didn't answer me!'

'Answer you about what?' he said, looking puzzled.

'About bloody Geraldine, the nun, the doctor?'

'Oh, you do remember *her* name!'

'Yes! So come on, surely you were not living like a bleedin hermit!'

'Of course I was not!' he snorted.

'You weren't?' I said, getting a fright and feeling annoyed all at the
same time. Immediately getting a picture of him and the nun with
the rustle of habits and all that hot weather!

'So, what happened?'

'About what, darling?'

'Oh, Ralph, you are pretending to be pure stupid just to annoy me!'
I shouted, losing the rag.

'Darling, I really do not have the slightest idea what you are
prattling about!' he snorted, getting annoyed himself.

'How dare you? So, is that what you think I am doing, prattling?'

'No,' he said slowly, looking at me, wondering how this all started
and got out of control so quickly.

so just shook my head, concentrating on getting the last cough, to take me first gasp.

'*Qu'avez-vous?*' she said, coming over to stand in front of me as I sat myself down in a heap on the chair.

'*Ohh! Je ne me sens pas bien!*' I groaned, wanting a hot drink. '*Madame . . .*' I was about to ask her for tea when the coughing and spluttering started again. Oh, where the fuck is Ralph? He can get me one. I'm not in the mood for messing.

She turned away and went straight for the boiling kettle on the stove and made me a hot tea with honey and fresh lemon, then put it down beside me.

I sipped the hot tea, feeling it slide down, easing my raw throat. Then I heard him coming just as the door opened. I looked up just as he was saying, 'Good morning, darling!' Then watched as his face dropped, taking me in.

The humiliation hit me. I hate to be a nuisance. It embarrasses me. I feel under obligation and just hate the tension. I wish now I had gone home last week. But Ralph suggested I stay on longer, besides, I need the rest, he said. 'Let me take care of you. I want to spoil you.' I was only too happy to agree. Now look at the fucking state of me. I'm just letting myself down as usual. I wanted to burst into tears because I couldn't cope. There was no way to escape this. I lowered my head as his voice faded away. Then he was putting his hand on my forehead, saying, 'You look dreadful, darling, quite the colour of parchment. Good God, you are burning with fever,' he muttered, lowering his voice to talk to himself. 'How do you feel? Are you aching all over?'

I shook me head agreeing, not knowing if I was or not, the pain was all in my back and it kills me when I cough.

Then I started a fit of coughing again, not able to get a breath with the pain. I lifted my head, gasping, feeling I'll never get another breath. I heard him say, 'Yes, I think you may have a chest infection, darling.' Then he turned to Madame Bouclé, who was standing listening and looking at me. I knew she was wondering how she could help.

'Oh, I'm sorry to do this to you, Ralph,' I said, not looking at him, feeling foolish I was making such a fuss.

'Darling, please . . . Do not say these things,' he muttered, letting his voice fade away as Madame dropped what she was doing and wiped her hands, leaving the room.

'We must get you back upstairs at once, darling. I need to examine you before I can prescribe something. You will need an antibiotic. What did she give you? Here! Drink this, darling,' he said, lifting the mug and putting it to my mouth.

I held on to it, and he sat down, pulling the chair over beside me. Then he rested his arm gently around my shoulders, leaving his other hand to rest on my knees, saying nothing. He just looked at me and sat thinking, looking worried. I said nothing, feeling too shaky and shivery and weak. Not wanting to make things worse for myself by making my presence felt.

I put the mug down and he took my hands and held them together in his own, saying quietly, 'Madame is gone to prepare your room. She will make up a fresh bed for you. Then we need to get you out of these clothes,' he said, feeling the hot, wet pyjamas steaming off me. 'Come on, darling,' he said, getting me standing on my feet. 'Let us get you back to your room,' he said, leading me out the door as Madame came down the stairs, saying something in French. He nodded at her, replying in French and thanking her. Then she headed to the kitchen and Ralph led me up the stairs. Then he suddenly stopped and lifted me in his arms, saying, 'Come, darling, I will carry you.' Then he bent down and swooped his hand under me, lifting me in his arms and taking me up the stairs with the greatest of ease. I let my arm hang around his neck, glad I was off my feet and heading back for my bed.

'Here we are,' he said, opening the door and carrying me straight over to the bed. I could see it was made up with lovely crisp white-linen sheets and embroidered pillowcases to match. The bedclothes were folded back ready for me to lie in.

He put me sitting at the end of the bed and took off my dressing gown. But it was his, really. Then he said, 'I will get you a fresh pair,' heading over to the wardrobe. He took out a pair of cotton pyjamas I hardly wore but had brought anyway just in case I might need them. 'Now, darling, strip off your things and sponge yourself quickly. Then give yourself a good rub down with the towel. I will go and get my medical bag. Do you need any help?'

'No,' I shook me head, just wanting to get back into the bed. I dropped the flannel into the hot water in the big washbowl and drenched my face. Then I wrung out the cloth and wiped down my neck and arms, squeezing and washing. Oh, I feel dizzy and cold, and it hurts like mad trying to take a breath. Now I feel like getting sick. Oh, let me get out of this. I just want to get back into the bed, I shivered, dumping the cloth in the water and lifting the big white bath towel, wrapping it around me.

I took up the hand towel and started to dry my face and arms. Ralph knocked and came into the room, seeing me shivering as I tried to dry myself with the towel wrapped around me.

'Darling, come quickly! We must get you into bed,' he said, rushing over to drop his brown Gladstone bag, leaving it sitting next to the big, old heavy press pushed in against the far wall. Then he lifted me off my feet and set me sitting on the end of the bed again and started rubbing my back and arms with the towel. A red-hot pain went through my back and chest, cutting me like a sharp knife. I moaned, trying to push him away.

'Oh, Martha! Do you have pain? Is it in your back?'

I nodded.

'Do you feel it in your chest?'

I nodded again.

'Does it hurt to breathe?'

'Yes,' I gasped.

He threw down the towel and pulled the fresh pyjama top over my head. 'Now, my sweet, into bed quickly,' he said, lifting me up and putting me lying on the pillows.

I sat up coughing and he turned to look at me before opening his bag and taking out his stethoscope. He listened to my chest, putting it inside the top with the four buttons opened at the front. Then he pulled up my pyjamas at the back, examining my lungs.

'Breathe gently, darling, it will ease the pain,' he said, listening.

I started to cough, then he tapped my lungs.

'I hear some crackling, darling,' he murmured, shaking his head and looking very worried. 'Perhaps we should get you to hospital?'

'No, no,' I barked, coughing and shaking my head.

'Yes, OK, it was a suggestion, darling, that is all. But I do think hospital may be the best place right now. They will be better equipped to take care of you, darling. They have all that is necessary to bring you back to health, my love! That is why I am suggesting it. No?'

I shook my head.

'OK,' he sighed. 'Now let me take your blood pressure, darling. I won't take long. I know this is distressing for you,' he said, looking very worried as he pulled the strap off my arm. Then he lifted my wrist to check my pulse. 'OK,' he said, standing up and wrapping the bedclothes over me, covering me up and settling them around me. 'You get some rest. I will tell Madame to come and sit with you while I take a prescription down to the pharmacy. I will not be long, darling. You try to sleep.' Then he went over and drew the curtains together, blocking out the light, leaving the room in a golden glow of dimmed darkness.

I snuggled my head, letting it sink into the pillow without moving myself, then lay on the side that was hurting me, and it eased the pain. I feel so weak and exhausted, but I'm a bit more peaceful now. The crisp clean sheets and the warm gown against my dry skin made me feel a little easier in myself. Within seconds, I felt myself sinking off into a deep sleep.

I woke up to hear Ralph's voice as he sat down beside me on the bed, shifting the mattress with his weight. 'Darling, open your mouth and take this pill.' Then he held a glass of water to my mouth. 'Now, I want you to drink this,' he whispered, holding the back of my head as he put a glass of brown, sweet syrupy stuff to my lips. 'Drink it all, Martha, It will ease your coughing.' Then he stood up after lowering my head to the pillows, taking up the glass and little measuring medicine cup, and switched off the light. 'Do go back to sleep, my love,' he whispered, closing the door quietly behind him.

'Martha, darling! Are you awake?'

I opened my eyes to see Ralph looking down at me. He was sitting on the side of my bed, gently stroking my face.

'Sweetheart! Here, let me put this in your mouth. I want to check your temperature,' he said, sticking a thermometer in my mouth. Then he lifted my wrist, checking my pulse as he stared at a silver watch that was hanging out of his pocket on a chain.

He just kept staring, saying nothing. My eyes wandered to the bedside lamp, seeing it glow a dark orange around me. The rest of the room was left in dark shadows. It must be night, I thought, feeling so very tired and weak.

'You have been coughing up a little blood,' he said, checking the Styrofoam cup sitting at the bedside table. He left that there so I could cough up anything coming from my lungs.

I didn't bother to ask about the blood. I was too tired, and just closed my eyes. I felt him pulling up my sleeve and opened my eyes, seeing he was checking my blood pressure. Then he lifted his stethoscope from the night table and wrapped it around his neck, saying, 'I am sorry, darling, but I must get you sitting up,' he said, throwing off the bedclothes.

He lifted me up, sliding me down a bit to make room for himself. Then he sat behind me and pulled up my pyjama top, listening to my breathing. He took in a slow, deep breath, saying nothing, then took the stethoscope out of his ears and eased me back on the pillows, covering me up.

'Darling,' he whispered, sitting on the side of the bed, stroking my hair and face. I opened my eyes, barely able to keep them open, struggling to look at him. He stared at me for a second, getting ready to say something. I held my breath, waiting. It eased the pain in my back and lungs.

'I would like you to have an X-ray. I can wrap you up warmly and take you there myself. We can have it done immediately. I will telephone the hospital and tell them I am taking you in. It will not take long, then I can take care of you myself. But I do need to see that X-ray, darling. We need to know what we are dealing with. You have pleurisy, my love, but it would be good to know the underlying cause. But of course that would mean taking tests,' he sighed, thinking about it.

I shook my head, feeling myself panic. I don't give a fuck about any pleurisy. I've had pneumonia a few times, I thought. To hell with it. I just want to be left alone. If he takes me there and they end up wanting to keep me in, then it will just make things complicated. Everything will change. He will see me as a complication in his life. A nuisance guest now turned out to be a patient in the hospital.

No, fuck them and their tests! And their messing! I just want to stay here, or I wish I was at home in my own bed with no one to bother me, and me not being a bother to anyone. I hate it when people wander into my life, taking over. Deciding what's best for me, when I'm nothing but a job for them and it makes them feel self-important having that power over me. That's what will happen if the hospital get their hands on me. I knows he cares, but if I make problems, then it will isolate us. He will withdraw from me. Just like he did that first time. It doesn't make a difference what the problem was then, the bottom line for me was that he could walk away from me because I was just a passing interlude in his life. Someone he could leave behind. It will happen all over again. No! Not this fucking time. I will not put myself into his hands, or any hospital he wants to drag in. Curse it, I will stay here, get better. Or bleedin drag myself home under my own steam. I'm in charge! So he can like it or bleedin lump it.

Then I felt myself raging because I couldn't be normal. I can't fucking get up and be on me feet. My good-for-nothing lungs are fucked from all my smoking. I did it to myself. Ohhhh! I just want to be on my feet. He's going to see me differently now. He won't want me any more because I come with nothing but trouble! I felt myself so tired, and there's nothing I can do about it. I started to heave with the sobs and the crying, feeling the rage at my helplessness. Why did it all have to end so suddenly? I was so happy. Now I'm just a fool he can't wait to get rid of. The tears and snots started rolling down me face and I didn't care any more, I just want to be left alone. I don't want to be with someone I love more than life itself and have them act like a stranger. Someone cold and distant.

I gasped, not able to get a breath with the sobs trying to escape out of me. I lifted my head, trying to get my hand under me, and the bleedin pain knifed through me!

'Darling! Take it easy. Don't get distressed,' he commanded in a whisper, suddenly moving and grabbing me to a sitting position, with his palm holding my chest, supporting me while he stroked my back, murmuring, 'Breathe out slowly, darling. Come on, breathe, ease it out, let go, you are doing fine. Don't be frightened now. I am here with you, my darling.'

I caught a breath, trying to grab hold and let it out on a searing pain, then my lungs jerked in and out, getting ready to let me breathe.

I held myself, concentrating on letting go. All the time hearing his voice whispering softly and feeling him holding me against him while he stroked my back very gently.

I started to breathe, feeling the sharp pain with every breath, but at least I wasn't suffocating. I slumped back into his chest and he pulled himself further into the bed then rested himself against the headboard and held me lying against him, stroking me.

'There, darling, hush, we will say no more. I will look after you, my sweet one. You just feel secure in my love for you,' he murmured gently, whispering so softly while he held me against him, all the time stroking me.

I let out a big sigh, feeling all the air and the tension sink out of me. I let my head sink into the warmth and safety of his chest, while the rest of me sank into his stomach, giving me a wonderful sense of peace and being loved and protected. Then I felt my eyes growing tired, knowing it was safe to sleep. Nothing bad would happen to me.

I sat with the tray on my lap, letting the legs sit each side of me, and sipped on the chicken soup then nibbled on a bit of home-made bread. I smiled at Madame Bouclé, who was standing and watching me with her hand over her mouth and her elbow resting in her other hand.

I put the spoon down, feeling I had eaten enough. My mouth felt like straw and I couldn't taste the food. I had no appetite. '*Merci!*' I whispered, waiting for her to take the tray and let me slide down and lie on my left side, where the pain eased.

'*Bon!*' she said, looking at what I had left. '*La poitrine!*' she said, pointing at her chest, looking concerned.

'*Oui!*' I muttered, then closed my eyes, slipping down in the bed and inching myself onto my side, feeling the pain ease. Then I was dozing off into a deep sleep.

8

I was sitting up, sprawled against a huge mound of pillows, feeling like Cleopatra as I chewed away on a box of chocolates, wondering which one to guzzle next. I let my fingers walk around in the air, hovering as I decided where to land next. I picked up a toffee one, seeing that's what the picture says, then changed my mind with the mouth still open and decided at the last minute to give it to Ralph.

'Open your mouth,' I said, lifting my head and looking up at him. I was lying with the box on his stomach, while he lay on top of the bed with his back resting against the headboard and his arm wrapped around me. He was reading *Madame Bovary* aloud to me while I contented myself making short work of the delicious handmade chocolates.

He stopped reading and looked at the chocolate making its way towards him, then opened his mouth. I shoved it in, gasping, 'Oh, these chocolates are delicious. It must be love, Ralph, or there is no way I would even share one, never mind let you have four!'

'Three!' he said. 'You let me have three.'

'Are you sure?' I said, looking down at the box, trying to think.

'Naughty sausage,' he grinned, planting a kiss on my nose, then saying, 'It must be love or I golly well would not have given them to you!'

'Oh,' I sighed, 'love is a marvellous thing. We could gauge it by the extent on how much we share,' I gasped, shoving another chocolate into my mouth on top of the one not even getting a chance to finish.

'Steady on!' he laughed, pulling away the book to look down at the near-empty box. 'You will be sick!' he said. 'I did not intend for you to polish off the lot in one sitting!' he said slowly, lifting his head to stare at me with a half-grin on his face, the other half looking a bit annoyed.

'Why not, Ralph? I have starved long enough!'

'Yes, but I think I made a mistake with those,' he said. 'It is wonderful to see your appetite returned, but, goodness, you are not quite out of the woods yet!'

'Whadaye mean? You were the one said I needed fattening up!' I snorted, raging he thought I was being a glutton.

'Uh-oh! Are we going to have a sulk?' he said, throwing down the book and turning around to wrap himself round me.

'No! Of course not! But I was enjoying those,' I whined, feeling sorry they were nearly gone now. Then I lit into him. 'I think it's bloody mean to give them to me then take the goodness out of it by complaining when I eat the bleedin things!' I snorted, turning away to look at the wallpaper and have a sulk.

'Oh, darling, I am sorry,' he laughed, lifting himself back to find the chocolates. 'Here, come on, eat away,' he said. 'They will do you good,' he laughed. 'Or at least they will do me good,' he said, shoving one in his mouth then trying to put one in my mouth.

I turned away, feeling hard done by. 'No, eat the bloody things yourself. Pity I ate the lot, otherwise I could have belted them back at you,' I sniffed, still feeling raging, because I knew I made a show of meself, dipping in and out of the box until the lot were nearly gone. 'And what do you mean, they will do you good? Oh, so it's OK for you to do what you like, my lord and master. But your aul chocolates are too good for me! Is that it?'

He stared at me, then threw back his head, roaring laughing. 'Oh, you are so funny, Martha!' he roared. 'I meant the bloody chocolates would keep you quiet if you were to eat them. Not have you go off on a tirade at me. So, yes, it would be good for me,' he said quietly, making a grab and squeezing the life out of me, then burying his head in me, making quick, noisy little kisses on my face and neck, whispering, 'If you don't behave, darling, then I shall eat you bloody up. I fancy something tasty, soaked in chocolate!' he said, lifting his face to look at me, with his eyes dancing alive in his head.

'Oh, I do love you,' I mewled, sounding like a cat as I snuggled myself into him. Then we went quiet, with him running his hands around my lower back and landing them on my leg, then up again with a big sigh.

Then he closed his eyes saying, 'I do feel lazy, let us take a nap, darling.'

'Yeah,' I muttered. 'It will be the first time we have slept together.'

'Hmm! Not quite, darling. You are under the bedclothes. I am out in the cold.'

'What cold? The room is blasting with heat.'

'Shush!' he said, resting his face on the side of my head. 'Try and get some rest, darling. I don't want you over-exerting yourself.'

'*Merci beaucoup, Madame,*' I said, seeing her take off out of the room with the shining dishes. 'Ah, that was just gorgeous,' I muttered, smacking my lips as I slid down in the bed, thinking, Gawd! She is a marvellous woman, just marvellous! I sighed, still relishing the taste of that delicious lunch. A fabulous bowl of creamy asparagus soup with hot rolls and butter. Then a lovely fluffy mushroom omelette and fresh fruit cut up in a bowl with vanilla ice cream. I think she definitely made that, too. Lovely, I thought, as I slid happily down in the bed for an afternoon snooze.

Wonder where Ralph is? I only saw him before breakfast, then he disappeared! Hmm! It's lonely without him, I thought, feeling me heart want to sink. Ah, he'll turn up later. Funny, but the house seems quiet. Like I can't sense his presence, big and all as the place is. He must be gone out, I thought, just as I started to doze off.

I woke up, seeing the day was nearly gone. The trees that were being blown about by the wind outside were throwing shadows against the far wall. I sat up and switched on the bedside light, and the room warmed up in a lovely orange glow. I sighed with contentment, feeling lovely and rested, then peeled my eyes to the wardrobe. Ralph had gotten Madame to wash all my clothes. All my good blouses, skirts, frocks and trousers were sent out to the cleaners. Then they were all put away, left hanging in covers in the wardrobe. I had watched her put away all my night things and underwear, beautifully pressed and looking like new. They were all sitting now in the lovely mahogany shelves inside the big rosewood press. Then my eyes lit on gold and blue shopping bags with rope handles sitting next to the alcove beside the wardrobe. I stared for a minute, wondering where they came from. How did they get there? I wonder if they're for me?

I threw back the bedclothes and swung my legs out, feeling how weak they were. But, Gawd, am I not a million times better than I was a couple of weeks ago? I made my way over and lifted one of the bags. I looked in, seeing lovely night things with what looks like a dressing gown.

I picked up the bags and walked back to the bed, dying to see. 'Ohh! This is lovely,' I gasped, lifting out the dark-green dressing gown with two pockets and a belt. It was so soft and made of pure wool. I put it down and went through the bags. A cream pair of silk pyjamas, a pair of fur-lined, slip-on leather slippers. A gorgeous pale-blue silk blouse, and a long, heavy royal-blue skirt. Then I lifted out a beautiful pale-yellow cashmere polo-neck jumper, with a heavy pure-wool wine jacket for outdoors. 'Oh, these are gorgeous,' I muttered, with me eyes on stalks as I fitted them up to myself one by one.

That's it, the lot! Then my eyes lit on the little box. I lifted out a lovely big bottle of Christian Dior perfume. God almighty, he must have bought these for me and left them when I was sleeping. I tried to take that in, not able to get over it. Me heart was leppin with excitement. Oh, he was thinking about me. He must really care about me! Maybe that's where he was today when he went missing. Ahh! I wish I could do something for him! He is so very, very good to me. I felt like crying with his goodness. Oh, Ralph, if only you knew how much I love you. I would give the world just to be with you always, I thought.

Right, have a bath and put on your new stuff. Wait, better not get dressed. It will only upset him. I'm hardly out of the bed that long. Never mind, I can put on the new pyjamas and dressing gown. Good idea, and I'll wash my hair while I'm at it. Jaysus, you could fry sausages on this hair, the grease is that thick.

I had just plaited my hair and wrapped it at the back of my head, securing it with a big gold slide, when I heard a noise on the stairs. I gave myself a dash of perfume and looked in the mirror, seeing how I looked. Ah, lovely, I thought, smiling at the sight of myself standing in the silk pyjamas with the belt hanging down behind my gorgeous new dressing gown. I won't fasten it, because I want to show off the pyjamas. Then I looked down at my feet, admiring the new slippers. Yeah, they're lovely and warm, making me feet feel nice and cosy. Right, you're looking grand now, Martha, nice and fresh and squeaky clean. Pity about the skinny look, though! Yeah, me curves are all gone, and now I'm looking all washed out, a bit too pale for my liking. Never mind. Sure, that's nothing a bit of fresh air won't solve.

Jaysus, I feel like a cigarette now! Ralph will kill me. Kill me stone dead! Fuck! I'm an addict! Now, where's me bag? Oh, happy days! Life's a bowl a cherries!

I made my way down the stairs and into the kitchen. '*Bonjour, Madame Bouclé!*' I said, making a sudden appearance, giving her the fright of her life.

'*Oh! Sacré bleu!*' she puffed, then panted with her hand on her chest.

I grinned at her, seeing her face light up with a smile. She was speaking away in rapid French. I hadn't a clue what she was saying. But I kept shaking my head and smiling, saying, '*Oui, oui! Oh! Oui, oui!*' Then for a change, I dropped me face and hesitated with a shake of my head saying, '*Ah, eh, non! Non!*'

'*NON?*' she screeched. Then the door flew open and Ralph stood there trying to take in first me then her standing there looking shocked. She babbled to him, then he spoke to her in French, then the pair of them looked at me.

'Martha! Why are you out of your bed?'

'What? Why not?' I said, looking puzzled.

'Madame is upset. She asked you how you felt and if you were much improved. You said no. But of course I told her you are recovering quite well. What is wrong? Are you feeling unwell?'

'No! I never felt better,' I said, trying to digest how this bleedin trouble flared up so suddenly. He started speaking to her in French again, then she looked at me, putting her hand on her chest, giving a half-laugh and cry at the same time, much as to say, 'I do not understand these foreigners and their ways!'

'Martha, you look nice,' he said, putting his arm around me and kissing me on the cheek. Then he pulled away, letting the light go out of his eyes, saying, 'You have been smoking! Martha, I am not impressed,' he said sadly, shaking his head.

'No, nor me either. I'm sorry, Ralph, but I'm a bloody addict. I have been on them too long,' I said, thinking I have left me smokes upstairs and I better go and get them. I can see Ralph is disappointed. I had been off them until now, but I have to have something to keep me going. Then I said, 'Ralph! God knows I don't drink much, I don't manhunt, I might as well be a bloody Carmelite nun!' I said, as I made my way out the door, raging with myself for letting him down and most of all myself.

I headed up the stairs and into my room, making straight for my bag and the smokes. I sat down in the low armchair close to the window and looked out at the lawns sweeping into the distance. The nearest house was miles away. I could see a puff of smoke wafting up through the trees on Ralph's lawn. It was coming from a field close to a house that looked miles away. This place is so magnificent, I thought, staring out at the beautiful greenery. Then I sighed, thinking Ralph is very annoyed with me. Rightly bloody so, smoking is a killer. But it is a vice I cling to. I felt my heart down in my chest at the coldness I had created. But there's nothing I can do about it. Kill me or not, I'm in no hurry to give them up.

I better move and see the lie of the land with Ralph. He's leaving me to stew! I thought, seeing it was nearly completely dark. I had only the little bedside lamp burning. The rest of the room felt cold without the light but it's actually very warm. No, it's the coldness in me without Ralph, I thought, wanting to go and find him.

I stirred myself, feeling a bit tired, and picked up my tobacco and lighter, putting them in my pocket as I made for the door. I came down the stairs and stood outside the kitchen. Maybe he might be in the sitting room, I thought, not wanting to have any more say to Madame Bouclé. I was in enough trouble with her after annoying her.

I opened the sitting-room door and looked around, seeing Ralph sitting on his favourite sofa, leaning himself against the backrest, reading the newspaper. He looked up, keeping the paper in front of him, and just stared.

'Hello,' I whispered. 'I'm terribly sorry I have upset you, Ralph. Can you not try to understand? I know the risks,' I said, making my way over to him, seeing him staring at me with his face closed down.

'Darling,' he sighed, folding and putting the paper down. 'I am frightened for your health. I can't possibly dictate your decisions but please do try to give that habit up!' he said, shaking his head at me, looking very sorrowful.

'Yes, I'll try,' I said, planting myself next to him and wrapping my arms around his neck.

'When?' he murmured, with a half-smile on his face as I brought mine close to his.

'Oooh! Just you wait and see! Any day now,' I said, thinking about it.

Then he laughed, giving me a slap on the arse, saying, 'You are bloody impossible!'

'I know,' I murmured, working me nose around to his ear, breathing in and out, getting ready to rest my lips sucking the skin off him.

I had just made my way round to his neck when he whipped me round in his left arm, holding me across him. Suddenly there was a knock on the door and he looked up, saying, '*Oui?*' Then the door opened and Madame put her head in, seeing me hovering across his lap, getting held in his arms. She smiled, saying something in French, and he said something back. Then she was waving, saying, '*Au revoir. Bonne nuit!*' Then she was gone.

'Dinner is served, darling. Let us go in.'

'Oh, good, I'm starving,' I said, getting to my feet. I waited for him, putting my arm around him, and he held me to him as we made our way to the kitchen. 'You have a lot of rooms in this house, Ralph. Do you ever use the dining room?'

'Of course. But it is nice to eat in the kitchen. I find it comfortable, much more cosy,' he said. 'Why? Would you like us to eat there occasionally? I suppose we could,' he said, talking more to himself.

'No, no, absolutely not. I love the kitchen. It is very cosy, Ralph. Oh, what are we having?' I said, seeing the big deep plates that looked like soup dishes, only bigger. They had been left sitting on top of a dinner plate.

He lifted the lid on the big casserole dish, saying, 'Fish stew, your favourite, Martha. My, you must have impressed Madame Bouclé! She wants to please you,' he grinned, pulling out my chair and holding it for me to sit down. Then he pushed me in, whipping open my linen napkin and smacking it in the air before landing it on my lap with a flourish. 'Would m'lady like a little wine?' he said, making for the fridge.

'Yes, indeed, sir, she most certainly would. I have been deprived long enough!' I said, thinking how bloody long it took me to get my appetite back.

'Yes, this will do you good in a measured quantity,' he said, pouring a drink into my glass.

I watched him filling it, wondering if he was only going to give me a half-glass, because the glass was big and he might monitor that as well. No, I got a full glass and picked it up feeling delighted to be back on my feet.

I sat smoking and sipping my wine as Ralph cleared away the dishes.

'Why don't you put them in the machine, Ralph?'

'Good gracious, no! Ridiculously awkward trying to get the stuff to fit. Besides, it makes a dreadful mess when it spills,' he said, clearing and wiping, landing dishes in the sink. Then he swung on his heels, taking in the room, seeing if anything else needed ordering. 'OK, sweetie, time for beddy-byes for you,' he said, making to grab me up and march me out the door.

'Not on yer nelly,' I said, twisting away from his grasp. 'No, Ralph, I am tired of the bedroom. I want to relax,' I said.

He sighed, saying, 'Darling, you would be more comfortable lying in your bed. Come on, Martha, we will lie together and do something.'

'Like what?' I said, gaping with me mouth open and a ready laugh on my face.

'Naughty, naughty,' he said, laughing and pointing the finger at me. 'Are you after my virtue?' he said grabbing out at me again, this time catching me.

'No,' I said, 'you may keep your virtue.'

'Good!' he said crisply, raising his chin and looking disappointed, but accepting the decision was settled.

'I want your manhood,' I said, looking up into his face, seeing him grinning at me.

'Martha! I need it for myself,' he said quietly, looking shocked.

'For what? Stirring your tea?'

'Ohh! You jezebel!' he said, grabbing and lifting me off my feet, nuzzling my face and neck.

'Come on, carry me away to paradise,' I said, making it sound like an order.

'The lady has spoken. I am your slave, madam. At your service,' he grinned, marching out the door then stopping to whip it open and boot it closed with the back of his heel.

'Wait!' I said, waving my hand in the air.

'Yes, m'lady?'

'The wine! We forgot the wine, Fitzgerald! Back at once!' I said, waving him back into the room.

He stopped for a minute, thinking about this before saying, 'Well, yes, of course. I shall need sustenance to give me the strength to get you up those stairs.' He laughed, putting me on my feet and rushing back into the kitchen, then flying back out and whipping me up again.

We stopped on a wide landing with a long window looking out over the lawn, and two doors, one on each side, facing each other. Ralph landed me on my feet and I stood looking around.

'Do you know, believe it or not, I forgot to take a look in your room,' I said quietly, wondering why that had happened.

'You want to see my room, Martha?'

'Yes, let me be privy to all your secrets!' I droned, sounding like Lady Muck. 'One cannot allow one's servants to take the upper hand, my good man. Good gracious! You could be hiding the family silver in that filthy little hovel, for all I know! Shocking! Goodness! Where's me smelling salts!' I puffed, looking around with my hand on my chest. 'Call the butler at once. Tell him to get here immediately! We must have a search, and tell him to bring my salts!' I screeched, looking up at him with a deadpan face after pinching my nose and breathing in and out with the drama of it all.

He watched me with a huge grin ready to break out on his face as I stood snorting and staring daggers at him. 'But, m'lady, I am the butler!' he said plaintively.

'Then hurry, you silly man!' I said, giving him a clatter on the shoulder. 'Let us get in there at once! We must do a search.'

He hesitated, wondering if we should go into his room.

'Do move!' I screeched, then said cautiously, lowering my voice, 'You go first, Fitzgerald. The man may be armed; he could have a shotgun in there. I do not want to have meself injured,' I said, grabbing hold of my chest.

'But m'lady! Who are we supposed to be chasing?' he said, hesitating at the door handle.

'The Fitzgerald man, of course! Who else, you silly creature?'

'M'lady, if I may be so bold as to suggest, but I think you may be a little confused. I am the Fitzgerald man!'

'What? But you just said you were my butler! Then who is this Fitzgerald person? How did he get into my house?' I snorted.

'But . . .' Then he suddenly started roaring laughing, saying, 'Oh, you are a clever one! Very amusing, you win!'

Then his face went serious. 'OK, if you insist,' he said, whipping open the door into a huge room twice the size of mine. Mine was big but this one was enormous!

'Look at the size of your bed,' I whispered, taking in a sharp breath, seeing a huge bed even bigger than a queen size.

'Yes,' he laughed, 'this is the master bedroom. This was clearly my uncle's boudoir.'

'But the bed, Ralph! The bed!' I screeched, staring at the size of it.

'Yes,' he grinned. 'Quite big,' he mused, looking at it as his head moved around the room. 'I think perhaps he needed that for his entertainment. I am sure he would have had quite a few fillies frolicking about on that,' he grinned, throwing his head back and roaring with the laugh.

I stared at it, seeing the lovely, heavy, carved bed ends. It was lower than mine and you could get lost in it without anyone knowing you were there. 'You sleep in this all on your own?' I said, looking at him, then at the bed and around the room.

'What a silly question!' he said, looking at me like I was mental.

'Well, it's too big for one!' I huffed, annoyed I had said the wrong thing, and raging with him knowing that!

He had a big picture window through which you could see the side of the house and then far into the distance, for miles without seeing another house. 'This is beautiful countryside, Ralph,' I said, staring out to the horizon, thinking, how lucky to spend your life here. To wake of a morning and see that view. It's heavenly, I thought.

He switched on the two bedside lamps and one sitting on a low table in front of a comfortable armchair. Then he switched off the main light. It looked so lovely and warm and airy, and the big, heavy antique rosewood chests of drawers and wardrobes made it look very grand and elegant.

I couldn't get over it. I wandered over to look at a long mirror supported by a mahogany frame on legs. Then I opened his wardrobes, seeing all his coats and jackets and suits. Some looked like priest's black suits, which made my heart fall and I closed it quickly, not wanting to be reminded.

'Drink, Martha!' Ralph said, handing me a glass of wine. Then he switched on a radio that was sitting on the bedside table nearest to the wall. Immediately the room was alive with soft classical music, then it suddenly reached a crescendo as the music become wild.

Ralph saw me listening with my head tilted to the sound. He laughed quietly, saying, 'You like that, Martha, do you not?'

'Yes,' I whispered, 'do you know what that piece is?'

He smiled, looking at me with his green eyes penetrating, making the blood rush through my veins.

'They all sound very familiar,' I said, feeling my heart go faster as the tempo of the music increased, letting the drama unfold.

'What we have heard so far is "The Ride of the Valkyries", "The Rape of the Sabine Women" and Beethoven's masterpiece, the Fifth Symphony,' he said, slowly enunciating each word very softly. I watched as his chin lifted and he rocked gently on his heels, straightening himself. Then he stared at me, taking in a long slow deep breath as we listened to the tempo quicken as the crescendo increased to a crashing roar. I felt mesmerised and our eyes locked as we took in the drama and fury of the violent, passionately fiery music. It raged through me, exciting every nerve in my body. I stood rapt, listening as the passion reached its peak, held, then faded out slowly, the anger having spent its fury.

I let out my breath, feeling my body flop, and eased my stare with a blink before settling my eyes on him again. He was breathing fast but quiet with his mouth closed. Only his heaving chest gave the game away. Then he smiled at me, giving me a knowing look, like we both shared a secret. I watched him turn and wander over to the window before flopping down on a chaise longue. My gaze followed his movements as his arm swung back, propping the cushions behind him and under his head. Then he lifted his legs, stretching them and letting them rest the length of the chaise longue, before resting his arm behind his head and taking a sip of his wine.

I was still staring at him when he caught me. I didn't waver as he lifted his head, letting his eyes linger on me, exposing me to the inner fire burning deep in him, showing me he was still caught in the passion of that music, and now it all poured out through his eyes. I could feel the power of it. The tension was thick in the air, making it hard for me to breathe. I opened my mouth, still staring at him, seeing his face melt into softness as his mouth slackened, letting it drop open. My heart raced. The blood pulsed through me, making me feel warm and soft, and I wanted to take the few steps and lie beside him and have him melt into me.

'Darling!' he whispered. 'I do love you so much,' he said, looking like he wanted to get up and come to me.

I felt speechless. I couldn't move. I didn't want this moment to end. I didn't want to do something that would take it away. Then I heard myself whispering, 'Ralph, I love you. I have never stopped loving you or wanting you. I waited all these years for you, Ralph. I have waited a lifetime for you, then some more. I have been waiting a whole eternity for you, Ralph, my darling man. Now I have found you again. I have come to you! Your letter brought me here. Have you come back to me?' I said softly, almost in a whispered breath, feeling totally naked and exposed, knowing I could be brutally crushed if he turns away again. I have nailed my colours to the mast. There can be no turning back, I thought, feeling myself shaking all over.

Suddenly he stood up and walked over to me, standing in the centre of the room. 'Oh, my darling,' he said, looking into my eyes as his hands lifted and fell, not knowing what to do with them.

I stared up at him, not able to breathe. I waited for him to tell me, to show me, to make a declaration that I was the centre of his life. That he would never leave me again.

His eyes stared out of his head, boring into me. 'Darling, I . . . My God, we are both roused to a passion,' he whispered, half-laughing half-crying. Then he suddenly whirled his head, saying, 'I need a drink.'

'What?' I said, looking at him then looking around. 'It's over there, on the table beside the chaise longue,' I said quietly.

He looked, seeing it, then looked back at me. 'Jesus! I need something stronger,' he whispered, running his hand through his hair, then slamming his fists down by his side. With that, he took off, flying out of the room.

I stared, going into shock, then shouted, feeling a rage pouring through me as the heat of it hit my chest. 'You damned bastard. Have you not heard one word I just said?'

There was a silence as he stopped outside the door, listening. Then he came back in, looking white as a sheet, with a rage pouring out of him. 'Yes, of course I heard you. Hell's fire and all damnation! Do you not know I feel the same? I have always felt this way about you. I have been tortured with my longing for you. Now you are here, I am crazed with my love for you! It has nearly driven me bloody mad, woman!' he shouted.

'THEN WHY DON'T YOU MARRY ME?' I exploded, screaming at the top of my lungs with my eyes closed and my fists held tight by my sides, shaking with the fury. I wanted to cry with the frustration, the misery and the hopelessness of it.

'Oh, you don't know,' he whispered, letting his breath come as he lifted his head, clenching his fists, then shouted, 'I do want to marry you! God knows I do! Yes! Of course I want to marry you!' he roared, shaking his fists then slamming them against his sides.

'THEN DO IT! MARRY ME!' I screamed, putting up my fists to hit him.

He grabbed my hands and held them, shouting, 'I cannot, because I am a priest! In here!' he said, letting me go and tapping his chest with his fist.

'But . . . So where do I fit in?' I whispered, feeling the wind going out of me, letting my heart sink into despair.

'You fit in,' he said quietly, 'the priest does not.'

'I see,' I said, for the want of something to say. Not seeing or understanding anything. I was worn out. 'So tell me,' I coughed, trying to get a breath from the exhaustion suddenly knocking the life out of me.

He stared at me, looking weary, breathing in and out, trying to steady himself. He looked white as a sheet. 'Oh, darling, please believe me. I am torn in half,' he said quietly, trying to explain. Then his eyes softened and he took me in his arms, looking down at me as I stared up at him, wondering where it would all end.

'You look terrible,' he moaned.

'I don't care,' I sighed, saying, 'What does it matter?'

'We are . . .' he said, letting it trail away. Then he just crushed me to him, burying my face in his neck as he leaned into me.

'What? We are what, Ralph?' I muttered hoarsely, listening with my eyes closed and my head resting in his arms, feeling his heart pounding and my own keeping up.

'I don't know,' he said. 'I want . . .'

'What! What do you want? Tell me!' I shouted again, opening my eyes, seeing him let me go and take off, muttering, 'I need a bloody drink.'

'Yes!' I shouted, going after him. 'So do I.'

Then he stopped and looked at me, saying softly, 'No, darling, drink your wine. You are not well enough for all this.'

'I want a bloody drink! A proper drink,' I snorted, glaring at him.

He looked at me, wondering about that. Then he laughed and grabbed my hand, saying, 'Come then, let us both get bloody drunk together! Or, sorry, darling, I shall have to rephrase that. You may have a measured quantity. I must take care of your health, look after you, my precious. Whereas I? Well, I need to be rendered helpless, or you may end up like the Sabine Women. I do not trust myself tonight,' he muttered, steaming off down the stairs.

'It's mythological, Ralph,' I said, feeling very aggrieved, not believing he would lay a bloody hand on me.

'What? What is?' he said, looking back at me.

'The bleedin Sabine women! "The Rape of the Sabine Women." That's what!' I snorted. 'No such thing ever happened!'

'Oh! Of course not! But . . . Oh, Martha! Do come on, darling. Let us not start another bloody row over balderdash!' he snorted, turning away and shaking his head with the annoyance.

9

I lay back on the sofa, feeling the tiredness hitting me. Jaysus, I think I pushed it a bit too much today. I should have taken it more easy, I sighed, taking another drag on the cigarette. My lungs burnt a bit, warning me they are still too delicate for this caper. I lifted my head, stubbing the butt out in the ashtray thinking, Gobshite! Now you won't live long enough to collect the bleedin pension. Ahhh! I snorted, dropping the elbow onto my lap and the fist under my chin, getting fed up with my own company. I looked at the door, wondering if Ralph was finished clearing away the dinner dishes yet. It's no company without him, I puffed, feeling not in the mood to entertain myself.

My eyes peeled around the sitting room then landed. Ah! A bit of television, I thought, spying the box hidden away in an alcove. I switched it on to see a very serious discussion going on between a crowd of young ones and a shower of aul ones. They were all staring daggers and shouting at each other. But I couldn't understand a word. It was all in bloody French.

I stared anyway, seeing the heated row was getting even louder. The young ones seemed to be getting the better of the aul ones. Now they were losing the rag. One aul fella wearing a black wig lifted his arse outa the chair, making a run at a young fella. The interviewer leapt up and grabbed him back, shoving him sitting down in the chair again. Then all hell broke loose. The aul fella clattered the interviewer, knocking off his glasses and destroying his lovely hairdo, making it stand up and go in all directions. The young fella got hysterical, hopping up and down in his chair, clapping his hands and screaming with the laugh. An aul one sitting next to him picked up the jug of water sitting on the low table in front of her and landed it smack down on the young's fella's head. He leapt up, dripping with the water, and an aul fella sitting opposite, thinking he might let loose and dig the woman, leapt on him, tearing the shirt off his back. Then another aul fella sprang up and joined in the fray. There was murder! I started screaming with the laugh just as the door opened and Ralph came in.

'What is it, Martha?' he said grinning, looking from me to the television.

'Ahh, you're missing it,' I laughed, looking at him as I screamed me head off, then back to the television, seeing the screen had gone blank. Then the adverts whipped on.

'Ahh! It must have been live! They cut it dead!' I moaned, feeling let down there was no more to see. I looked mournfully at him, saying, 'It was a shower of aul biddies and young ones having a row, then all hell broke loose. It was brilliant. I thought there was going to be killings,' I sniffed, staring at some young one now showing off her arse with her flying along on a bicycle and the short skirt whipped up into the air. She was enjoying herself, letting the world and his wife see the long skinny legs and the big knob on her navel button. It must have happened when they hauled her into the world. I stared sourly, seeing Ralph's eyes on stalks, with him milking the sight of her for all he was worth. Her and her bleedin short skirt and her bony arse, I sniffed to meself, looking at him.

He finally tore himself away and peeled his eyes on me, seeing I was giving him dirty looks. He gave a big grin, cocking his eye at me, muttering, 'No, darling, I was studying her, noting she is not a patch on you, my lovely.' Then he grinned, examining his shoes, knowing he had been caught.

I said nothing, just sniffed, then muttered, 'Just as well! You might lose yer teeth chewing on that bag a bones.'

'What! Good heavens! You are the only bag of bones I want to chew on,' he said, throwing his head back and roaring with the laugh.

I looked at him, sighing, letting him see I had forgiven him.

'Oh, come here, you silly goose,' he said, taking hold of my feet and resting them in his lap.

'So, I missed the excitement!' he said.

'Oh, yes, you did, the French are bloody mad,' I laughed, thinking about it again. 'Pity they ended it. I wouldn't mind, but it was just getting really good,' I said, wishing he could have seen it.

'Never mind, darling. The French love a good row! But it can't be so public and certainly not televised!' he grinned, looking at me and blowing me a kiss.

I stared at him, feeling my insides melt. 'Ralph, I love you so much,' I whispered, lifting his hand and kissing it.

Then he took my hand in the palm of his, saying, 'Darling, I do love you so very much. You are my most precious treasure.'

'Oh, I feel so happy just to be here with you,' I said, letting my head slip onto his shoulder. Then I started yawning, feeling the tiredness really getting to me now.

'Oh, Martha, you look positively drained,' he said, lifting my chin to stare into my face, not liking what he saw. 'I have allowed you to stay up too long today,' he said, shaking his head, staring at me. 'I should have insisted you get some bed-rest. This is not good. You will have a relapse if I don't keep a careful eye on you. Come on, darling. I am taking you to your bed,' he said, standing up and walking over to switch off the television.

We took off walking along the hall, then I stopped at the stairs. 'Do I have to face those stairs?' I said, staring at him with a grin on my face but feeling my legs like iron bars.

'No, my love. Allow me! I shall carry you.'

'Oh, good,' I sighed happily, as he swept me off the floor and into his arms. 'Let's go to your room, Ralph. I didn't get to see too much of it last night. We were . . . Or you were! Too bloody busy fighting with me,' I said, seeing him hesitate, then keep going.

'I think we both got carried away, darling,' he murmured.

I decided to keep quiet. We had said enough. Things take time, I know that. Last night I told him exactly how I felt, and I understand him a little better now. He wants me, but the priest in him is very strong. Two highly conflicting and opposing forces. Each with their own powerful drive. So best back off, Martha, you know that instinctively. It really is a waiting game, one that is killing me. But all will be revealed in its own time, one way or the other. Ralph is a man of action when he gets going. He does not shy away from making difficult decisions. So at the minute he does not know where he is. As he said, he is on a sabbatical. That's it, just leave well alone and let him get on with it.

'Here we are,' he said, landing me on my feet. Then he opened the door and switched on the main light in his bedroom.

'Did I pull the heart out of you, carrying me up those stairs?' I grinned, still keeping my arms wrapped around his neck as he lifted his hand, pushing back the hair landed over his eye.

'Of course not, there is simply no weight in you,' he snorted, holding my waist to look at me. Then he shook his head saying, 'Martha, we are going to have to build you up again. You are positively wasting away on me. Goodness! You have become so terribly frail,' he said, letting his voice soften as he took me in.

I stared at him, saying nothing. Just looked down at myself, thinking, Yeah, I lost a lot of weight all right, and it was in no bloody time at all. 'That sickness really took it out of me,' I sighed, missing the loss of the time when I never had a day's sickness. Well, I did, but it didn't bother me. I was used to keep going. But now!

'Ah, I'll be OK, Ralph,' I said, thinking, I'm over all that now. The thyroid operation is well behind me. This was just unlucky. It's the bleedin smoking trying to eat my lungs alive.

'You go along in. I shall go back downstairs and get some wine. Would you like another glass?' he said, seeing me make a beeline to nosey around his room.

'Oh, I don't mind. Maybe half a glass,' I said, looking back at him. Then he was gone.

I wandered around, picking up books left lying on shelves, presses and tables. I wanted to look and poke and examine everything in great detail. I wanted to get inside Ralph, touch his private inner self. The side he keeps well hidden. I want to know the man behind the priest, the doctor. The man from a wealthy family, with the aristocratic bearing, who hides behind impeccable manners. I want to peel away those masks he uses as a barrier and see the raw, naked, vulnerable Ralph. Because we have both touched it in each other. I sense his fears and he senses mine. Our souls have touched each other, but we don't let them free. We keep hiding, saying one thing and thinking, wanting, another.

I looked around as he came back into the room.

'Your drink, Martha!' he said, handing it to me, then turning away and sitting on the chaise longue, crossing his legs and stretching them on the floor.

I looked over at him, watching, seeing him sipping and letting his eyes wander along the books lying about. He handed me that drink, I thought, and called me 'Martha'. Hmm, I sense he's closing down. Yeah, he's putting distance between us, because I am in his inner sanctum. It's uncomfortable for him. He doesn't want me getting too close. He would prefer to have me somewhere neutral, preferably the sitting room or even my bedroom.

Then he let his eyes rest on me, seeing me watching him. He looked serious as his eyes took me in. Then he smiled, letting his eyes soften, whispering, 'Yes, you look terribly frail but very lovely, my darling. I find you quite alluring in those silk pyjamas,' he murmured softly, sounding very sensuous as he slowly stretched his legs and took a sip of wine, keeping his eyes on me.

I could feel the nerves in my body tingling, getting drawn over to him like a magnet. But I stayed still, letting my head rule, and decided not to play his game. He will back off as soon as I declare my interest. He is frightened of losing control. OK, let him enjoy himself. I enjoy it too. I'm beginning to see this like those ballerinas dancing on the stage, flying with wings towards each other, then taking fright and flying away again. They even do it in the animal kingdom. It is all part of the mating process between male and female. *I want you! Come to me! Get away! Prove yourself to me! No! Not yet! I am not ready! I need more. Let this last. Or then it will be over. And we may not be the same.*

Yes, right, Ralph! Let's play the mating game like the young buck driven by his powerful need to impregnate a herd and spread his seed. He will limber up, then roar in, ready to take on the strong male who controls the females. Then, driven by a passion that sends them both into madness, they will fight to the death, if necessary. The docile females stand by watching. They will only go with the strongest, most powerful male in the pack. The winner takes all. The strong buck will give them healthy young like himself, ensuring their survival and the continuation of their species. It is the law of the jungle. Well, Ralph, I have chosen you to give me young, but I don't want to make it easy for you. It may just deflate your male ego, getting me handed to you on a plate. You need more substance, something that is a challenge and will keep you challenged. So, I'm not making you privy to my knowledge. It is all part of keeping ourselves hidden. The mating business is a long process. Let the games play on!

I picked up a book, seeing it was Voltaire. 'Ah, the rabble-rouser who caused the revolution,' I laughed, putting it down and picking up another one. 'Marcel Proust! Hmm, you like zee French. So do I. We ave so much in zee common!' I said, looking at him staring but not seeing me. 'Monsieur! Please to listen!' I said, walking over and giving him a tap on the skull with the book.

'Oh, my dear! That was a fatal move,' he said, lunging at my legs and barely missing as I shot back.

'Ah-ah! Temper, temper, padre! Remember! I am zee invalid.'

'You will be in-valid when I catch hold of you,' he warned, pointing his finger at me.

'Oh, well, keep your threats, I can have fun by myself,' I said, rummaging in my pocket for my tobacco.

'Martha, please, no!' he said, waving a finger at my tobacco.

'What?' I said, looking at him in surprise.

'I really would like it if you could choose not to smoke. I am concerned about your health.'

I hesitated, looking at them, then said, 'Sorry, I need it,' rolling one and lighting it up.

He lifted his head and turned away in disgust. 'What shall I do with you?' he muttered, examining his fingernails and going into a sulk.

'Do we have an ashtray?' I said, looking round the room.

He shook his head, looking a bit pleased, with a smile playing around his mouth.

I sighed, looking around for something to use. 'Ah, perfect!' I said, picking up a tiny little pale-blue dish that looked very fragile. It was probably for holding sweets or something. Then I walked over and laid myself down in the middle of the bed. Then turned and pulled down the cover and lifted the pillows, stacking them against the long bolster, and lay back, feeling the essence of comfort.

He sipped on his wine, watching me, then said, 'Martha! I absolutely forbid you to smoke in my bed,' lifting his chin and glaring over at me.

I stared at him, with the cigarette halfway to my mouth, then took a big suck on it, saying, 'I am sorry, Ralph, but you do not forbid me to do anything! Yes, I am taking a liberty smoking in your room, but you have two hopes of stopping me, Bob Hope and no hope!' I sniffed, lifting up my wine from the bedside table and taking a big swallow. Then I glared back at him. 'In fact, you will now find it impossible to get me out of this bed, because I have taken up squatters' rights,' I grinned, then put down the cigarette and dived in under the covers. 'Hmm, very comfortable,' I said, wriggling around and enjoying the lovely silk sheets. 'You do love yourself. Silk! Very sexy, Ralph! I didn't think you had it in you!' I said, wanting to draw him out and get his male pride rearing up.

I watched as his face suddenly lit up in a gorgeous smile then broke out in a laugh. Then he started roaring laughing, thinking it was hilarious. 'Oh, dear, please do not make me come and remove you. I will not be kind,' he said, lying on his couch, sipping his wine and watching me lazily.

'Threats – you are all puff and hot air,' I said, lifting myself up, propped on my side, sipping wine and watching him.

'You are teasing me,' he muttered, watching me with his eyes half-closed.

'Is that what it is? My, you do fancy yourself, Ralph Fitzgerald.'

'I fancy you, darling,' he muttered under his breath, blowing me a kiss.

'Really?' I snorted, at a distance. 'You are terrified to get too close. Are you frightened you may not be up to the job?' I said, tilting my head, keeping my eyes on him.

'You are goading me, darling. Wanting to be cruel. Forcing me to the challenge,' he said, speaking quietly and slowly.

'No,' I shook my head. 'I don't want to see evidence you may not be able to rise to the occasion!' I said, giving him a long, slow, knowing smile. Then I threw my head back, roaring with the laugh at the sudden audacity of me.

I watched as he drained his glass then leaned back to put it on the table. 'Have you finished your drink, darling?' he said quietly.

I looked at the empty glass sitting beside me on the bedside table and nodded, seeing him stand up and slowly make his way towards me. He had a glint in his eye and I followed his movements, watching with a smile on my face. Then he stood looking down at me, saying, 'You are a femme fatale.' Then he suddenly whipped down the bedclothes and put his arm under me, swooping me out of the bed.

I grabbed hold of him, wrapping my arms around his neck, giving a little squeal with the laugh out of me. Then he stood still, holding me in his arms, staring down into my face with a glint of deep sensuality, making his eyes swim with longing. Then I watched his face bend closer and suddenly he was kissing me hard, letting his passion soar as his lips opened and he went deep down into me. Letting his tongue draw mine to him, then plunge deeper until our breath was one sound. I could feel the heat of him and the rise of every nerve in me screaming to melt into him.

He suddenly pulled away and looked at me, saying with a smile on his face and his eyes glittering with passion, 'I do not take advantage of invalids. Besides, you are still my patient,' he grinned, taking off and marching away with me. 'I am taking you to your bed, darling. You need rest,' he said, bending down and whipping open the door, then heading me up to the next floor.

I felt my heart dropping and the life leaving me as a sudden weakness hit me. The extreme tiredness was suddenly catching up on me. 'Yes, Ralph,' I whispered, feeling very weary. 'You are right.' Then I wrapped my arms more firmly around his neck, stroking the softness of his skin and pressing myself into his warm body, feeling him holding me close to his chest and stomach. I could feel his strength through the soft wool sweater, and the power of his masculinity made me feel safe and warm and cherished.

IO

I watched Ralph drinking from the last of his brandy snifter then he laid the balloon glass down on the white-linen tablecloth and wiped his mouth with the heavy linen napkin, leaving it sitting on a side plate. 'That was a fine dinner,' he said, sitting back and giving me a smile.

I nodded, smiling back at him, saying softly, 'Yes, it was very fine,' feeling very relaxed and content. 'The lobster was delicious. It takes the French to sate the senses. They do everything so well and have developed their appetite for all good things to a fine art. Especially the senses,' I purred, giving him a slow smile, letting him see what I was thinking.

He looked at me, giving me a long, lingering look that spoke volumes about just how sensual he was feeling. My heart turned over at how incredibly handsome he looked. He was totally at ease, lying back in the chair with one hand sitting on the table while the other rested on the back of his chair. He looked so distinguished in his black evening suit, wearing a crisp linen Charvet dress shirt and black bow tie. I looked at his hands, with the gold cufflinks showing just below the sleeve jacket, then smiled up at him, thinking, I must be dreaming. A man with his looks and calibre feels I deserve his attentions.

Suddenly he leaned towards me and whispered, 'Darling, you look absolutely enchanting. Really, I have never seen you look more beautiful.'

I smiled, whispering, 'Thank you,' suddenly feeling shy. I dropped my eyes, not wanting him to see how overcome I was. I was being fast swept away into another world. His world, and he was laying it at my feet.

'Darling! What is it?' he said, lifting my chin.

I couldn't speak or meet his eyes.

'Are you happy?' he whispered, taking up my hands and examining them.

'Yes, very happy,' I murmured, overcome with the way he is giving me his full attention, like he is losing himself in me, and I felt lost in him. It was like I was taking his masculinity and letting it swallow me up, leaving me soft and warm and filled with a sense of my own femininity. Serene, gentle and happy to delight in being a woman. I had a quiet sense of knowing my worth and did not have to prove myself.

Then he pressed my hands to his lips, sighing. 'You are positively ravishing,' he murmured, as his eyes left my face and travelled down my body, resting on my breasts.

I was wearing a long, pale-green and grey chiffon dress that clings. A string was drawn across and tied just where I wanted the frock to sit on my breasts, then drawn around to the back, tied high up with a ribbon, emphasising the cleavage while leaving the rest to flow and sweep away. When I walk, it leaves a billowing mass of chiffon floating out behind me. It was light as air and made of pure chiffon. The design was from the early Georgian period and like something from the Russian court of the Tsars when the nobility of St Petersburg were at their dizzying height, enjoying a period of immense power and privilege, bought with a fabulous store of wealth. Now here I am, wearing the same kind of frock, feeling I have gone into another world and it will end soon when I wake. I felt myself shiver inside, feeling as if someone had just walked over my grave.

'Are you cold, my love?' he said, running his hands along my bare arms. 'Would you like me to move closer to you? Keep you warm?' he grinned.

'Yes, lovely,' I smiled, wanting to feel his closeness. He lifted his head to the waiter, who was standing at the ready, keeping a discreet distance.

'*Monsieur!*' the waiter bowed.

Ralph said something in French and instantly the table was lifted, swung and Ralph's chair was moved closer. Then we were alone again.

'Is that better, my sweet?' he said, resting his arm along the top of my chair, leaving his fingers dangling and rippling along my shoulder, sending shivers of delight up and down my spine.

I sipped my brandy liqueur, feeling the heat fill my chest, making me feel intoxicated from the sheer happiness of being wrapped in a mellow haze of love and warmth. 'You have spoilt me, Ralph,' I sighed. 'After all this, I will sure have a long way to fall,' I said, sweeping my hand around the restaurant with the glittering chandeliers, the bow-tied waiters, the tinkle of crystal, the subdued laughter and the controlled quiet conversation rippling around the dazzling room. The other diners were among the very sophisticated and well-heeled elite of France.

'Do you know, Ralph, I have seen Paris as I have not seen it before,' I said. 'I have been many, many times to France, and especially Paris. But I was always slumming it,' I laughed.

He grinned at me, listening.

'Oh, yes, the backpackers' hostels out in the suburbs, or the flea-ridden *pensions* down the back streets of Paris. Once I ended up in Pigalle! But I didn't realise it was the heart of the red-light district until that night when the sex shops opened,' I laughed, 'and the women lined up against doorways all along the street. I was a right bloody eejit, Ralph! But it was great! Have you ever been there?' I said, suddenly thinking it was a ridiculous question. He was always busy doing something more serious.

He shook his head at me, saying quietly, 'No, but my uncle wanted to take me when I joined the priesthood. My mother learned about it and thought it was a ridiculous idea! I did not become privy to that until years later,' he grinned, throwing his head back and roaring laughing.

'Would you liked to have gone? A huge blowout before you gave it up for ever?' I said, grinning at him, watching his face.

He thought about it, staring at me, keeping himself very still. Then said, 'No, darling. It would not be me. I would prefer the real thing, like you, my divine woman!' he said, leaning over me, whispering into my neck.

I stared at him with a smile on my face, sipping my liqueur, then said softly, 'Now, with you, I have seen Paris at its grandest. I have spent two glorious nights in a top hotel close to the Arc de

Triomphe and the Champs-Elysées, attended the theatre with all its glamour, then dined magnificently along the Seine. Wonderful,' I sighed, thinking of the magic of it. 'Then that first day you took me shopping! Insisting I needed something "suitable" to wear, you said. I didn't really understand. I thought I had perfectly good stuff to wear. "Oh, no," you said. "We must get you something special." Then you took off, waltzing me through the incredibly expensive shops. *Voilà!* I end up with this frock,' I said, staring and smiling at him, seeing him look very amused.

'You have wonderful taste, Ralph. Remember I refused to look at this frock when you whipped it up, telling me to try it on?'

'Yes, I had to march you to the changing-rooms,' he laughed, shaking his head at me. 'Or goodness knows what you would have chosen.'

'But how did you know this would suit me, Ralph?' I said, looking up at him. 'I mean, you don't even think like that. You have never really been involved in women's doings!' I said.

'Nonsense! I had sisters, remember? I learned all I need to know about your species from them,' he laughed.

'But you were all away at school, so you didn't exactly grow up together, did you?'

'Oh, darling, we had summers and winter holidays together. Of course I did!'

'Yes, I suppose so,' I said, thinking how close they all were. 'Oh, yes, then, the *coup de grâce*!' I laughed quietly, still not able to take it in. 'When you swept me into Cartier and sat choosing diamond earrings for me,' I whispered, then roared laughing, getting the picture all over again with him and the very proper Frenchman discussing what would suit me and my earlobes best. 'Then I walked out with these,' I said, putting my hand up and gently caressing them, feeling a million dollars with my ears flashing and sparkling, glittering when the lights hit the diamonds. 'I'm ruined,' I laughed, shaking my head and leaning into him. 'There's only one place for me to go now and that's down!' I said, wondering if I was speaking the truth. 'They cost you a bloody fortune, Ralph!' I said, getting a bit worried. 'Are you sure I didn't break the bank with all this extravagance?' I whispered, looking at him seriously.

'Don't fret, you silly goose. This is simply a bauble! Designed to bring out the best in you, darling. You look divine! Now, no more of this. Let us relax and enjoy,' he said squeezing my waist and planting a kiss on my lips.

'Yeah! But now this!' I said, looking around at the chic sophistication of the women and the men holding themselves with a haughty indifference while the waiters beetled about making sure they had every comfort and convenience. All they were short of doing was standing behind them and fanning away the cigar smoke that wafted up like Indian smoke signals. The men and women sat impervious to all this, arrogant in the safe belief they were born to rule. They were so in command of themselves it sent out a silent message saying, *You may speak to God, but you will need an appointment to speak to me.*

My breath caught as I slowly let my eyes wander around, taking in the grandeur of the place. Chandeliers hung on long chains from high ceilings. Statues of women leaned off the walls, lighting the way. Candles and flowers graced white-linen covered tables, gleaming with silver, and crystal dazzled with sparkling light. An intoxicating diffusion of scents and sounds all mingled, sending me messages of being in an exalted place with exalted company. It was the perfume of the women, including my own, the smell of the candles and the flowers, and the steam from the food as it was suddenly produced from under silver serving dishes. Not to mention the cigars and the crinkle of silk and the smell of freshly coiffeured hairdo, including my own, of course. My coiffeured hair, done by a Frenchman at a fancy hairdresser's, had left me looking breathless at myself in the mirrors. Gawd, there's a lot to be said for having money. And for this moment, I was part of it all. I was sitting among the great, the good and the glorious, especially Ralph! I thought, sliding my eyes to take him in. He was nodding at the waiter, who appeared in a flash, bowing and ready to do Ralph's bidding. The whole thing was going to my head. Jaysus, I thought. When I wake from all this, I hope the Samaritans are still in business. I will have enough woes to keep them on the line for the next month.

Ralph said something and the waiter was back bowing and producing a big cigar box for Ralph to peruse. He pointed one out and the waiter bowed then took off, coming back in a jiffy to cut the cigar and hand it to Ralph, producing a light he seemed to whip from behind his back like a magician. It was all theatre, the carry-on of the waiters, with the waving of their arms and the bowing, keeping the back straight. I felt as if we were all like actors somehow. Oh, I had the better part. I was being waited on hand and foot. I only had to raise a nod – well, Ralph did – and whatever Madame desired it was produced. I wonder how long it takes you to get fed up with all this?

Then I woke up, realising I was missing out on something. 'Ralph! I would like a smoke too. What about getting me something for a lady?' I said, looking into his smouldering green eyes that were alive with his heightened sensuality. I wanted to dive in and swim in them. Bury myself inside his lovely green eyes that were like deep pools of raw sex.

'Like what, darling?'

'Oh, you know, something long and slim and sexy-looking,' I mewled. 'I need something to go with my new image. I can't very well take out my roll-ups now, can I, sweetie darling?' I demanded in my best new voice. Sexy, smouldering and definitely sounding like the 'Hooray Henry Brigade'. Terribly upper class. Jaysus, I'm a smashing mimic!

I saw Ralph grin at the allegations of me, then straighten his face as he nodded to the waiter. He spoke a few words and another box was produced for my perusal. I stared in and decided on a couple, then thought maybe I should have three – that's better. I lifted my fingers, pointing them at the waiter, then decided it would be better to refer the matter to Ralph. After all, it was most definitely not the done thing for a lady like me to be fraternising with the serving class. No, no, I am to stick to my own now! Yes, it's not taking me long to learn the ropes. Keep the nose in the air, look bored, sated. When you've money, you can do anything. Jaysus! I was born to rule.

'Would you like another drink, darling?' Ralph said, as the waiter finished lighting me up, then whipped up the silver bucket with the bottle of ice-cold wine, cooling for our delectation. I had refused champagne. 'Don't like the stuff,' I told Ralph.

He was astonished. 'Darling, you should try a little! We are ideally placed here in France to have some good vintage! Shall I order a bottle?'

'Yes, OK, thank you.'

I still didn't like it. So now I have my very own bottle while he drinks his champagne. I sipped on my dessert wine, enjoying the sweet taste after the liqueur. I wondered if I would be able to stand straight when I got up, and decided Ralph could carry me to the car! Ah-ah! Behave, Martha! You are a lady now! Yes, Ralph is a stickler for decorum and good manners.

I leant back into him, enjoying the strong comforting feel of him. Then he lowered his head, whispering into my ear, 'Darling, I cannot take my eyes off you. You are deliciously ravishing,' he said, dropping his lips and breathing his way down my neck.

I gave a sudden shiver and laughed, looking up into his face, saying, 'Sir, I do believe it is safe to say you are . . .' I stopped to think of the right word.

'Darling! I do think we may leave if you are ready! What do you think?' he said.

I looked at him, wondering what he was thinking. 'Is that a proposition?' I said, breathing into his mouth with my lips close to his.

He smiled, giving a slow blink, then let his eyebrow raise a fraction, still staring at me.

'I think this frock has gone to your head, Ralph! Now I know why women were mad for diamonds,' I said, patting my ears. 'It really does work! I have a feeling you would eat your dinner off my belly if I asked you to, Ralph.'

He let out a roar, laughing his head off, then breathed in and rested his eyes on me again. 'No, darling, not dinner. I would fling that to one side and simply start with you! Then,' he said, 'if music be the food of love, then play on, maestro. Let us go home and relax with some music.' Then he lowered his head to me, waiting for my answer.

'Yes, Ralph, I am all yours to command.'

He took in a deep breath and smiled without parting his lips. Then he nodded at the waiter, who rushed off and then came back with a leather book and the bill inside. Ralph took a second to examine it, then slipped money out of his wallet and stuck it inside the leather book. The waiter materialised like he was on wheels, bowed solemnly and skidded off with the bill and the money hidden inside.

Ralph turned to me nodding and saying, 'Your coat, darling.'

I turned and there he was, the waiter, waiting and bowing. '*Madame!*' he said, giving a little wave, with my fur coat hanging in his white gloved hands, ready to drop it on my shoulders and allow Ralph to take over the business of getting me well settled inside it. Then Ralph's coat was produced. A long, black cashmere one that buttoned up to the collar with an extra flap down the length of the coat, hiding the buttons.

Then Ralph nodded, and the waiter bowed again then stepped aside as we went past. Ralph was standing back to allow me to start walking, then he put his hand lightly on my elbow, guiding me towards the door, where another fellow, this time the doorman, saluted to Ralph, gave a little bow to me, and the door was whipped open.

The French air hit me straight away. I could get the smell of sulphur in the humid, damp night. I pulled up the collar of my fur and snuggled myself inside. We were now into the dark night, lit up by the glittering lights from the restaurant.

'Here we are, darling!' Ralph said, opening the car door and holding my back, then supporting my arm as I climbed into the front seat. Then he slammed the door shut and smartly walked around the front of the car, sitting himself in.

'I don't like the look of that sky,' he said, bending his head and looking out into the pitch-black treacherous night. 'We should be home within the half-hour,' he said, switching on the car engine and pulling off, heading us for home.

The car radio was playing and Paul Robeson crooned softly, making me sigh out in deep contentment. I inched closer to Ralph and snuggled in beside him, resting my hand on his leg and then moving it gently, caressing the softness of the trouser material and feeling the strength of his muscles and the heat of his thigh underneath. Then I let my hand wander up to his chest, feeling the hardness of it, and slowly went around and down to his stomach. I could hear Ralph take in a deep breath. 'You are so manly,' I murmured, speaking into his neck.

'Darling,' he whispered, laughing. Then he slowed down and dropped his mouth against my ear, breathing, 'If you keep that up, we will both end up wrapped around a tree.'

'OK,' I sighed, leaving my hand resting on his chest.

He turned slightly, giving my head a quick kiss while keeping his eyes on the road, then slammed the gears up a notch and we roared off into the night.

The car purred up the drive and Ralph stopped, getting out to open the front door. Then he came around to my side and opened the car door, helping me out. 'You go along in, darling. I will drive around the back and put the car away,' he said, walking quickly and getting back into the car.

I walked into the hall and looked back, seeing a flash of lightning. Then suddenly I could hear a roar of thunder in the distance. 'Right, upstairs and out of all this finery,' I muttered to myself, making my way upstairs. I stepped out of the dress and stood in my long petticoat that goes with the frock. Hmm, that's even lovely enough to go out in, I thought admiringly, looking at myself in the full-length wardrobe mirror.

I hung up the frock carefully on a wooden hanger that was covered in a thick cloth, then stripped out of the rest of my clothes. Then I put the black-satin shoes in the shoe rack at the side of the wardrobe and took out my earrings, putting them back into their little satin-lined Cartier box. Right, what will I wear for bed? I thought, going through my night things. No, not them, no cotton stuff for me, I thought, fingering the pyjamas and nightdresses. Not after having my body caressed by that delicious silk all evening. Then I lifted up the box with the long silk nightdress and matching gown. Perfect, I thought, lifting it out of its box and letting it waft to its full length. I put it against my face, feeling the soft silk melt into my skin. Lovely, I'll wear this. Anyway, it will be nice for Ralph to see me in it. I put my eye on it as we strolled around that very expensive shop in Paris. He bought it for me, grinning, saying, 'You do appreciate the fine things in life, darling. No matter what you may say to the contrary.'

'What do you mean?' I had said, glaring at him.

'Well, you complain how frightful the prices are, but here we are, I am happy to say. You appreciate one must pay for quality, that is all, my love!' he said, staring at me until I understood. Then he went marching off through the store, keeping a hold of me on one side while the other was weighed down carrying all my lovely-looking and very expensive stuff. It was all nestled inside a load of smashing-looking carrier bags. Pity I can't bring them back to Dublin with me. 'Shopping in Paris, darlings!' I could tell the neighbours as I swan up the street with my nose in the air. That should put a sock in their gob. I'm not exactly their favourite neighbour. Well, I wasn't when Sarah was young. Not with the crowd of kids around the house and all the shouting that used to go on. My voice being the loudest. Hmm, they would love to have gotten a petition up to get rid of me, only I own the house. They must be bored these days; it's too quiet!

Right, enough letting the mind wander. Get going and have a quick freshen-up, a nice hot bath before I climb into these divine things. 'The latest silk nightwear from gay Paris!' I sang, then grabbed up my wash things, making my way out the door, heading for the bathroom.

That's better, I thought, looking at my scrubbed face shining back at me in the mirror. Right, now to take the hair down. Pity, but it's had its day out, now get back to normal. I took out the diamanté slides I bought . . . *Ralph* bought on our shopping trip, and loosened the curls, letting it fall down. Yes, that is better. Gawd, I am going to have to get used to it looking this length. Myself and the gorgeous gigolo hairdresser had an almighty tussle. '*Non!* It is impossible to do something with diss! You must cut!' I was outraged and caused a scene . . . Lucky Ralph was not there! It was most unseemly! Dearie me, he would not have approved. Meself and the gigolo were dug out of each other with the whole salon, all the madames, staring on in horrified silence at the foreigner with the hair nearly trailing the floor! Oh, well, it's gone now. It hangs just above my waist. Hmm. I like it! I thought, staring at the back of myself. It feels lovely and light.

Right, twist it into a knot and pin it on the back of my head. Lovely, I must say, I do look . . . a bit more polished! Parisian! Hmm, I better get a bit more poise to go with it, though. That would mean keeping quiet, smiling enigmatically like the *Mona Lisa*, developing a bit of grace . . . Jaysus! I would be dead and buried by the time I get that far. Forget it. I am Martha Long, a woman of many faces. I can be what I want, when I want. But only when it suits me! I am capable of all these things when necessary. But I am what I am, I am Martha Long. So fuck it, the world takes me as I am. I can stand with the best of them, and I have. Good! Be yourself. Now for a dash of perfume, seeing as the feminine side rages madly at the minute!

I looked at myself in the mirror, seeing a softness in my eyes. They glittered! Passion! I thought. Yes, that's what love does to you. It softens you up in preparation for motherhood. Wily old nature! Well, I'm not going against it. Oh, no! I most certainly am more than ready to have myself impregnated with Ralph's babies! But so far – nothing. It may be he does not want marriage! My heart did a nosedive. No, chin up, as the old British would say. It will be what it will be. I am ready for anything.

I wafted down the stairs, feeling the silk cling to my curves as it slinked around me. Then it hit me! Wonder should I wear the diamonds? They'd go with the silk? No, don't be daft. I'm supposed to be dressed for bed. Anyway, you took the hairdo out and scrubbed all the war paint off. Forget it! You look a million dollars in this thing.

I made my way along the hall, listening to the wind howling around the house. It rushed at the heavy front door, clawing its way underneath, then whooshed its way down the hall, catching my negligee at the ends and swooping it up, sending it billowing out behind me. I could hear the rain beating down and I gave a sudden shiver. Jaysus, I'm glad I'm not out in that.

I could hear the sound of soft classical music coming from the sitting room and saw a light showing under the door. Good, he's still up. I opened the door, feeling a smile instantly on my face. It was the sight of the room looking so warm and cosy and welcoming. I looked at the fire, seeing the logs glowing red and the flames shooting up as the wind caught it, sending out the delicious smell of country pine. The room was shaded in a lovely rosy-pink glow coming from the two lamps sitting on tables, one behind each sofa. Then the music changed, lifting the soft, gentle atmosphere of the room into a more strident feel. It was Vivaldi and *The Four Seasons*.

Where's Ralph? I looked around and saw him standing at the window, staring at me with a slow smile on his face. He was smoking a cigar.

'Oh! I didn't see you for a minute. I must be going blind!' I said, getting a shock at seeing he was suddenly there.

'Yes, darling, I was simply admiring how heavenly you look,' he said, letting his eyes travel the length of me before coming to rest on my face. I watched as he slowly lowered his head back, taking a deep puff on the cigar, then blew the smoke out, never taking his eyes off me. I knew he was roused by the way he was acting, slow and sensual. But he hasn't made a move to come and greet me with a kiss, or touch me. That means he doesn't trust himself.

I knew I could go to him but immediately I could feel myself filling up with emotions going in all directions. It made me feel shy. Yet I felt I could be the one in control. But I don't want that. I don't want to seduce him. I want him as a husband. He has to come to me. I felt tongue-tied. Not knowing how I should behave. My emotions are going crazy. I want him to grab me. Well, not that. But I want him to make passionate love to me and declare his undying love. Ask me to marry him. Bloody hell, my heart is flying. The man must be made of bleedin steel! No, he is highly disciplined. Very mature, knows what he wants and is, above all, a gentleman. A good old-fashioned knight in shining armour. Bloody hell, don't stand like a fool, Martha. Do something! Wonder do I look a fool?

I took in a deep breath, saying, 'May I have one of my cigarillos, please?'

He looked at me, raising his eyebrow, then let a little smile part his lips. That came out wrong, I thought. I sounded like a bleedin schoolteacher!

'Yes, of course,' he said, walking to the mantelpiece and taking one down. 'They are here, waiting for you, darling! I didn't forget,' he said, shaking his head and giving me a smile. The sudden smile showing his dimples and white teeth, and the lovely green eyes looking so soft and sexy, nearly buckled my knees. I could feel myself begin to sink down with a bit of weakness and flopped down on the sofa.

Suddenly a flash of lightning lit up the window as the rain tore against it.

'Shall I draw the curtains, darling? Are you frightened of the storm?'

'No, it doesn't bother me,' I said, not wanting to talk about a storm. I wanted to talk about love!

'I see you have slipped into something more comfortable,' he said, grinning down at me from his place now leaning on the mantelpiece, with the elbow resting there.

'Yes, very comfortable,' I sniffed. 'But I see you don't like it. It seems to keep you away from me,' I heard myself say, wishing I could keep my mouth shut.

'Oh! Oh, darling, I am so sorry, please forgive my rudeness. Would you like a drink?'

I looked up at him, seeing him now in his gentleman role. Good manners! But where's Ralph the man? He still hasn't even given me a hug! 'Yes,' I sighed, feeling fed up. I suppose after that big dinner in that very grand and incredibly expensive restaurant I thought he was feeling very amorous towards me. But no, it's keep the bleedin distance time!

'Won't be a tick, darling,' he said, taking himself out of the room.

I snorted out me breath and lifted my legs, flinging them onto the sofa. The silk swam away and drifted down to land in a liquid pool of sheer shimmering mass. Then it clung to me, outlining every curve I had. I dropped my arm behind my head and sucked on my cigarillo, thinking I look like a dying swan when I really want to look like Mae West in one of her Hollywood 1930s films. How would she have handled this? I know. She would have gone over to him, slowly smoking and stood blowing it in his earhole, saying in her husky voice, 'Well, honey, how do you want me, lookin like this?' she would say, whipping her arm, pointing at herself. 'Or would you like me with nothing on but the radio?' Then blow the rest of the smoke in his face and stand back waiting. Fuck! I'm no good at that!

The door opened and he appeared in carrying a bottle and two glasses. His eyes lit on me. I heard his sharp intake of breath. 'Goodness, you look . . .'

'What? What do I look?' I said, not able to take the tension. He wouldn't bloody finish!

He poured the drinks, saying nothing, then handed me a glass of wine.

'Thank you,' I muttered, now completely fed up.

He saw this and moved over to his own spot on the sofa, pulling up his legs and stretching them. Then he pinned his eyes on me, thinking. 'You look very desirable, darling,' he murmured, smiling as his eyes wandered down me.

I took a sip of my wine and sucked on my cigarillo, thinking of

Mae West. I blew the smoke in his direction, saying, 'Is that why you are keeping your distance, honey?'

He looked at me with a sudden grin on hearing the American accent and seeing the pose I struck. Then he laughed and said, 'Who are you now, my love? This is not you speaking!'

I spluttered on the drink, feeling a drop go down the front of my chest, and hopped up. 'Feck ye anyway!' I shouted, rubbing it with my hand before it ruined the silk. Then glared at him with the rage for spotting quick as a flash I was 'Abbey Acting'.

He roared laughing, saying, 'Darling, I always told you, you should be on the stage! You are a natural!' he roared, throwing his head back, giving an almighty laugh.

Then another flash hit the window and with that there was an almighty roar of thunder. I looked, and his head went to the window, seeing more lightning.

'Yes,' he said, shaking his head. 'It has been coming all day.'

'That sounds like a bloody hurricane,' I said, 'not a simple storm!'

He sighed, then said, 'You are upset with me, darling. Is it because you think I am neglecting you?'

'Yes!' I roared.

'Oh, darling, look, look over there. You see, I have prepared that for us.'

I looked over to see the round supper table set with a white-linen tablecloth. A tray sat on top covered with a white-linen cloth, and the table was set with plates and cutlery.

'Madame Bouclé prepared us some supper, darling. She knew we would be dining out, so she assumed we would be having a late night,' he said, sounding like his heart was breaking after all the efforts he went to.

I looked, seeing it now. 'I never noticed that before,' I said. 'Oh, thank you, Ralph. You are very good to me, and that is really very thoughtful of her,' I said. 'Yes, I'm actually feeling a bit hungry now,' I said, getting up and sashaying over to take a look.

He came up behind me and stood while I pulled off the cloth. 'Delicious! A lovely cheese tart and some sandwiches,' I said. 'We can have it with our wine.'

'Yes, darling. Take a seat,' he said, pulling out the chair for me and sitting me into it. Then he bent down and kissed the back of my neck. 'You look like a goddess, my darling,' he whispered into my neck, letting his hands slide on my shoulders, feeling my skin under the silk.

My heart did a tango and instantly my body went mad with the heat as my passion roared back into life. Then he went to the window, drawing the drapes across, leaving the storm to get on with its business without us seeing, only hearing the muffled sounds that were dulled by the thick walls. The fire crackled in the grate, hissing from the sap in the wood, and soft music wafted over from the radio. It filled me with such contentment I felt like I was in paradise.

'That was lovely,' I said, sitting back in my chair and sipping on my wine. 'I think I will have one of my roll-ups,' I said, getting up to collect them from the mantelpiece.

'I shall remove this and clear the table. You sit and relax, darling. I won't be long,' he said, stacking everything on the tray then heading out of the room.

The thunder seemed to get louder and I could see streaks of lightning beaming a shadow across the wall as the sky lit up behind the curtains, showing a shock of blue and white. I sat smoking, looking over to the window and staring at the drapes. I could hear the dulled sound of the thunder getting nearer as the storm seemed to draw closer. Fuck! I hope the house is not hit! Ralph better put down that cutlery. I should go and see what's happening! Don't be silly, he's knows better than you. The man is an experienced doctor. Right!

Suddenly I wished he would hurry up. I didn't feel so comfortable any more. I was just about to get up when the door opened and he appeared. I smiled happily up at him. 'Do you hear that storm, Ralph? It sounds closer and it's getting worse! Do you think there is any danger of the house being hit?' I said, looking up at him, feeling very worried.

'No, darling,' he laughed. 'We are perfectly safe here. The house is fitted with a lightning rod! Oh, you are frightened, my poor love. Come here,' he said, sitting himself down beside me and taking me in his arms.

'Oh, that's better,' I said, curling into him as I lifted my legs, throwing them across his lap.

'You are lovely,' he said, lying back and resting his eyes on me.

I had my face very close to him and I stared at him, examining the shape of his face and the colour of his skin, and his lips that screamed for me to kiss them. I lifted my hand and stroked his cheek, feeling the soft texture, yet getting the manly feel of him. His hand was resting on my thigh and he started to stroke it, saying, 'Darling, I want to be close to you. Tell me about you.'

'What is there to tell, Ralph? I have told you all that happened since you dumped me,' I said, half-laughing.

'No, please, don't even jest. I would never abandon you. I have always wanted what is best for you, my love.'

'No, OK. Let us not bring that up again,' I said, thinking no good can be had from dragging up the past. 'Yes, I understand, Ralph. It all happened with the best will in the world,' I said, getting the picture of that black period as it tried to wash over me. I pulled away and lifted my glass from the table, sipping on my wine and rolling a cigarette.

'Darling, if I may ask a question?' he said, looking at me, sounding very cautious.

'What? Ask me what, Ralph? Go on!' I said, seeing him hesitate.

'What about your family? What happened to you, to them? You have never spoken to me about them or even mentioned anything about what might have happened beyond the point of when we first met.'

I stood up and walked away, sipping on my drink, then stopped beside the fireplace and looked at him. I could feel a hard knot of rage twisting itself, wanting to explode out of me. But I held it down and just stared at him. I could feel the colour draining out of me. 'Family!' I said crisply, staring at him, feeling hard as nails. 'I will say this and please don't interrupt. Do you mean the people who live in the hovel where you dropped me one winter night? The people you insisted were my family because that nun, Sister Eleanor, told you they were?' I nodded my head briefly. 'That family, Ralph?'

He stared at me, shocked at the change in me and seeing a hard side he never saw before. I didn't give a damn. He wanted to know, because clearly he has no idea of the dark side of life.

'In that hovel lived my mother. She was breeding like a rabbit for a man who was pure evil and psychotic! Oh, yes, quite clinically so, Ralph.

He was not my father. Nor was he the father of one of my half-brothers. His name is Charlie. Now, you want to know? I will tell you. My mother was an unmarried mother. She had me at sixteen. Does that give you the picture, Ralph? Then five years later she had Charlie, my brother. From the age of five years I was an old woman living in the body of a child. I looked after my mother. She could not fend for herself. We walked the streets homeless. That man took us in, and he was raw and brutal and hated me with a pathological hatred. So much so, I learned to always sleep light for fear of losing my life, Ralph!

'I was the sole provider in that family. I took care of them all from the day she gave birth to his first child. I was not a part of that family, neither was my brother Charlie. We were known as the two bastards. I continued to provide until I was sent away to that convent. I escaped at sixteen when they opened the doors. Then, a few months later, you took me off the streets for one night. Then you fucking bunged me back! I tried to explain I did not have a family. But you were so self-righteous in your belief that you and that fucking nun knew best. Her, she fucking knew, but she was prepared to have me dumped back there rather than reach out a Christian hand to help me. I understand you knew nothing. So, what was I to think? After putting my trust in you, and believing you cared and you would help me. Fuck you, Ralph. I learned a lesson from that. I saw how charming and caring you seemed to be, yet when it came down to it, you were no different to anyone else in the world. You saw what you wanted to see, and you believed what you wanted to believe. Like the three wise monkeys – see no evil, hear no evil, then fear no evil. That's what makes the world a very dangerous and threatening place for vulnerable people, Ralph, especially children. The world does not care.

'You wondered why I was so cold and indifferent when you turned up to see me in that hospital? When the hospital telephoned you after finding your phone number in my suitcase? After I collapsed on the streets suffering from exposure and pneumonia? Well, that was the reason. I had nothing to say to you. I certainly did not trust you. Then you took me to live with your mother. Well, you redeemed yourself. I slowly grew to love and trust you. You were the first person in my life who had ever put their arm around me in a kindly way. It had never happened to me before.

'Yes, Ralph. I loved you, then you left me again. But of course I survived. It broke my heart but not my spirit. That took an awful long time. That was triggered when my young brother Harry killed himself. So I ended up in the mad house. I am only out a few months. Now, don't ever bring this subject up again! You have heard all there is to hear!'

I stared at him coldly, seeing him turned to stone with the shock. No, I thought to myself, he had that coming. He fucking let me down. He dumped me when I needed someone most. I could have died on those fucking streets! Just another nameless bastard. Ireland was full of them. We were a hidden lot.

I went over to the bottle and filled my glass with wine. Then I grabbed up my tobacco and walked out of the room, saying, 'Please say nothing, do nothing. I need time to calm down.'

I went up to my room and sat in the easy chair by the window, sipping my wine, smoking and looking out at the madness of the storm. Lightning streaked across the sky and the thunder roared and the rain lashed the window. I felt it was right – in harmony with the rage tearing around me. I took another sip and looked at the half-empty glass. Fuck, I should have brought the bottle. Lovely, I really must be on the tear. I never drank or wanted so much like I do this night. I suppose he's down there wondering, *By Jove! I say, old bean, where did all that come out of?!* Huh! Fuck him. It was the word 'family' that enraged me. He still thinks I have a 'family'. I wanted to lash out and hurt him. Just like he hurt me that first time. I never realised how badly it hurt until now. He wouldn't listen to me; he didn't want to hear. I tried to explain I didn't belong there. It hurts even to think about it now.

I had sat in the priest's parlour all day with him, watching the snowstorm outside. We sat by the fire and I felt safe and warm. He had said such soothing lovely things to me, I thought he was going to help me. That maybe I had met someone who cared. He had filled me with hope. Then that night it was all dashed. He dumped me outside the house of 'the family'. I had ended up back on the streets and it was that very same night I ended up with pneumonia. I must have been sick all along. I thought it was just exhaustion from hunger and the cold. My brain wouldn't work. So it appears when he brought that back up again, the rage I didn't know was there blew up! So now he knows. Jesus, I have never let anyone know anything like that before. It never even occurred to me to mention it. No, Jackser had me too well trained.

Anyway, he thinks he knows all there is to know about me now, but that is only the start of it. Jaysus, if only he knew the half of it! But he won't, ever. No, that is the past and that is where it will stay. I will take it to my grave with me, like many a one before me. There are some things you just never talk about. So let him make what he likes out of it. Fuck him. At least I got the opportunity of giving him the full works. Yes, I loved him. I do love him. More than I value my own life. But he hurt me, and I wanted to hurt him back. I don't think I could have let that lie between us. He needed to know how badly I took that.

Right, I don't suppose there's any chance of getting another drink? I thought, draining my empty glass. Anyway, it looks like the night is over. Pity, it had such a promising start!

I sat on, staring out the window, listening to the rumbles and then the crash of thunder. It sounded like a very angry God was tossing huge boulders at the earth. If I was an ancient Roman, I would probably believe that.

My eyes settled on the tobacco pouch and I stretched out to lift it from the little table and rolled one. Suddenly there was an almighty bang followed by a flash of lightning that lit up the pitch-black night. Then the door opened and Ralph put his head in, followed by his body.

'May I come in?' he said. 'I have been knocking but perhaps you did not hear me.'

I turned my head slowly, looking up at him. He looked pale and the light was gone out of his eyes. But I didn't care. Somehow I felt numb inside now. I had no feelings left to connect to.

He shut the door and came walking slowly towards me with his hands in his pockets. 'Darling, may I sit down?' he said, making to sit in a chair by the dressing table.

I stood up. 'Yes, of course you may. It is your room, your house. You may do as you please,' I said coldly, getting up to walk out. 'May I ask you, is it OK for me to go downstairs and refill my glass?' I said, holding out the empty glass.

He stared then jumped to his feet. 'Yes, of course! Please, allow me,' he said, making to take the glass from me.

'No, I am perfectly capable of getting it for myself, thank you.' Then I turned and walked out the door with him coming after me. I wanted to turn and tell him I didn't want his company but somehow I missed the opportunity between thinking it and telling him, so I went on silently.

I went into the sitting room, seeing the fire had died down to a lovely red glow, the music was still playing and the lamps still burned a lovely hue of rosy pink. But I could feel the tension in the atmosphere I had left behind and I wanted to get out. I grabbed the half-empty bottle and rushed out the door, leaving him behind.

'Wait, darling! Where are you going?' he said, calling me from the hall.

'To get drunk!' I said, waving the bottle at him. I was half-plastered once, but I still knew what I was doing. So this was something new for me. Anyway, he said the same thing to me a while back ago!

'No, darling, please. I know you are upset . . .'

I kept going. Suddenly I heard him taking the stairs two at a time. My reflex was to run, but what the heck, he is wasting his time. I have shut down for the night. He will get no more out of me. Let him go to hell!

He came rushing at me, wrapping his arms around me, trying to stop me getting to the next floor.

'Let me go, please. I do not want to talk to you. I would like my own company. If you insist, I will pack and be out of here first thing in the morning. I can catch the next plane out of here. The train, then the plane,' I said, giving a slight nod of my head, correcting myself, thinking of the exhausting, bloody awful long journey home.

'Oh, my heavens, what Pandora's box have I opened?' he said, letting go of me and stepping back. 'I had no idea,' he whispered softly, talking to himself as he slowly pushed his hair back off his forehead. 'If only I had even the remotest idea . . . You were not ready! I should have known! How bloody stupid of me to go stumbling blindfolded into something that has been a hellish thing for you! Oh, but really I did know! Of course I bloody knew! I saw it so often in your eyes, that terrible haunted look you had, it crept in when your guard was down.'

I turned and walked away, heading up to the next floor and into my room.

12

I woke up plastered to the bed. Something had disturbed me. I opened my eyes, seeing Ralph lifting me and putting me under the covers.

'What happened?' I said, looking around me, wondering what was going on. One minute I was sipping . . . guzzling what was left of the wine, the next he's here.

'Darling, you will catch cold,' he said, covering me up and moving close beside me, leaning over me. 'How do you feel? Do you have a headache?'

'No, but my face feels a bit hot. I'm a bit dry,' I said, seeing he was in his nightclothes. I never saw him wear those. He is always dressed.

'Wait, darling. Let me go down and get you a hot drink. But first I think you should drink this,' he said, handing me a huge tumbler of water. 'Sip this. It will rehydrate you,' he said, putting the glass to my mouth, getting me to drink. Then he got up and padded out the door in leather slippers and what looked like a silk dressing gown and light-blue cotton pyjamas.

I drank away at the water and finished the lot. 'That was good, I really was thirsty,' I muttered to myself. Then I got up out of the bed and grabbed my wash things. Bloody hell, I need to cool myself down. He is right. I am probably dehydrated!

I went down to the bathroom and splashed cold water on my face, then soaked my facecloth and washed my neck and down my chest. Then I brushed my teeth and put cream on my face. That's better. I went back to my room and put away my washbag and lit up a cigarette.

'Here we are,' he said, sounding cheerful and smiling at me.

I looked up at him, still not over my row with him. But he did look lovely. The colour of the dressing gown suited him. It was a deep red and, yes, I could see it was pure silk. Oh, nothing but the best for our Ralphie! I sniffed to myself, still feeling aggrieved, but I couldn't drag myself out of it. There were things now coming to the surface. Things that had clearly been eating away at me.

'Hot chocolate and chocolate biscuits,' he said, grabbing my pillows and slapping them into place, then leaning me back and handing me the mug.

I sipped on it, munching the biscuits. He did the same, saying, 'Hmm, these are quite delicious, wouldn't you say, darling?'

'Yes, awfully good!' I mimicked.

He looked at me, shaking his head, looking a bit hurt but trying to smile. Then he said, 'Darling, we need to talk.'

I felt my heart jump and didn't want to hear any more of whatever he was going to say. I knew it could only lead to trouble. I shook my head, saying nothing, making it very clear I did not want to discuss anything.

He sighed, putting down his mug, and just looked at me, then looked around the room, wondering what he should do next.

'Whatever it is you want to say, why don't you let it drop? I have said enough,' I hissed, turning away and staring at my drink.

'But I am devastated by what you have told me,' he murmured, looking ahead, making it sound like he was talking to himself. 'Firstly, of course I should have recognised instantly you were ill. But I just assumed . . .' he said, letting it trail off.

I watched him out of the corner of my eye, listening. Waiting to see what he was saying.

'But I thought it was simply . . . You looked so wretched! Yes, of course you were ill!' he said again, getting very annoyed with himself.

'Please let it go, Ralph. Frankly, I am not sorry I said it. It hurt, you let me down, but that is history. It has been said, now we both know. So it is over,' I said, feeling cold and annoyed. It was now too fresh in my mind. I didn't want to drag it out.

'But it was more than that, darling,' he said slowly, turning to look at me. 'It was all that horror you experienced. Then I inadvertently sent you . . . bloody dammed you back to that hell! My goodness,' he said, thinking. 'It was so bad, you chose to brave the streets, wandering in the dead of night, exposed to that dreadfully awful weather, with heavy snows, rather than try to seek shelter with them.'

'Fuck off, Ralph, I told you! Forget it. I did bloody try! I went to the house and my mother was looking for money from me. She had nothing. I had nothing. So I wasn't fucking welcome. She wanted to use me. I wouldn't agree, so . . . Let it go! It is not your bloody business,' I said, suddenly feeling myself losing control. 'You weren't to know that! It wasn't really your fault! It was nothing to do with you. But bloody yes, you did take me there! You wouldn't listen, you wouldn't believe me. Now get the hell out or I will leave. I can't take any more! In fact, if you must know, while we are on the subject . . .'

The next thing I knew he was holding me, pinning my arms with his arm wrapped around me, pulled into his chest. He was stroking me while holding me against him. 'Please, darling, don't! Say no more. Believe me, I do understand! I love you. I always knew you were very special. I saw that in the first moment I met you. You had such dignity! I could see how proud you were. My God, the world is indeed a cruel place. I was cruel simply by being indifferent. Yes, I was smug and self-righteous. Quite a bloody prig, really. Darling, listen to me. I want to say I am so terribly sorry. Yes, I did turn my back on you. In fact, I saw you through the driving mirror watching after me. You looked so terribly young and bedraggled, and so frightfully vulnerable. I choose to drive on. I was already late for my meeting,' he said slowly, shaking his head, sounding so very regretful. Then he sighed, looking down at me.

I stared at the colour of his pyjamas, not really seeing them. I was somewhere I didn't want to be. Back with him standing on that road, feeling terribly tired, lost and lonely. But trying to muster up a bit of strength to move on, telling myself, forget about it. Ah, well, that's life! Then go in and see the ma.

But he did come back into my life. I did reach out to him, and he still let me down a second time. Now I don't know. I feel like it may happen again. I think I have tried and failed. Ralph is not going to marry me. I am on a fool's errand. Oh, well, at least I tried, I thought, pulling away from him, saying, 'I need a cigarette. No more, Ralph. Let the past now rest in peace. I have to think of the future.'

'Pop into bed, darling, I will get them. Where are they?' he said, looking around, seeing them on the table.

'Were you in bed?' I said, looking pointedly at his pyjamas.

'No, I took a bath, but I was concerned about you. I wanted to check on you.' Then he half-smiled, saying, 'I did come in at one stage. You were asleep even then. But I dare not tread where angels fear to go! So I thought it best to wait. So, here we are, Martha,' he said, not knowing what to say any more. There was a wall between us; a new barrier had gone up. I could feel the tension in the air. It felt like there was a lot of things unsaid, but should be said. The time was drawing close. I could feel something myself, tugging away at my insides. A sense, a knowing, something was going to come to a head. I think he sensed it too.

I pushed back the bedclothes and threw my legs out of the bed, seeing the silk float, admiring it from a distance. It didn't seem that important any more. I walked over to the window and looked out, seeing the storm was still flashing lightning, but it wasn't as powerful, or maybe I had gotten used to it. Then I turned and saw Ralph looking at me like he was trying to figure me out. Staring with his brows knitted, thinking hard.

'Ralph, you have managed to find a way in to tear down my defences, temporarily anyway, leaving me exposed. I think as we are on that path we should continue. What about you? You have taken vows. What are they? Poverty, chastity and obedience. Let us take the obedience. Yes, you take orders. You must do, and go, where you are ordered. I would say you do. Poverty! How do you rationalise, reconcile this –' I said, waving my hand around the place, taking in everything, including what we were both wearing '– your lifestyle, Ralph, with your vow of poverty?'

'This is not my lifestyle as a priest,' he said quietly. 'It is as I told you, Martha. I am on sabbatical. So technically I am keeping my vows as a priest. Whilst now I am living as a private person,' he said.

'Hmm. Very Jesuitical, splitting hairs, as the Dominicans would say, Ralph. What about your celibacy? That is a Church rule also, a man-made one. It is not the teaching of the Christ I follow! He said nothing about this when he asked his followers to grow his kingdom here on earth. Begin the first Roman Catholic Church. I don't know what kind of God you pray to. But mine is a lot kinder. He is much more benign and loving, more forgiving. Your God is a very cruel

God. He terrorises you into an unnatural way of life. You believe you will what, Ralph? What will your God do to you to wreak vengeance down on your head if you break your vows?'

He looked at me, saying, 'You are right. It is vows I have taken as a priest. I am a member of the Roman Catholic Church. I do believe I am anointed by God to do his holy will.'

'I already said, Ralph, this is not the word of God. He did not ask his followers to take a vow of chastity. So what is it you are about, Ralph? You want to do good? Let us see, you abandoned me twice when I needed your help. Not knowingly. It was simply pure ignorance. You looked at me but you did not see me. I spoke to you but you did not hear my plea for help. So why? Because you have spent so many bloody years closeted away in an institution studying for an elite order of priests who practically rule the Church. Oh, yes, Ralph. Very elite, your order. It takes years before ordination is even considered. You leapt the years because you were already a doctor. But do you know? Your ignorance came from too much bloody learning! You spend too much time thinking. You have educated yourself out of the real world. Everything is so complicated, you believe what you have been brainwashed into believing. I believe if you really wanted to do good, and I do not question your integrity for one minute, but I think quite simply you would have been better served as a married man.

'You could have done good with a wife. Had children, helped them to grow and develop, and sent them into the world as caring, loving people who would make a difference simply through their kindness, caring and even your good manners. It would all help to make the world a better place. I think you hide behind your chastity just like you do with your poverty! Your obedience? Well, you have told them to go and fuck themselves, because here you are taking private time for yourself, doing what you want to do. Oh, you can cloak it in more technical terms, call it a "sabbatical"! But it is the same thing. A married woman or man can't tell their partner, "Sorry, dear! I am off for a sabbatical! See you in a year!" Because it is not part of the marriage contract. The Church can bend and go whichever way the wind blows them good fortune. That is why they have survived for over two thousand years! They are the masters of Machiavellian skulduggery!

'So, to sum up, Ralph, I believe you are afraid of life! Oh, you say you want me. You want to make love to me. But that is all in your head, Ralph. I have no doubt you desire me, you love me. But it is at a distance. You do not really love me, you do not really desire me. Not me, Martha Long. You want me because I am a woman, I am here and I am available to you! Because you are a hot red-blooded male. But that is it. You cling to your vows because they are your saviour. You spent too many years locked away in a boarding school as a boy. In your own way, you are no different to me. The poor little rich boy, while I am the poor little street kid. You got the privileges; I got the street sense. But we both have a lot in common. Neither of us had a home life. No, very few of the wealthy ruling classes did! So you are playing games with me, Ralph. Well, let the games end. I am going home to start my new life. I will probably marry before the year is out and start a family. So enough said. I bid you goodnight,' I said, looking at his struck-dumb stone face.

He just sat and stared, wondering where I came out of and where is Martha Long? I felt like laughing.

Suddenly he blinked, raised his eyebrows and said, 'I am going for a drink. Please excuse me.'

I watched as he stood up, taking to his heels, and marched out the door, leaving a draught behind him he swung it open so hard. I could hear the thud of his footsteps on the carpeted stairs as his presence faded out of the room, leaving only a cold sense of foreboding in its wake.

I sat still, staring at the door, not moving. My hard shell that had masked my inner softness, my deep love and need for him, started to crumble. It is happening almost as quickly as it appeared. I could feel a panic begin to raise itself. I had spent my anger. Now I wanted him back. I need him, but a terrible fear was hitting me. We have crossed a line too far. I have moved into territory where I didn't belong. Tapped into something that was too private for him to even acknowledge. He did the same to me, so I went straight for his jugular. I homed in on his weakness. Yes, I may have spoken the truth, but what has the truth to do with anything? I have laid us both bare. Left us naked. Now we are both exposed. The relationship we have developed slowly, coming from our past history together, had accelerated very quickly in the weeks we have spent together. We had grown very close, developed a bond that tied us almost like a couple but without the deep intimacy of sex. Yet in spite of that, or perhaps because of that, we had grown very close. We were almost inseparable. We only parted to sleep, each going to their own room.

I have grown to love him very deeply. I admire him in so many ways. I know he feels the same. He has really cherished me. I have grown as a woman, become much more aware of my own deep femininity. Something I was not really conscious of before because I was always running to provide. Since I was a young adult I have been a responsible mother. I didn't have time to think about my own needs. I didn't have a man in my life to bring out the woman in me. I was simply Martha, the person, the mother, the woman, who wanted to get on in life. Now that side of me has run its course. My days of mothering ended when Sarah grew wings and flew the nest. My past caught up with me, and I faced it in a mental hospital. Or rather managed, I think, to acknowledge I do have problems. So be it, I am moving beyond that now. I needed to look to the future. Start a new life. The old one is dead. It is all now part of my experience. It has gone into what I have, and will, become.

Sergei asked me to marry him. It was then the realisation hit me. Yes, of course, I do want to marry again, I do want a family. I desperately want that. I desperately want a man in my life to love and make me feel loved. So I took my courage in my hands and came here. To meet the only man I have ever loved. I knew it was a huge risk. I could have made a thundering fool of myself. I could have been rejected. I was not sure if I could handle that. My near fast exit from this world is still terribly fresh. I could relapse with maybe no way back. But I feel an inner strength, a drive to push and take risks, and the devil may care! I was back to my old nature. Be afraid but do it anyway! Because the rewards are great.

So here I am. It was better beyond my wildest dreams. I have been so happy. I had a growing awareness he may yet choose to marry me. I understood perfectly he needed time to arrive at such a decision. His life as it is did not happen overnight. It took years for him to arrive where he is now. He has been a priest for a very long time but now he is here to question his way of life. He was trying to work out if it held any real purpose for him any more. But you put the spanner in the works by accelerating the whole process. Not just that but you confronted him about things on a very deeply emotional level that he was not anywhere near to even recognising! He has a deep inner loneliness that he covers up through being a caring doctor, the ministering priest, by helping others. He reaches out to people. But he does not recognise he is not helping his own inner deep emptiness. He must have been a sad little boy, only seeing his family during holidays. His mother was away a lot. She was not exactly the maternal type. Very lovely but a bit of a social butterfly. The children had Nanny!

Martha, you are a fool. Your relationship was most certainly not strong enough, or cemented enough in time, to allow you to push that far. Now you have thrown down the gauntlet to him. You have shown a side he was not aware of. He still sees you in his mind's eye as the little waif. The young girl who grew to become his lovely young 'rosebud'. He used to call you that. He thinks now you are the same girl who has grown into the woman he thought he knew. The soft, loving, feminine, vulnerable woman who has been ill in a mental hospital. But she has pulled through. I am still the same Martha he has always loved, the one who does not make too many demands on him. The one who shares his loneliness, but he is not aware of that bit. It is not something he would dwell on as a public schoolboy – stiff upper lip, old chap. A mature man, a doctor and a priest of a very elite order! They are certainly trained to keep the old stiff upper lip!

So you blew the whole bleedin thing up with a keg of dynamite. You are not the woman he thought he knew! You who has stirred up a whole hornets' nest! He has no choice but to tell you, *I am sorry, dear, but I cannot meet your need for a commitment. No, I do not want to marry. Frankly, my dear, I would find it difficult to handle you. You reach into places I would not care to tread, thank you very much. Good day to you! Please shut the door on your way out! You may ask directions in the village to the train station. The locals are very helpful around here. Nice to have met you again,* as he smartly produces his hand to give me a firm handshake, then turns on his heels, leaving me to shut the door after me. I make me way down the drive, getting buckled over with the heavy suitcase.

I stopped to think about this, getting that extreme picture. But it would be all the same – rejection is rejection. Then I suddenly roared laughing at the picture, more out of fright than anything. I could feel the panic of loneliness, of being lost, getting abandoned – the terrible fear of it hammering inside my chest. I wanted to jump up and run down the stairs, crying, *No, don't leave me. I'm sorry! Please, I didn't mean any of them things! I don't know what came over me. I am a right eejit! I do push like that; it's the only way I know. Believe it or not, I did it because I love you. I actually said all those things because I wanted to get close to you. I wanted us to push our relationship to a deeper level! The problem is, I have always known what I wanted from you. I have always loved you. But you are ten steps behind me. You always were. I wanted to tear the priest away from the Church and even fight God for you! Your God! Because you belong to me and you need me. I understand you. I have had glimpses of the man behind the masks. But you do not know or understand any of this. You think the priest in you is the only way for you to be happy. But that priest makes the man you are barren. He does not allow you to live and love and take risks and cry like a man. You could do this with a woman! Me! Because I would devote my life to making you happy. Because you would be my whole world! With you by my side, I would fear nothing. I would reach for the stars, taking you with me. We would carry each other. I could make you happy, or die trying.*

But I did not run or say any of these things. I sat still, staring at the floor. No, I can't run to him screaming in terror. *Don't walk away and abandon me! Please! Don't leave me all on my own! I can't bear the empty silence in a world where I don't belong. I don't matter. I have no one to call my own.*

No, because that is the child screaming in terror. I am not a child; I am a woman. But not even the woman can tell him her real reasons for doing that to him. Because we had not arrived at that intimate point where he knew it was safe to listen, because he trusted me. No, he had opened some very deep old wounds and I turned around and knifed him back, killing our relationship before it had a chance to strengthen.

I lifted my head, feeling the tears running down my cheeks, and wiped them away with the back of my hand, looking around me. I listened to the silence, hearing the emptiness and knowing it was telling me I was now on my own. Nobody is going to come, there is nothing to expect. I stirred, then it hit me. I can have some comfort, have a cigarette.

I got up and grabbed my smokes, rolling one up and lighting it. My mind flitted on the idea that maybe he will come to me and it won't be so bad. Maybe it is just the fear in me that thinks I have pushed him away. Then my heart started to drop. No, I saw the look on his face. He was icy cold. I had shocked and pushed him too far. I know him, he has iron discipline. He will react as he has been trained to do. Look coldly and clinically, deal with the facts. *This woman is now making complications in my life. She is getting too close. She wants marriage. This is impossible. I must be free of this.* So, yes, no doubt about it, Martha, you will be given your marching orders.

You fucking eejit! Or are you? Think again, why did you really push? There are a million reasons for doing just one thing. I have looked at some of my reasons. But the bottom line is, Martha, you pushed because you are here to see if Ralph wanted to share his life with you. That is the real reason you went for the jugular, knowing it was the wrong time, but you were not out of control. You knew exactly what you were doing. Yes! You damn well faced it head on, which is the person you are! Good, bad or indifferent, you face things head on. He does not! He could afford to toy with you, he thinks. He knows he can go back to being a priest, but he also thought perhaps marriage was a possibility with me. So how long would it have taken him to arrive at his decision?

Yes, Martha, that was the unspoken question. You knew it but did not push yourself to face it. But it was there, and you knew if you did not face him with it, you could have been left waiting at his pleasure only to be told sometime in the future, *Sorry, Martha. I have decided to remain a priest.* By then I would have lost the opportunity of moving on. It would be too fucking late! Right! So face it, Martha. You have done what you came here to do. Find out if the man wants you! Tomorrow is another day. Prepare yourself for the worst. You know what you have to do then!

Right! Good! I thought, putting out my cigarette butt in the ashtray and climbing into bed. I switched off the light and slid under the covers, enjoying the silky warmth of the gown. Suddenly I realised just how tired I was. My eyes started to feel very heavy and I was out like a light.

13

I woke up to see light streaming in the window. The storm was over. It looks like a nice morning now, grand and calm.

I looked around the room, feeling something strange. Then it hit me. Ralph! I have to face him. Oh, dear God, grant that everything will be OK. If I have to go home without him in my life, I will get on with it. But me heart was leppin at the fear. I hope there won't be awful tension, a terrible atmosphere, with us creeping around each other. That would come to no good end.

I lay still for a minute, waiting for my heart to slow down, then put my legs out of the bed and made to get my wash things. Madame Bouclé always leaves out lovely big fluffy towels. So maybe I will take my time in the bath and try to relax myself. Find an inner place where I can get a bit of peace and deal with whatever happens. Take it all calmly, yeah, resigned. Then move on to Plan B – Sergei! He knows I don't love him but he is willing to make a go of it. OK, why not? Love grows out of respect and a willingness to work together towards a common goal!

Ah, fuck, Martha! Will you stop your carry-on? Of course love matters! Ah, shut the fuck up, Martha. That's only Plan B. Look at that when you have to! Snort! I was beginning to feel really annoyed with myself. Jaysus! My nerves are gone!

Right, take it easy. Have your lovely bath, take one thing at a time. OK, good plan! I headed myself off to the bathroom feeling better with that thought. It managed to get me moving.

I put on a pair of jeans and a black polo-neck mohair sweater; it was lovely and big and went down past my arse. Then I put in my gold stud earrings. I have worn those for years. I bought them for myself as a present for my eighteenth birthday. I brushed out my hair, seeing it was lovely and shiny. Still not a grey hair and me now hit the thirties. Right, I decided to leave it down and just pulled it up at the sides, sticking a long brown hair slide across to keep it in place. Then I made my way cautiously down the stairs. I need time to get my bearings, see the lie of the land before I come face to face with Ralph.

My heart thumped as I stood ready with my hand on the doorknob to open it. I took in a deep breath, lifting my chest, and pushed open the door. The room looked empty! Madame was at her usual place over by the stove but there was no sign of Ralph.

I went in slowly, closing the door, feeling my heart begin to thump then a sinking feeling as it hit my stomach. He's not here! Wonder where he is? Suddenly I felt very anxious to see him. I made to turn just as Madame looked straight over at me, saying, 'Bonjour, Madame!'

Oh! I forgot to greet her, very bad manners. It wouldn't do to upset her as well. I walked back into the room, saying, 'Bonjour, Madame Bouclé!', giving her a little bow of my head.

She put out her arm with a tea towel hanging off it, waving me to sit. I hesitated, wanting to get out and look for Ralph. But then I just smiled and sat myself down. Maybe he will come in, he might have heard me. But I didn't hear any sound of him. Wonder what the fuck he's up to? Maybe he's gone to the village to get a newspaper. He's always around when I come down for breakfast! He never leaves the house without telling me.

Right, calm down, take it easy, I'm in a worse state than I thought I was.

'Madame!' she said. I looked up to see her with a steaming hot plate in her hand. She was holding it with a tea towel. I leaned back and she landed it in front of me. Then a basket of hot rolls. Lovely with a mug of tea.

I was just reaching across the table to get the sugar bowl when I saw a white envelope with my name on it leaning against the fruit bowl. I stared at it, my mind trying to take it in. I slowly reached across, checking it was really for me. Yes, there's my name with a line flowing underneath. I opened it, taking out one sheet of paper. A note was written in his beautiful script. It was folded in half. I opened it, reading, then read again. I couldn't take it in.

Martha, I will be away, I do not say when I shall return. In the meantime, do please feel free to make yourself comfortable. I have asked Madame Bouclé to take care of you. She will remain on in the house during my absence, as she would normally do. If you need something, please, do just ask. I have left you a French phrasebook, which might be of help. It is on the kitchen table next to this envelope. Martha, I would suggest, you must do what you think best for you.

My deepest regards, Ralph.

I felt an almighty panic hitting me but it stayed down. My heart was sinking all the way to the floor; it was leaving me. A terrible feeling of dread hit. I could hear the roars in my head of the panic. HE'S GONE. HE'S LEFT YOU, MARTHA! He was too polite to tell you to leave, so he just upped and left himself. He probably told Madame Bouclé to phone him when I have left. He doesn't want to face me. He's not up to that. He couldn't deal with the pain he would see no matter how much I would try to hide it, and hide it I would. I can never admit humiliation to go with my rejection. Chin up! Smile! Be polite, that would have been my way. But he would have known, he would have seen it in my face, showing through my eyes. He spotted it that first time he ever met me, as he said himself. Yes, he was the first one to ever notice my pain and that added to me falling body and soul in love with him. Now it is over. OK, time to . . . Is it?

I read the letter again. No, it doesn't say get out of my house, my life. Just 'Do what is best for you'! Oh, Ralph! Where are you? No, I can't just walk away! Can I?

I can't breathe. I need air. I got up and made my way out the door, hearing Madame calling me.

'*Oui, Madame?*' I said.

She said something about my untouched breakfast, pointing at it as she lifted her arms with the eyebrows standing up.

'*Non, merci!*' I said, trying to lift my face in a smile. Then tried harder, '*Merci, Madame!* I have a headache,' I said, putting my hand on my head.

I saw the look she gave me as her eyes took in the letter hanging out of my hand. I stalled for a minute, taking in that look, wondering if I had insulted her. I didn't want to be rude and upset her. She has been terribly good to me. I caught the way her eyes looked at me after she lifted them from the letter. They moved, then changed, showing a look of sympathy. Then her mouth fell and she waved, turning away slowly. She knows! She knows he has dumped me. Fuck, that makes it worse!

I took off heading for the stairs and into my room, shutting the door behind me. I have to go. I better get packed. Jesus, what times are the trains? How will I get my plane ticket? I missed my return flight weeks ago but I thought Ralph would be able to organise it. Tell me what to do, go to a travel agent's or something. Fuck! What a mess. I could feel myself shaking all over and my heart was flying. I spotted my tobacco sitting on the low table. I must have forgotten it in my worry to get downstairs. Jesus, little did I only know.

I sat down and rolled a cigarette, thinking, take it easy. Think first. You are just feeling humiliated. You are no longer wanted in this house, you don't belong. But fuck it, that doesn't mean I have to rush out headlong into the middle of nowhere! Jaysus! It was bad enough getting here. But at least I had my train and plane tickets. Now I have nothing. I have no times of trains or even the bleedin planes. I could get stranded anywhere. It's the middle of the bleedin winter here. The weather can be worse than Dublin! Right, so take it easy. Don't panic! Sit, do nothing.

I lifted my head from the window. I had been staring for hours out at the lawns but seeing nothing. I now feel numb. The loss of Ralph had shut me down completely. I couldn't take the pain. I felt like nothing mattered. I would be better if I got moving out of here. Then I could put distance between him and me and this place, with all the memories here to crowd in on me and drive me mad. There are too many happy memories! They are twisting my guts.

I started wringing my hands, trying to make a decision. I could feel my breathing coming heavy. It was the need to run, take off! Make a decision – but, no, something would not let me.

I knew it was too late to start going now. No, it takes hours to get across France from here. Nearly a whole fucking day! I will have to find some way of organising it. Right, the phrasebook. Madame can help me. I will ask her, but not now. When I am ready, tomorrow.

Right, so that means I am staying for today at least. Anyway, the afternoon is nearly gone, I thought, seeing the day was now turning grey, with the bloody country mist starting to rise. It's very damp out there, that wouldn't do the aul lungs any good! No, that's definitely settled then, I thought, making out the door.

I stopped on the landing, looking at the door into Ralph's room. I wanted to put my hand on the knob and open it, just to get a sense of him. Look and see his things, remind me of his presence. But I hesitated, listening and looking down the stairs. Madame would think I am snooping. It wouldn't be right. She knows my status in this house. He has gone off, leaving me here. He left a letter for me and I reacted badly. Oh, yeah! You gave that one away nicely, Martha! Well done, you need now to look before you jump. But fuck it! I needed an answer and I got it! So fuck him, the bastard. He spends his life running. The cowardly bastard wouldn't tell me to my face.

On the other hand, I forgot, no. It isn't actually cowardice with him. It is sheer fucking arrogance! I have seen over my time how they can cut you dead when they have no further use for you. That is what he is doing. Simply dismissing me, because his decision is made. The thundering fucking bastard. If I could only get my hands on him this minute, I would give him an earful! Huh! He thinks he heard enough last night, does he now? Fuck, that was nothing. He has not experienced me when I really let rip! I could feel the rage beginning to roar up in me. I wanted to do him damage.

My head peeled to his door again, with the chest flying up and down. Where does he keep his fucking cigars? I could mash them and stick them in his bed – that would discommode his lordship. No Madame Bouclé around to change his bleedin sheets when he decides to take himself to bed! No, he would have to do it himself, the slithering, slimy, good-for-nothing, chinless, waste-of-space bastard! I will kill him! Wonder does that Madame one know where he's gone? Yes, fuck that! I could turn up and make an absolute show of him. Give him something to remember me by when I'm gone home. Yes, off to have me new life, thanking my lucky stars I wasn't landed with a . . . 'Oh, the bleedin bastard,' I moaned, running out of air. 'Fucking men! Useless bastards,' I muttered, nearly crying with the rage, then making my way back up the stairs.

I don't know what to do with myself, I thought, heading back into the room. Go for a walk? No! Too damp. Talk to Madame? You can't speak French. Listen to the radio? No, too many happy memories. See if she has something to eat? No, not hungry. Pack? Fuck that! Have a smoke? Yeah! Great idea.

I walked up the drive huddled into my fur coat, listening to the crunch of my soft leather boots walking over the mulch thrown up by the storm several nights ago. Jesus, that seems an age ago, I thought, thinking about that night. I stamped up to the front door and stood looking at it. No, don't bother knocking. It might torment her. I get enough of that in the morning when I come in for me breakfast. She gives me a polite, '*Bonjour, Madame,*' then the guarded look as the eyes peel away, much as to say, *Are you still here?* But then she gets back to her work as if it's none of her business.

The French are great at that. Lots of shrugs, then it's *Merde*! The world is crazy! But we do have our routine, Madame and me. I have settled in nicely since Ralph flew the coop. So now, I might as well be getting meself a bit of French country air while I'm at it. I need to recover my equilibrium before I start my journey home. I don't want to have another crash before I even get started on my new life. No, good food, plenty of rest and the good fresh air will do me all the good in the world. I need all the good that's going. I'm sure Ralph would agree with that. After all, he is sworn to make well and do no harm. Or is it, if you can't do good, then do no harm? Yeah, Hippocratic oath! Jaysus! That man is full of oaths and vows!

Right, I blinked, bringing back my vision, and looked ahead, seeing my way around the side of the house, and let myself in the side door. I slammed the heavy door shut and walked along the old tiled passage. I looked at the doors along the corridor and decided to take a look. I stuck my head in one of them and found myself looking at a big old study. Or more like a library, as a huge old bookcase stood in the middle of the wall behind the door. I went in, shutting the door behind me. It was filled with books. Some of them looked old and dusty. Probably over a hundred years old. Must belong to the relatives who are pushing up daisies by now. I looked around, seeing the two lovely old high-back, leather-winged library chairs sitting one each side of the big fireplace. They both had a table standing next to the wall, with lamps sitting on top, and a box of cigars sat on one of the tables. I opened it, seeing Ralph's cigars! Ah-ha! So this is where he keeps them! I lifted one up, smelling it – very nice. Then sat down in the chair, sucking on the cigar without lighting it up, and lifted up a book. Tolstoy's *War and Peace*! Jaysus! I read that years ago, definitely not my cup of tea at the minute. My poor brain is laboured enough. It needs rest.

This place needs air. It's a bit stuffy. Ralph must come here for his smoke and do his reading, relaxing, and write letters, I saw, looking at the big old roll-top desk with the round leather chair sitting in front of it. Bet that's where he keeps all his papers and private stuff!

Right, get the hell outa here before Madame thinks you are up to no good. It would be embarrassing, seeing as I am an unwanted guest. Ah, fuck the begrudgers! I've been rapidly developing a brass neck over the last few days since he left. Yeah, once the shock wore off, I settled in nicely.

OK, time to get moving upstairs and out of these boots and fur coat, then down for dinner. Wonder what she's dishing up tonight? Jaysus, pity I can't bring her home with me, she is a marvellous cook, not to mention the polishing and cleaning she does. Oh, how the mighty have fallen. A week ago I thought I was going to inherit her when I got me hands on Ralph, now look at the state of me! A bleedin nomad, wandering around in a foreign land, looking for love! The only difference between me and the nomads is that they move on, looking for leafy bushes for their goats, or whatever it is they breed.

Right, up and out, get moving. I shut the door behind me and made my way back up the by now familiar stairs. Pity, I felt so much at home here. I will miss the aul place, I sighed, making for my room.

I gave myself an extra polish in the bathroom, soaking for at least an hour. No more slobbing; no, today I am going to do something special, I thought, hurrying meself back to my room and dropping my wash things, digging into my make-up bag. No, today is 'make-the-effort' day. Right, just a little make-up; it is morning anyway. Or nearly, well, maybe a bit into the afternoon. I decided this morning I would have a lazy morning. Well, most days have been lazy, but I did get a bit windblown when I showed my nose out in the grounds for an airing. Jaysus, the weather here can be very treacherous. Biting cold winds! Anyway, the Madame is fed up looking at me appearing down in my pyjamas for breakfast. The same pair for the last few days. Maybe she wasn't fanning the cooking smells with that dishcloth after all! Anyway, I gave her a big smile this morning. It made a change from the usual grunts we give each other. She smiled back. Things are looking up!

Right, what's special on the agenda today? Oh, yeah, I am going to take myself off down to the village and sit in one of the bistros. I passed them a few times. People seem to meet and chat over their coffee and cakes, very sociable. So I better get down there and start to mingle with the locals, meet a few real French, get myself into the holiday mood. So long as Madame does not put the boot under me . . . She can't, she takes her orders from himself, and he doesn't look in any hurry to get back. So, in the meantime, I'm making the best of a bad situation. I'll just have to enjoy meself. Oh, yeah, that's a good idea I thought up for myself when he gets back and sees I haven't shifted myself. No, not the squatters' rights one, because it's not just about him any more. I like this house and the way of life. I'm very fond of Madame Bouclé and I think she might grudgingly like me too. But himself is a fucker. He would just grab me by the neck and fuck me out with the cat.

I shall simply tell him, *Sorry, old bean, but no mon, no fun. I didn't have the loot to buy myself a plane ticket! So got marooned here, old sock! What, eh! Damn unsporting of you not to cough up and leave the old first-class tickets! Eh! What? Shocking bad form, I say! Oh! One more thing, old sport. I think it is awfully bad manners to send me packing with a load of old baggage! Have you seen my suitcase, old bean? Bloody disgusting! How can you possibly expect me to travel first class wearing diamond earrings carrying a Dunnes Stores suitcase? I mean, it is worse than the Woollies' best! Woolworths! For gaud's sake! No, has to be Louis Vuitton. Good old Louis goes well with diamonds, old sock!*

Come to think about it, he did give me diamonds! I did get diamond earrings! Yeah, I thought, feeling my heart sink again, remembering how much I love him. We were so happy. Fuck you, Ralph! I miss you terribly!

Right, but forget it, Martha, the bastard didn't think twice about dumping you! Oh, yes, the fucker has been ruthless with me, so two can play that game! Gone over a whole bleedin week! Right, my claws have had time to grow! I will be bleedin dug outa him if he comes the high and mighty with me! I will even insist on a taxi to the train station and one to the airport! Oh, yes, pride has nothing to do with this. Oh, no, this is a case of 'Hell hath no fury like a woman scorned' – sniff. He won't forget me in a hurry!

Right, a little lipstick, not too much, this is France after all. They invented beauty! Well, the 'chic' look. That's the one I'm going for. Now for the daywear. What does one wear to a French village bistro? Never know who I might meet! Ahh, the very thing. A lovely polo-neck black-wool frock, just about covers me arse. It looks more like a jumper. I'll wear that with a leather belt. Oh, black winter tights and boots. Hair down or up? Hmm, up looks better with fur, that's all I have! Perfect, that's all I need. Now for a squirt of perfume. Oh, and my real pearl earrings. I looked at myself in the mirror. Good God, woman! You look smashing! I would marry you myself, if I wasn't meself!

OK, time to perambulate down yonder village. I opened the door, making my way down the stairs in a whiff of perfume and fur. I decided to pull up the collar and hold it, it definitely gives me the 'chic' look. Now I'm ready for anything.

I made my way along the hall, listening to my boots make a muffled thud on the rugs then thump along the floorboards, sounding purposeful, a woman who was going somewhere. My hand was on the doorknob getting ready to turn it when I heard the whish of tyres and a car stop just as I was opening the door. Before I had time to think, the door was opened and I was stepping out. I saw a blur of dark-green Jaguar, a car door fly open and a man in a long black coat with a leg encased in black pristine trousers with a very sharp crease down the centre emerge. The leg disappeared into a handmade, narrow-fitted, black shiny shoe tied with a lace. The sock was black cashmere, of course.

I recognised the owner. I stood gaping, trying to correct my vision as Ralph whirled and stood erect to attention, taking in the sudden sight of me. I stared, seeing first the whole of him – the long black

for him. The fright and fear and the humiliation at being a nobody in somebody's life and house was making me feel like a child again. An outcast, an outsider. Then that very old familiar strength started to hit me again. Suddenly I had a buzzing feeling going through me of being saved. I was all right. I could get on the train and go away from here. I had a life waiting for me back in Ireland. In Dublin I had my own home and a man who had asked me to marry him. I have a dog, yes, Bonzo. He will be missing me. The neighbours know me. I am nearly one of them. I have lived among them for years. I belong to Dublin. I am somebody. I am Martha Long, mother of Sarah. I am successful. I am somebody to be respected. I have come a long way. I am not the bastard of the ma and Jackser's slave.

No, I thought, pulling out my tobacco and deciding to head for the bistro. Ralph Fitzgerald, yes, he has worked and achieved through discipline. But it was all laid out for him. All he had to do was follow orders. So, fuck him. I have outstayed my welcome in his house and in his life? So what? Fuck him! Hard cheese, aul sock! No, I will have no problem facing him. In fact, I will humiliate him by saying quite crisply, *Would you mind awfully organising my trip home? Unfortunately I do not have your financial resources. I missed my flight, so it is going to be expensive. Would that be a problem?* I shall say, looking at him with a fixed, indifferent look on my face. Oh, yes, the great mimic me! Fuck them. The bastards in this world who think they are one cut above me! 'No, Martha, you are forgetting who you are. You are worth a thousand of them arrogant, chinless bastards,' I hissed, gritting my teeth as I turned and headed off in the opposite direction, making my way to the bistro.

That was a brilliant idea, Martha, yeah. I enjoyed myself in there with the two old ladies and the man. He spoke a bit of English and acted as the translator. Most of the fun was when we suddenly understood what the other was saying. Then the roars, shouts and laughs went up, with the hands rising to land a slap on the table. Yeah, we all laughed, looking and nodding our heads at each other when the penny finally dropped. It was the reward after much hard work. With me at the ready '*Oui, oui!* That is it!'

It didn't matter what we were saying, only that we finally worked it all out. It was the discussion between them, and me diving in on the odd word I recognised! I passed the time for them, giving them something different to think about, while they had all the time in the world to sit and indulge me. With me trying to escape, for a while, the horror of what I was now losing with Ralph.

Yeah, they were lovely old people, not too much different from my own lovely old Dublin people back home. No, we're all the same under the skin. Only the colour or the language might be different, but we still want the same things. We just want to be loved and to feel we are somebody because we belong. 'Yeah, that was grand, lovely! I enjoyed that,' I sighed, pulling up my fur collar and digging my hands deep into the pockets as I made tracks back to the house.

14

I turned in the gates, looking ahead to the wide expanse of fields and lawns, with huge old trees spread out on the horizon. I walked on, finally getting sight of the big house in the distance. Hmm, I thought, lifting my eyes taking it all in. Yes, everything he surveys is his for the taking. All for the benefit and glory of him, and his family when he is not using it. Right, Ralphie, I do not intend making it easy for you. No, two can play your genteel game of politeness. I am going to draw you out, all the way to the wire. No polite hints will shift me. I will make it very uncomfortable for you. Because I am now brimming with confidence. I know who I am and I have my own life back in Dublin. But I intend having some fun at your expense while the going is good. I shall continue to have a life of ease and the comfort of a wonderful holiday with everything a body could want, until you tell me otherwise. I am in no hurry. This is actually the start of my new life. I am living it now. It will continue when I get home. Sergei will wait; he has been waiting. If he does not, then it was not intended. No, philosophy is the order of the day. I shall take life in my stride. So, Ralphie, the ball is in your court. You have to tell me to leave.

I looked at the front entrance and decided to keep going. Walk ahead, Martha, round the back and in the side entrance. I walked along the side passage and through the door leading into the main hall, then turned and went up the stairs, seeing no sign of Ralph. Good, I am not ready to meet him just yet.

I went into my room and took off my coat, hanging it up in the wardrobe. Then I took off my boots and left them at the bottom in the shoe rack. I checked my hair in the mirror, seeing I looked fresh and healthy. I had certainly filled out again in all the right places, I thought, feeling delighted at how sexy I was looking. I looked grand in the knee-high soft-leather boots with the wool frock clinging to my curves and the wide leather belt strapped around my waist.

OK, head for the kitchen and get something to eat. I wonder if he is there? Well, I doubt I will be leaving today. It's too bloody late. It must be around the four o'clock mark.

I headed into the kitchen, seeing nobody there. But the smell of gorgeous cooking hit me straight away. The kitchen was lovely and warm, with the heat coming from the Aga. A light burned over it, sending a lovely muted yellow glow into the room.

Right, let's see what's to eat. I opened the oven, seeing big casseroles slowly cooking with the steam and heat escaping as I opened the door. I shut it fast. Nothing in there for me by the looks of it. But Madame Bouclé is thinking of producing a big spread tonight. Must be in honour of the wanderer's return. Good, got that to look forward to, I thought, opening the lid of a pot. A clear soup was simmering away and in another pot vegetables sat waiting. I turned around looking, seeing nothing I could eat now. Right, have a bit of bread from the basket and a bit of cheese from the dish sitting on the table. Make a drop of tea and what more could I want?

I opened the kitchen door, making my way out, heading for the stairs, when I heard a door opening behind me in the hall. I could hear the rattling of dishes and the clinking of glass. I stopped and waited to see who it was. Madame came out of the dining room looking very busy with a big, empty, brown wooden tray in her hand and a duster and cloths hanging off her arm. I went up a bit and turned to look from the landing. She didn't see me as she busied herself with the stuff in her arms. I turned and kept going. Oh, she must be doing a cleaning job in the big dining room, I thought, heading for my room. I turned onto Ralph's landing and stopped to listen, not making a sound. No, it's very quiet in there. Wonder if he's gone out? I shrugged my shoulders, thinking, Oh, well, the longer I keep out of his way, the longer my holiday will last.

I lay on my bed reading but not really able to concentrate. I sighed and threw my legs out of the bed, wondering if I should just change into my night things. It doesn't look like I am going to run into

Ralph any time soon. The bastard has been hiding himself since he got back. I went down for dinner last night and no fucking sign of him. I ended up looking down at a bowl of stew. She must have made that using the consommé soup and stuck some vegetables and bits of meat into it. I was told to help myself to the cheese and fruit, and that was my lot. No big dinner in his honour, whoever she was doing the cooking for. But it fucking wasn't for me. Worse! Not a hair, sight nor even sound of him, wherever he got himself to. Never clapped eyes on the bastard. Not even today!

Worse again! When I went down for me dinner tonight, Madame looked at me as if to say, *What do you want?* I stood looking and smiling, then sat down, waiting to be served. She started babbling about something, pointing at the pots and all the stuff bubbling away everywhere. I kept nodding, following her and her busy hands with me eyes and head. Then she slammed the oven door shut and looked to see did I understand. I nodded, letting her think I did. I didn't give a damn about what she was saying, I was waiting for me dinner. But then she turned and went back to her business, getting on with her mound of cooking. So then I was left looking at the empty place where a dinner should sit. I got up and went to the stove, trying to ask her, with me pointing at the pots. Then she started again, nearly getting into a rage this time. Me nerves went. I was looking at the door, afraid of me life. I was worried Ralph would come in and march me out, putting his boot under me arse as he sent me flying out the door. So I just nodded my thanks with a sick, weak smile and took myself off up here without any grub! It looks like he has decided to starve me out.

Jaysus, I thought I was prepared for him but it's looking like I'm no match for the likes of Ralph. He must be deciding to freeze me out as well. Get me on all fronts. I should have fucking known. You can't get the better of these bastards. The aristocracy have it down to a fine art. They know exactly how to bring you to your knees without making it look like they even raised a muscle. Usually it's all in the raised eyebrows or the look in the eyes. Or rather the lack of it. They can look right through you, as if you didn't exist. Ah, well, fuck off, Ralphie. Jaysus, oh man alive, am I glad I didn't end up with you! It would be hell on earth. The wintry silences if you crossed him would freeze the marrow off you. Right, so go fuck yerself, ye chinless bleedin wonder, I thought, giving the air a kick, wishing it was his arse.

Right, better get ready for bed and forget the rest of the night. It looks like I'm stuck with the bread and cheese and the bit of fruit. Not to mention the half-bottle of wine whipped from behind her back. It was left sitting on the windowsill. Jaysus, lucky I changed me mind and went back in to grab that stuff.

Fuck it, I'm the one down to the wire! Now I probably have to slink in and rob the kitchen to feed meself. Still, I'm not moving. He has to tell me to go himself. It's the least he can do, face me like a man. Mind you, if this is a Mexican stand-off, I'm not going to be the first to give in! Imagine, Martha! All this since that night I gave him an earful! It was right what I said about him that first time after he dumped me and then disappeared. It was when I was on my way to that convent, the one for unmarried mothers, I said he was a man of straw! Oh, was I right? Indeed I was, so bloody right. Pity, though, I don't listen to me fuckin self!

Right, get into the pyjamas and dig into the grub. It should go down nice with the drop of wine. No, Ralphie! Yer not goin te best me, ye fucker!

I woke up seeing it was dark and hearing the noise of banging and loud voices drifting up from somewhere in the house. I sat up listening, hearing a buzz of voices and footsteps. I held my breath, wondering what is happening. My head felt a bit muzzy and my eyes were foggy. I looked, seeing the empty bottle sitting on the low table. Jaysus, I drank the lot. Keep this up and I'll have . . .

Suddenly I heard a woman's laugh, then more voices getting louder. I looked out, seeing people getting out of big cars, and they were all dressed up to the nines. The women had long frocks and some were in tight evening dresses that clung to their bodies and came just above the knee. Yeah, I thought, staring out with the mouth hanging open to me belly button, the women are dressed to kill and the men are all in suits and dickie bows.

Fuck! The swine is giving a party! My heart starting hammering and me head flew one way then looked down at myself. So that's what all the grub was about! She was cooking for them! Where's my dressing gown?

I lunged for the wardrobe, then flew open the door. Immediately the tinkle of glasses and voices floated up from downstairs. I could feel myself shaking. I'm not invited! Course ye're not, ye fuckin eejit.

Oh, I can't be seen looking like this. I rushed back in and flew to the mirror. Jaysus, get dressed, wash your face, look at the hair. Then it hit me, no, don't be stupid, you will make a thundering fool of yourself, appearing down there out of nowhere. You will be laughed out of it.

I sank down into the chair, taking hold of my tobacco, and rolled a cigarette, lighting it up. Don't go out there, don't let yourself be seen, I thought, feeling the life going out of me. No matter what I think or say, it always comes back to the truth. I am sick with the longing to be a part of Ralph. But it's over. This is his life, Martha. You are very much not a part of it, I thought, taking a deep sigh and letting it out, feeling I have died and gone to hell.

I sat rock-still with my back pressed to the headboard, staring at the window, looking into the distance, seeing nothing. My insides were icy cold, feeling completely shut down. All the life was gone out of me. I could sense the hours passing and the night drifting away. The voices had dimmed to a more muted and lesser babble as the guests thinned out. I listened as more and more car doors opened then slammed shut. Their engines started and I heard them drive off, the cars slowly taking the guests away from the house.

I looked at the clock. Ten to two. The party is dying down and they are all going home, I thought, blinking and lifting my head, seeing the tobacco with the ashtray sitting on the bed. I sighed, taking in a deep breath, and reached to pick it up. I rolled a cigarette and lit up, taking a deep drag down into my lungs.

No, Martha, this is no good. It is time to call it quits and go home. This is doing me more harm than good now. Tomorrow I will talk to Madame and ask her to ask Ralph to sort out a ticket for me. I will pay for myself. Enough is enough. Leave well alone. I have nearly fallen so low tonight that it is just like the bad old times again. No, I better get moving. I can't afford to let myself fall again now I know the difference. I see the signs coming and I can take action. Right, so no more games. Time to be serious. He is entitled to do as he pleases. He owes you nothing and you owe him nothing. All that talk about love, well . . . it is human nature. People really believe what they are telling you at the time. But human emotions are very fickle. He has simply wiped you out of his mind and therefore out of his existence. I actually did bring him to the edge. That is why he ran, just like he did before, when I was eighteen. The man is a confirmed bachelor, never mind a priest. Anyway, the whole thing is academic now. It matters not one way or the other.

I finished the cigarette and got out of the bed, making my way down to the bathroom. It doesn't matter now if anyone sees me. I owe them nothing and I'm not their business. Anyway, I will be out of here soon. So that goes for Ralph too, if we happen to clap eyes on each other.

I came out of the bathroom and walked down the stairs, thinking of going to the kitchen to get myself a hot drink. But I don't want to meet any of them, not down there. I'll just see if the coast is clear.

I made my way cautiously down the stairs, seeing the house was lit up like a Christmas tree. Every light burned in the hall. Even the old candle chandeliers on the walls blazed in a glory of light. The crystals danced and sparkled, throwing shadows of diamonds into a darkened corner. I could see the glare of lights coming from the dining room, with the doors thrown wide open.

The sitting room door was half-open and I could hear voices and the tinkle of glasses coming from there. I could smell the heavy smoke of cigars and the pungent aroma of expensive cigarettes. Voices murmured then lifted, talking rapidly in French as others joined in, then there was a sudden burst of laughter. I held my breath, wanting to hear. Then I heard Ralph's voice. He was speaking French with the deep mellow timbre of an English gentleman. I listened, thinking it sounded like music. His intonation went softly up and down, like he was making love with the music of words. It sounded like he was gently scolding, then cajoling, then softly whispering words of love.

Other voices joined in, all adding their point. Some made it sound like they were crying out in hushed pain, then the voices would lift. I heard a woman's voice say something, then it sounded like she was pleading as she said Ralph's name. I heard him laugh, then he said something quickly, '*Non, non accord! Ohhh, ma chère Soviah!*' he pleaded. Then she said, raising her voice and making it sound like a cry, '*Ohhh! Que! Ohhh, mon dieu, Ralph!*' He laughed, and they all started shouting, with everyone talking at once.

I crept further down, finally arriving on the bottom step. I wanted to make it into the kitchen and walked slowly and quietly. It was the room closest to the stairs. Beyond that, further down the hall, was the sitting room and my eyes stayed peeled on that. Go on, just take a look, see what's happening. Be careful and they won't see me.

I hesitated, then started heading down, creeping slowly. This is fucking ridiculous. If someone comes out, it is perfectly obvious what I am doing. Sneaking around like a bloody fool. But I couldn't resist.

I held my breath as I got just within their sight. I slowly put my head around the door and found myself looking straight at Ralph. He was leaning against the fireplace with a woman standing close to him. She was leaning herself into him, then pulling away as she got her balance.

She was incredibly sophisticated. Her ash-blonde hair was cut in a wisp around her head. Long and short bits deliberately sculpted were now pasted to cling and frame her face. It was all intended to emphasise her high cheekbones. She wore a long silvery-black dress slit all the way to her thighs. Her black high-heeled shoes with the high back-strap emphasised her long legs. Her make-up was perfect, barely showing she wore any. Her high-arched eyebrows were perfectly shaped into a narrow line. Her beautiful blue-grey eyes sparkled with a light pink and grey eyeshadow that was intended to contrast with her ivory skin. The lipstick was dark wine, showing her white teeth as she smiled. She had the look of the 'Bright Young Things', the devil-may-care young aristocrats of the Roaring '20s.

She is beautiful! I gasped inwardly, letting my eyes gape, with my mouth hang open. I could feel myself wanting to get sick with the fear and jealousy filling me up with its poison, making me feel icy cold.

I watched as she listed to one side, leaning against Ralph while his arm went around her waist to steady her. He was wearing an evening suit with a white dress shirt and a black bow tie. I have never seen him look so handsome or remote from me. He didn't look like the Ralph I knew. He looked like somebody I would admire from a distance. Somebody who would not take me, as I am, very seriously. No, I don't have the sophistication of that woman, or move in his circles.

I watched as she touched him, then left her hand gently resting on his shoulder. That one fancies him, and he knows it, I thought. They are flirting but doing it discreetly. Everyone sees it, but it is nothing. These things are normal, it is expected between a man and a woman. Yeah, I thought, the French invented romance.

I turned away in case he saw me. It would be horrendously humiliating if that happened. It would really lower me to the point of having absolutely no dignity. It's not him I am thinking about; it is my own pride.

I went quietly into the kitchen, closing over the door, not shutting it for fear of making a noise, then looked, seeing the place stuffed with grub. Casserole dishes sat on the side with what looked like pieces of duck in an orange sauce. Bottles of booze were everywhere. I grabbed a plate, loading it with food, and picked up a half-bottle of white wine left sitting on the table. I sat down and started to make short work of it, gulping down a drop of wine filled to the brim in a big glass.

Suddenly the door pushed in with voices and laughing, just as I had half the duck to me mouth. I had given up on the fork. I looked straight into the face of Ralph as he stopped in shock. Your woman came right in behind him, stopping to look at him, then turn to me, seeing his eyes were landed in that direction. Then he recovered and walked in, looking at me, saying, 'Well, hello. It is nice to see you. Are you enjoying yourself?' he laughed, nodding at my plate. Then he whipped open the fridge, taking out a bottle of white wine and looked at the label.

The blonde minced her way over, standing close to him, saying something in French. He waved the bottle slightly, then she said something, keeping her eyes wide as she stared at him, looking like a little girl lost. He grinned, shaking his head laughing, saying, '*Bah! Au contraire! Non, non.*'

She pursed her lips, pushing her mouth out at him, looking like a little girl about to cry, saying, '*Auuh! Oui, oui, Ralph!*' as she landed her hands lightly on his sleeve, holding it and running her long red nails up and down his jacket, trying to persuade him of something. '*Oooh, Ralph!*' she moaned, then she lifted her head, planting a kiss on his lips, whispering, '*Oh, Ralph! Je me sens très seule. Dites oui! S'il vous plaît, Ralph!*'

I stared with the duck halfway to my mouth as it gaped wide open. I was going into spasms of shock. My body didn't know whether to drop dead or kick-start again. The heart was trying but missing a beat as the breath wouldn't come.

I saw Ralph grin, step back and flick his eyes to me, then he was moving out the door, holding the bottle of wine in front of him, with the blonde keeping up as she kept her hand lightly on his arm. Then they were gone.

I looked at my duck sitting in my hand and put it down. Then I looked at my wine and picked it up, swallowing half the glass, nearly choking. I staggered back to my room, deciding I had enough to eat and drink, I just wanted to get back to bed. Somehow I had lost my appetite. Now I felt very tired. It must be well after four in the morning. I felt like I had just had electric-shock treatment. It must feel something like this. Like someone blew me up, leaving me like a living zombie. Because I just had the soul sucked right out of me.

15

I woke up with my head a ball of cotton wool. I squinted my eyes round the room, landing on the window, seeing the sky is very bright, it must be late morning. 'I have slept too long,' I moaned, or maybe just caught up on my sleep. 'Right,' I grunted, pushing back the bedclothes, trying to get one leg out, then the other. I stood up, feeling my legs like jelly. Jaysus, I need a cold drink and a cold shower. OK, first things first. I lowered my head, looking around the room, wondering where my dressing gown was. That bleedin light is too bright, I thought, trying to keep my eyes away from that sun, beaming itself in through the window.

I stepped over the dressing gown lying on the floor by the bed. Jaysus! I never do that, I thought, picking it up and shaking it. I must have been really bad. I threw it around me and struggled my arms into it, feeling a dead weight, then tipped, nearly overbalancing, making for the doorknob to stop myself.

I was halfway down the stairs when I looked down seeing I was in my bare feet. Lovely, Martha, you make a grand picture if himself catches you. Who cares? I thought, landing in the hall and looking down to where the noise was coming from. It was the voice of women. Fuckers must be the leftovers from last night's party. In having their lunch – luncheon in the dining room no less!

Or maybe it's the blonde sex-starved vulture from last night. Then I stopped dead. Wonder where she slept? Suddenly I could feel myself erupting. The rage sent me going blind! 'Fuck this,' I muttered. 'This is adding insult to injury. That no-good, chinless, slimy, good-for-nothing toerag is rubbing my nose in it.'

I stood stock-still, panting, thinking how I would get my own back on him. He has been leading me on, making a fool of me. He's just a cheap chancer! All these years . . . He's not the man I thought he was. I have put myself through all this for nothing. Fuck it, I am going to lift a bottle of red wine and pour it first over her head, then upend the dinner on his fucking skull. I stopped my body as it reeled to get going, still rocking on my feet. Will I do it? YES! I roared in me head.

I took off walking fast and rounded into the dining room, coming to a dead stop and looking around. Two young ones were slapping each other with dusters. The grin was wiped off their face when they saw me rooted to the spot, taking them in. Suddenly they got busy, dusting around, lifting ornaments and furiously dusting the mantelpiece while another one grabbed up the Hoover, looking terribly busy. Oh, just the cleaners after last night's party, I thought, blowing trapped air out of my flared nostrils, letting all the fire escape out through me mouth. An intense feeling of pleasure settled in my chest, giving me a lovely sense of relief. So they weren't at it! Well, that's something anyway.

I took off again, heading for the kitchen this time, and breezed in, seeing Madame doing the last of the mopping up. The place was gleaming as she put dishes away, resting them on top of the dresser shelves. I suddenly felt very chirpy as I wheezed out, '*Bonjour, Madame,*' beaming over at her.

She stared, taking in the cut of me, looking down at my bare feet, then nodded, saying, '*Bonjour, Madame.*' Then she pointed to the stove, rushing herself over to grab a plate from the heating rack and serve me up last night's offerings. I polished off the consommé soup with chunks of bread, then made short work of a lovely fluffy cheese omelette she whipped up, then grabbed a banana. I need sustenance; I haven't been fed properly for the last few days.

'Oh, that feels better,' I gasped, lifting up my dishes and landing them in the sink. '*Merci, Madame,*' I grinned, giving her a cheerful wave as I took meself out the door, heading up the stairs.

I rounded my own landing and flew into the room. OK, what's next on the agenda? Take a good long bath. I need to polish up, especially after seeing that French vamp seducer of priests last night. Jaysus, the style of her! I wish I could get myself looking like that. But, no, I see where it comes from, I thought, getting the picture of her. She has spent thousands getting that look. Years getting blowed with the hairdryer, the hair cut, fingered, massaged and managed by George the gigolo hairdresser. Then, of course, there is the beauty parlour, or wherever they get their face done. No, years of pampering, a rich husband, and you have to be born in France to get that sleek, chic, casually beautiful-looking sophistication. Mind you, look more closely at that one and I'd be better looking meself. No, underneath all that she was a bit hatchet-faced looking. Take away the make-up, hairdo and eyebrow-do, and what would you get? Yeah! I thought, then still wishing I could look like that.

Then a thought hit me. Never mind that, I sighed, feeling a change come over me as reality began to hit. Hmm, you have more serious things you should be putting your mind to. Like it is high time now to start thinking about getting yourself back home. Yeah, first thing tomorrow get it sorted. Hold on, tomorrow is Sunday. Well, then, first thing Monday, see about getting the tickets. Tomorrow I can spend the day getting packed. Good, that's decided, so that just leaves me this evening to get through. I could do with a good bath, I thought, looking down at the scruffy pyjamas, feeling the greasy hair sticking to me scalp.

I came out of the bathroom feeling squeaky clean. Now all I have to do is get the tangles out of my hair and brush it out. Then I think I will go for a walk. Get some fresh air into my lungs and blow the cobwebs out of my head. I need to start focusing now and thinking ahead. I will write to Sergei when I get back and see what he's still thinking. Maybe I would be better throwing my lot in with him. Ralph is for the fuckin birds. Oh, well, it wasn't a waste of time, so now you know. It's a good thing in a way. Now I have cleared my path to move on, feeling easier in myself, knowing I am missing nothing. Good, I thought, nodding my head, feeling happy I am now seeing my way more clearly.

I threw on a pair of jeans, pulling a heavy navy-blue wool jumper over my head, then climbed into my boots and put on my fur coat, wrapping it up around me. OK, here we go, I thought, taking the stairs two at a time. I grabbed one of Ralph's scarves off the hall coatstand and wrapped it around my head, not wanting to get a cold with the wet hair streaming down my back. Then I pulled the collar up, thinking Ralph won't mind me borrowing this.

I made my way out the door and down the drive, heading off into the country, feeling I am now on the move again. I could feel a buzz of energy running through me. It was coming with the idea of getting myself geared up to start moving out of here and making my way home. The novelty had worn off and I was getting fed up with this place. It wasn't my own and there was no good in it without Ralph. I was beginning to come to terms with the idea that we were now like strangers. Whatever there had been between us was now over. Dead and gone. Last night proved that to me. It was like I didn't exist. Then when I saw him with that woman! No, enough is enough. I was glad today he hadn't been with her, or at least I didn't see them. That would have had me throwing my stuff into the suitcase and taking off in the middle of the night. It would have proved once and for all that I had been living in a fool's paradise with him. Yeah, even the letter showed a very ruthless streak. But a part of me didn't want to face up to that truth, it would have shattered my dream. Oh, well, that's over now. Just another couple of days and I will be home in my own place. It will take Monday to sort, then I can take off early Tuesday morning. I'll talk to him myself in the morning. I don't suppose I'll see him tonight for the bit of dinner.

Here we are back at last, I puffed, getting the feel of my hot, wet breath landing on my face as it hit the frost that was coming down with the late-winter evening. Bloody hell, that's some nip in the air, I thought, giving a sudden shiver from the cold damp air, with the night drawing in fast. I dropped my neck deeper inside the fur and pulled up the collar, wrapping it tight around me. Lovely, can't wait to get back inside, I thought, delighted to be passing in through the gates and getting back into the bit of heat. I stood at the front door wondering if I should knock or go around the side. It might be locked. No, leave the front door, try the back first. Don't draw attention to yourself. It's best to keep the head down now you're not bothered about this place any more.

I turned the handle in the side door and it opened. 'Great,' I whispered, letting myself in, glad to be heading off up to my room.

I was passing Ralph's study when I noticed the light on. I hesitated, wondering if I should knock. Ask him now and get it over with.

At least the sooner he knows, the quicker I will be out of here. My nerve failed, and I kept going. No, plenty of time. It's best wait until tomorrow. Or, the night is still early, I might run into him later.

I passed the door and was halfway up the stairs when I heard my name whispered softly. I looked back and Ralph was standing looking up at me. I stood staring, wondering what was coming.

'Hello,' he said quietly, suddenly looking like the old Ralph.

I said nothing, still trying to take him in.

'Have you been out walking?' he said, letting his face break out in a smile.

I nodded. 'Yes,' I said, standing very still, not moving a muscle.

'Shall I see you later? Dinner will be in about an hour, Madame says,' he said, looking with the brows raised and the head cocked to one side.

I said nothing. I couldn't find my voice. I felt suddenly cold inside. I had run out of feeling for him. It was the result of one too many shocks. I nodded slowly, saying, 'OK, cheers!'

'Good, I shall see you later then,' he said, smiling as he turned, heading back to his study.

I went upstairs and into my room, getting out of my coat and boots. I felt a bit chilled. Maybe I should jump into another hot bath, it will warm me up, I thought, pulling off my jumper and tugging out of my jeans. I slipped on my robe and took off to the bathroom, padding in the leather slippers Ralph bought me. I wonder will all this new stuff fit into my suitcase? I don't want to have to pay extra at the airport if it's too heavy. Them fuckers are bleedin robbers, I thought, running the bath, watching the steam rise, then pouring in the bath oils left sitting on the shelves. The place is well stocked. I wonder who organises the upkeep of this place? Probably some of the family. I can't see Ralph bothering himself with paying wages or even the bills! No, they probably have an accountant.

I got in, feeling the lovely heat, and lay back, getting myself a good soak. Ahh delicious, lovely and warm, this is more like it, I thought, closing my eyes and relaxing.

I stood in front of the mirror brushing out my hair and wondering what I would wear. OK, first get some make-up on, seeing as you are going to change into something nice. I looked at myself in the mirror, seeing my eyes were looking much brighter and my face was glowing from the fresh air.

The make-up looks grand. Right, what will I wear? I know. I will put on the new bra and silk cami knickers with the matching slip and mink stockings, with the little suspender belt to hold them up. Ralph bought them for me without knowing, when I slipped them in with the other stuff he was getting me. I kept disappearing around the shop with my eyes on stalks. I couldn't get over the amount of gorgeous stuff they had. But he won't get to see how sexy I am looking, I grinned, feeling a perverse, savage satisfaction with that thought. Yes, but I will bloody know just what he is missing. So thank you, sir, they are deliciously soft, with the way they gently caress my skin as they move with me.

I put on a light cashmere peach sweater that sits nicely hugging my figure, then a black-linen skirt that reached just above the knee with a slit up the back. It was fully lined and hung down without creasing. Then I put on black-patent high heels and stood back to admire myself. Yeah, they go very well. Now for the pearl earrings, and I think I will leave my hair out. I'll just pull it up at the sides and roll it to the back of my head, pinning it in place with the black slide. 'Ready,' I muttered, as I dabbed Chanel perfume behind my ears and wrists. That's better, lovely, I thought, beaming at myself in the mirror. I might as well look my best. It's nearly my last night here.

I looked over at the clock, thinking it must be nearly time for dinner but seeing it was just after six. It's probably a bit early but I'll go down and see what's happening.

I walked into the kitchen to see Ralph leaning against the windowsill with his feet crossed, sipping his gin and tonic. He likes that before his dinner. Himself and Madame were standing having a conversation. She was talking and shrugging, and he was nodding. Then they both turned in my direction as I shut the door.

'Well, hello!' he said, standing up with his eyes lighting up at the sight of me, letting them peel the length of me as I slowly sashayed my way across the room, wriggling my arse and mincing along on the high heels.

I sat down just as he sprang to pull out my chair. 'Thank you,' I murmured, lifting my leg and swinging it across, then letting the skirt ride up just below the top of the stocking.

I could hear his sharp intake of breath. 'You look lovely,' he murmured, then bent down to kiss my cheek. He missed when I moved slightly, letting his mouth land on my ear.

I looked up at Madame, seeing she was taking me in with a critical eye then throwing one at him to see what was going on. '*Bonjour, Madame,*' she said, nodding and smiling at me, actually looking happy we seemed to be making up until the kiss fiasco, then thinking how wrong could she be.

Too bloody right, missus, I thought, thinking I've had my fill of Ralph. He causes too much heartache. It's not worth it.

She had her coat and hat on, and moved herself off to the door, then turned to wave goodbye, saying, '*Bonne nuit,*' and nodding at both of us. Then she was gone out the door, leaving us together.

He turned to me with his eyes dancing in his head, looking very excited to see me. Yet his eyes were guarded, keeping his distance. I looked, seeing him smile, showing his dimples, and the green eyes flashing as he took in my stare. Normally, in another time, I would have melted at the sight of him. He looked so handsome, with the head of brown silky hair and a sprinkling of silver. It only added to his good looks, distinguishing him as a mature, handsome gentleman. His looks and smile, his bearing, his impeccable manners – yes, he is a real heartbreaker, I thought, looking at him clinically, feeling nothing inside now. No, he didn't move me in the slightest.

'Would you like a drink, Martha?' he said, making for the fridge and taking out a full bottle.

I nodded, remembering he did the very same thing with the vamp in only the early hours of this morning. It made me pull even further back into myself, thinking how treacherous he could be.

'Cheers!' he said, clinking glasses. I said nothing, just gave a half-smile. Then he put down his glass, saying, 'Shall we start dinner? Madame has served,' pointing to the casserole dish sitting on a heavy board on the table.

'Please,' I said, giving a nod of my head. It was a game stew cooked in red wine and it smelled delicious.

'There you are, eat it while it's hot,' he said, landing down the plate in front of me.

I started straight away, not bothering to wait for him. I was beyond caring about his concerns.

16

'So, how have you been?' he said, putting down his knife and fork then taking up his wine and sipping.

I did the same, then reached across, taking a piece of bread and breaking it, then chewing, taking a mouthful of stew. 'Fine,' I said, drinking and concentrating on my dinner as I gave him a dirty look.

He took in a deep breath, letting it out slowly.

'I got your note,' I said, giving him a brief cold stare before going back to eat my dinner.

He said nothing then muttered, 'Yes,' looking down at his plate and starting to eat again. 'We must talk,' he said quietly, looking at me.

I looked straight at him, saying, 'Yes, you are right. Would it be possible to arrange my travel to go back to Dublin?'

'What?' he said, looking up at me in sudden shock. 'When were you thinking of leaving?' he asked quietly, looking back at his dinner and slowly forking up a bit of meat, looking like he needed something to do.

'As soon as possible. I have been waiting for you to come back so I could get it organised,' I said, keeping my voice even.

'I see,' he said, putting down his knife and fork, and taking a long drink of his wine.

The silence hung heavy between us after that. The air was pregnant with words not being said. I concentrated on eating and finishing the dinner, and took long sips of the wine, feeling I needed it. This was becoming just too painful to bear. I couldn't take the tension and wanted out of it. Anything could happen. I don't know what is brimming underneath my cool feelings on the surface. I knew I had a lot of anger. But, wisely, my emotions were locked down at the minute. My nerves had been through too many up and downs, and it had left me feeling a bit numb. But I didn't trust myself. If something was triggered, God knows how it would end. I might even let rip again and where would that get me? No, keep it calm, Martha. Just use the head.

He finished his dinner, leaving a bit on the plate, with the knife and fork lying side by side, showing he had enough. Then he leaned back in the chair, taking in a very long, deep, slow breath and looked at me, saying nothing.

I broke some more bread and used it to mop up the gravy, putting down my empty glass and looking at him. His eyes sparked with interest, hoping I might want to talk. I took in a breath, opened my mouth and he waited, his eyes alive with interest. 'May I have some more wine, please?'

'What?' he said, swinging his head to my empty glass. 'Oh, I am sorry, yes, of course,' he said, whipping up the bottle and filling my glass, then his own.

'Thank you,' I muttered.

'The pleasure is all mine,' he said, smiling, sounding delighted he had something nice he could say.

I looked around the table wondering if there was any dessert.

'Would you like something else? Oh, yes, I do believe we have chocolate mousse and some biscuits she has baked.' Then he was up and over to the stove, lifting a cloth that was covering a tray. I watched as he took out the homemade biscuits, setting them in a basket, then served the chocolate pudding, putting a bowl down in front of me.

It was delicious. I munched on the biscuits then went for the cheese, cutting some to have with the bread. Ralph helped himself too.

I finished dinner and rolled myself a cigarette, sitting back enjoying my smoke.

'I do have some cigarillos, if you prefer,' he said, looking at me. 'Would you like me to fetch them? I actually bought them for you quite recently. Would you like to try one?' he said, seeing I wasn't answering him.

I shook my head, saying, 'No, thanks, I am fine with these.'

He started to clear away the dishes and I got up, wandering over to take a look around, and stood staring at the beautiful big old serving dishes stacked on the lower bottom shelves of the big old French kitchen dresser.

Oh, I am fed up, I thought, wanting to do something, but there was nothing to do. I was fed up with Ralph, him and his politeness, and all this pussyfooting around each other. I wonder what I ever saw in him. Particularly after seeing what he is really like.

I sighed and wandered out the door, heading into the sitting room, hoping something might get my attention. It smelled of lemon oil and the furniture gleamed with a burnished red, reflecting the light from the roaring-red log fire. They must have given it a good cleaning after the party, I thought, looking around, remembering I was not welcome here last night. Now here I am again. But somehow the good has gone out of it all. I feel very cheated. There's too many unresolved questions and there's been too much hurt. Oh, well, the damage is done now, there's no going back. So what are you doing here, Martha? You're only wasting your time and annoying yourself. Sure, you don't want to be with him, then why not just go to your room? Get easy in yourself. I thought about that as I lit up a cigarette. Then sighed out a breath, thinking, No! I'm fed up with that. Anything is better than that. Oh, but is it? Think again! No! Anything is better than this. You're just messing yourself up with him.

I was just thinking of walking out when the door opened. I looked over, seeing him come in carrying two glasses and a fresh bottle of wine. He turned, putting the bottle under his arm, and shut the door slowly, looking like he was thinking how he should handle the atmosphere. I wonder why he is even bothered! What's he after?

He looked up at me, seeing I was staring at him coldly, and dropped his head, putting the wine and glasses on the table beside his sofa, and poured the drinks. I stood in front of the fireplace sipping my wine, then turned my head to look at the window, seeing the room with the flames licking up the chimney reflected in the glass from the darkness outside. He stood for a minute, thinking, looking into the distance. Then he sat down on the sofa and turned, looking for something on the table.

'Please, may I?' he said, pointing to the mantelpiece behind me. I moved out of the way and he helped himself to a box of cigars.

I threw the cigarette butt in the fire, feeling restless again, and started walking to the window, looking out. I could see my own reflection looking back at me. I'm all dressed up, I thought, and nowhere to go. Jaysus, I will be glad to get home! I thought, seeing him sit down and light up his cigar.

'Martha!' I heard him say, and I turned around slowly, taking my time to look at him, saying nothing. 'I owe you an explanation,' he said, lifting his chin to look at me, seeing the stony-faced stare out of me.

I waited as he paused. He was trying to find some life in me – a way in. I could read it in the hidden look behind the steady stare. It was just a flicker, then his eyes would shut down as they stared, wanting to give nothing away.

'When that awful row blew up and you gave me some home truths as you saw them, quite frankly it did hit the target. You see, I have spoken a little to you about my time on the mission. Well, it was good, very good in fact, for quite some time. I found it challenging and I was totally absorbed, feeling I was meeting a need. Then it began to pale. I felt drained, my inner resources were drying up. I needed to get the hell out and perhaps seek a new challenge. I had been feeling that for some time. So I came here to rest and reflect on the future. I took a sabbatical from the order because I am not sure if that is now where I can best serve. Then you appeared like a bolt from the skies. Goodness,' he said laughing, with his eyes back there remembering. 'I thought I was seeing a ghost, Martha!' he said, laughing up at me, slowly shaking his head. 'I simply could not comprehend. But then the row,' he paused, thinking about that. 'I was extremely disturbed by some things you said, Martha. I cannot deny that it rocked me off my feet. I felt a great need to take myself away from the situation I was finding myself in with you. You see, it created a great conflict for me. I have fallen deeply in love with you. I . . .'

Suddenly I felt a rage fly up. 'Ralph, don't you dare say that to me! You took off without bloody word or warning. You left me a note telling me in no uncertain terms I was not wanted here in this house, in your life. You didn't even bloody bother yourself whether I had the means to get home. I had missed my flight!' I said, raising my voice. 'Then you come back and continue to ignore me like I really was a bloody ghost. To cap it all, you have a party last night and I'm not invited! Then you sit there now and tell me you love me? Did you tell that to the blonde bimbo last night, hanging on to your arm while you gazed lovingly into her eyes?' I said, my voice rising to another pitch as I leaned myself at him.

He stared, letting his eyes show pain and worry and concern.

'Remember the bleedin blonde with the red talons, the one who kissed you?' I shouted, wanting to remind him.

'Darling,' he laughed, 'do you mean Soviah?'

'Yes, whatever her bloody name is!' I shouted, feeling the rage roar up, getting really hot in me.

'But she . . . I have no interest in her,' he laughed.

'Then why were you all over her like a bleedin rash?'

'But, Martha, that lady is a butterfly. She flits hither and yonder, honing her charms, and is an outrageous flirt. My goodness, please, Martha, do give me some credit. Yes, of course I am entertained by her. She is fun and is indeed attractive. Of course I am flattered. I am a man first, you know, not a bloody eunuch. But for heaven's sake, there is no substance to that lady. I would not feel the slightest interest.'

'So why did you run away and dump me, Ralph? You were all talk about how much you care and love me. I don't understand,' I said, letting my voice trail away. 'No, you don't love me. You are in love with the bloody idea. Given enough time, you would be the same with Madame Butterfly! Soviah fuck-face,' I said, wanting to disgust him. He hates foul language, as he calls it.

'Darling, I do love you. I left because, as I am trying to explain, my mind and emotions were in turmoil. I have a complete split . . . a terrible conflict between desperately wanting you and my commitment as a priest. However one sees it, I am still a priest, but I want you more! Therein lies the difficulty. I can't give full commitment to either,' he said, looking at me with his eyes softening, letting all the pain and torment come through.

'I am sorry, Ralph, but I can't let you hurt me again. You have done this once before, when I was a young girl. In fact, Sarah can thank you for being born. Because if you hadn't dumped me, I would never have gotten involved with Ulick. No, you are unpredictable, Ralph, there is no denying that fact.'

'Darling, please. I have not even begun to explain what is happening with me. We need time to talk. It is not as you perceive it. Believe it or not, I went away thinking I was protecting you. I am so frightened of doing the wrong thing by you,' he said, standing up and coming towards me.

'No, don't touch me, Ralph! If I let you inside me again, well, I am definitely asking for trouble. Hurt me once, Ralph, shame on you. Hurt me twice, shame on me. No, keep your distance. I am afraid of you now,' I said, walking over to roll myself a cigarette.

'Darling, please,' he said, coming over to sit down beside me, resting his thighs against me. He put his arm along the couch behind me, letting it rest there. 'Darling, I dearly want to marry you. But I need time to make the right decision for both of us. Please be patient with me,' he said, landing his arm on my back then stroking me gently.

'No, I don't believe you. Anyway, another thing, did you sleep with the blonde?' I said, wanting to know. 'Would you tell me the truth?'

'Good heavens, is that part of your difficulty with me? You actually think I slept with that woman? Darling, believe me, it is so incongruous the whole idea. No, of course not! But it did upset me when she kissed me in your presence. I did not take kindly to it,' he said. 'Unfortunately it happened and I did not see it coming. I knew it would hurt you. I thought to myself, Goodness, my poor Martha is going to think I am a right bloody cad. But if it had happened another time I would simply have laughed it away, thinking it was fun then forgotten about it. This is all part of the cut and thrust of male and female interaction. It means damn all, not to me anyway.'

I sipped my wine, still not feeling I could trust him no matter how sincere he sounds.

'You look wonderful,' he said, running his finger along my knee and up as far as the hem. 'Honestly, Martha, if I wanted a woman, I would not pay you this much attention. For goodness' sake, I would be off gadding about, sleeping with one right this minute. Not sitting here worrying about you and I. I love you, darling, please believe me,' he said, lifting my chin to look at him. 'I want you, darling. It drives me to distraction. You have no idea how deeply I have fallen in love with you in this short time. I have always loved you. Now, when I think just how courageous you are . . . I have always known you had great depth. Your extraordinary wisdom came through even as a young girl. You were wise beyond your years and now I understand a little of where it all comes from. You have a great store of inner cashmere coat buttoned to the collar hidden by a flap to cover the buttons. He was wearing a dark-wine cashmere scarf loose at the neck, with the two ends snuggled side by side, hanging down the front, French style.

The sight of him took my breath away. I looked, seeing his well-polished face fixed rigidly into the settled look of arrogance that comes with his aristocratic bearing. His face bore a quiet certainty that all he surveys is his to command.

He looked startled, letting his green eyes shatter at the sudden sight of me. I stared in shock, seeing his eyes change to become fixed, rigid like his face, showing only a stone mask. Then he lifted his chin before lowering himself, tilting his body towards me, acknowledging my presence. I watched as he moved to the back of the car and leaned in, elegantly stretching with one leg just off the ground, and whipped out two leather bags. Then he turned and stopped smartly, saying, 'How nice to see you, you do look well.'

I heard the words coming to me like I was watching the scene from a distance. It looked and sounded like he was greeting a stranger he only vaguely knew. I couldn't move; my heart hammered with the sudden fright of him. I stood rooted, seeing how handsome he looks. Then an icy cold fear hit me at how remote and distant he is. All the power went from me. I could feel my legs buckling from the sudden fright of so much happening at once. So I just stayed perfectly still, keeping my face rigid, saying, 'Thank you, it is nice to see you, too.'

Then he marched towards the house, with me standing for a minute in the middle of the big door, and I suddenly stepped aside as he tilted his head saying, 'Thank you, I must get these upstairs,' giving a slight tug to the brown-leather travel bag and what looked like a big leather briefcase.

He disappeared in through the door and I stood stock-still, not knowing what to do next. My head turned for the door, then my heart dived with fear. No! I can't go in there. Then I turned, looking down the drive. My instinct took me that way. I headed off, walking quickly, wanting to make distance, be out of sight and get the hell away.

I got out the gates and around the corner, heading along the country road, wondering where I was going. I didn't want to go anywhere; I wanted to go back there and jump into Ralph's arms. My heart ached resources. You have yet to develop your potential, Martha. I do not want to hurt you, that is why I am being cautious,' he said, pulling me down across his lap and stroking my arm as his eyes softened, looking like they were going to melt with desire.

'Ralph, I am not convinced,' I said. 'I still feel myself holding back from you.'

'Darling, what can I do? Tell me, please.'

'So why did you ignore me when you came back? Huh?' I said, glaring at him.

'For the same reason, Martha. We needed to talk but the opportunity did not present itself. I couldn't approach you. I felt you were off limits after what happened between us. I needed to sort out some things in my head. I was simply overwhelmed. I couldn't think. I needed to be away, darling! Of course I thought about you. But my hands were tied, darling! Do you see what I mean?' he said, staring into my face, trying to get me to understand.

'I don't know,' I sighed. 'It's all too much for me. Just give me another drink, please,' I said, turning to get my glass.

He got up and poured more drinks, and I rolled myself a cigarette, holding that in one hand and the drink in the other. He came and sat back down and lifted my legs, looking at my shoes, then pulled them off, flinging them on the floor.

'You do look well, darling. You have beautifully shaped legs,' he said, running his hand along them.

'Are you after sex, Ralph?'

He stopped and gave me a look of horror, letting his brows knit and his eyes stare in confusion. 'What do you mean, Martha?' he said, moving away and sitting up straight, giving me a very serious look.

'Just what I said, Ralph,' I glared, looking at him coldly.

'With you, do you mean?'

'No, not just me, or in this given situation, with me seeming to be readily available to you! Would you want sex with me? In other words, is it simply because I happen to be available?'

'No,' he said, standing up and walking away, looking back at me outraged. 'Of course not! I do want you, I crave you. But I have already explained that. Soviah, for example, is a woman like many. For her, it is an exercise in fun. The joy is in the tryst! Then she would be bored and move on. Of course not, you bloody silly woman!' he roared, getting very annoyed. 'Do not insult me, Martha,' he said quietly. 'I do have principles. I would have thought you would know that. You know the emotional side of me better than most. I have shared that with you.' He looked hurt as he held his drink in his hand.

I stared at him, seeing I had gone too far. But why not? I thought. 'Well, Ralph,' I said, looking up at him. 'These things need to be said.' Then I took a deep gulp of my drink.

Then something else hit me. 'What was that viper after anyway?' I said, looking at him, seeing him still nursing his pride.

He gave me a quick look, then ignored me, taking a sip of his drink. 'Who would this viper be?' he said, looking at me but not really interested.

'Bloody Soviah! Who else, Ralph? What was she asking you for? I know enough French to know she was trying to wheedle something out of you. Now, you said talk, so let's talk, please. I really am curious.'

He looked at me, then a smile played around his lips and his eyes glinted with amusement. 'Oh, I see, you want me to tell you what she was asking of me?'

'Yes! Tell me,' I said, feeling my antenna going up. 'What was that one up to, Ralph?'

'She would like me to accompany her to the ballet, then she suggested supper at her house, with a few people gathering later. Today, in fact!' he said, grinning at me.

'I see,' I said slowly. 'So what did you say?'

'Well, darling, clearly I did not accept. I am here with you, my love!' he smiled, giving me a melting look, with his eyes feasting on my body.

'Would you have gone if I was not here, Ralph? Tell me the truth! It is not my business if we are not involved. So, would you?'

He shook his head, saying, 'No, darling, I would not. I think she perhaps had me on the menu for a late-night snack after the guests had all petered away,' he said, throwing the head back, giving an almighty roar, laughing the head off himself.

'Oh,' I said, thinking about this, feeling mollified, pacified even! 'So, it's only me you want, is that what you are saying, Ralph?'

'Darling! What have I been bloody telling you all this time?' he said, slowly walking towards me, then making a run and grabbing me to him.

I kept my arms hanging down while he had himself wrapped to me. I still held back, something wouldn't let loose. I could feel his neck on my face and feel the softness of his skin. Then he held me away from him, looking into my face, saying, 'You are impossibly lovely, my darling. Don't fret yourself about the Soviahs of this world. You are so much more than they can ever hope to be. Darling, please try to trust me,' he said, trailing off as his face came closer and his eyes looked like his soul was on fire. His whole face softened, looking like it was melting from a suppressed passion just waiting to erupt and tear free.

I could feel my breathing beginning to quicken and suddenly the ice running through my veins started to melt away, filling me with a sudden rush of heat as the passion started to erupt in me. It was now a fire racing itself around my body, making me want to flop, let myself melt into him, but I still held back, as I heard myself say his name. 'Ralph,' I breathed, whispering into his face.

'Yes, my darling?' he said, staring intensely.

'Look, you are holding me and I have a glass dangling in the air,' I said, moving my eyes to it.

He grinned, saying, 'Shall I take it from you?'

'No,' I said, shaking my head. 'It needs a refill.'

He stared at me, trying to work this out. I let a smile play on my face.

'If I move, darling, may we come back to this point?' he said, making it look like I would have to agree. I nodded. Then he sighed and put me lying back on the cushions, gently taking the glass out of my hand, and stood up.

'Now, where were we?' he said, handing me the fresh glass and taking a sip of his own.

'What about getting me one of those cigarillos you offered earlier?'

'Oh, yes, hang on, darling, I will have to go to my study. That is where I keep that stuff.'

17

I stood up, watching him shut the door behind him, feeling I'm all up in a heap. Listen, Martha, don't start again, getting all carried away. This time you really need to think, work it out.

One half of me is going crazy with excitement. I'm nearly suffocating with the happiness at seeing he still loves me. He told me he is madly in love with me! He might even marry me! Jaysus! Me heart is flying. I can't think straight. I'm going crazy for the want to just let go and bleedin drag him to bed if I have to.

But yet there is a little warning voice saying, no, it may come to nothing. I will end up in an awful state. Look at the first big and last mistake you made! Yeah, I fucking lost the head and ended up with Ulick! For the love a Jaysus, no! 'Step back and calm yourself,' I snapped, grabbing down and tearing up my high heels, putting them back on. I didn't want to run a ladder in my stockings, I thought, looking down to see they were fine.

I wonder, I thought, walking over to stare out through the window, looking into the darkness beyond, is he actually, in fact, the marrying kind? Given enough time, would he really be able to bring himself down that road? I'm not so sure. This could drag on for a very long time. I should really pin him down more. But I'm not in a position to do that. As he said, he's here now, trying to sort himself out. Then you come tearing in here on your mission like 'Attila the Hen', banging on his door, just turning up out of the blue. Expecting, well, if he still loves me he can marry me, no less! Because I'm waiting a lifetime for him, so he can get on with it! Jaysus! Think, Martha, that was the first he heard of it! Then what happens? You discover he still loves you then lose the head. You put the fuckin skids under him. No wonder he ran for the trees. You frightened the life out of him! What choice did he have? Poor Ralph didn't know whether he was coming or going. So, yeah, he made a wise move. Get the hell out and say nothing to me. Otherwise we would have had it out there and then, and that would have been the end of us. As it was, by doing that, he still left us with an opening. I even understand now what the letter was about. By telling me to do what was right for me, he was saying, *If you insist now on making demands I can't meet, then there's nothing I can do about it.*

But he didn't tell me to go, because the decision was mine, and I think he hoped I would stay. But if I did, it would be on his terms, as he needs time. Of course I stayed. Underneath all that bravado and fear and anger, I was secretly hoping he might still love me and we could make it up. So we have! But what now? Do I go home and wait for him to decide my fate? Or stay and let Sergei wait for me to decide his fate? Fuck! I'm caught between a rock and a hard place. Ralph may never decide. Then I'm fucked, up the creek without a paddle. I will end up haunted and hunted without man or child! No, I have my mission to get married. I want more children while I'm still young enough to have them. But I am in my bleedin thirties, that's not exactly a spring chicken! No, if only there was a way to speed things up. Sergei won't wait for ever.

Gawd, if only he knew what I was up to. I wrote and told him I needed time to think, telling him I would write to him sometime in the next six months, letting him know one way or the other. Because it was all very sudden. So that's where it stands at the minute. But, anyway, this is not his business. He knows I don't love him. But I am considering his offer. So here I am.

Oh, bloody hell, all I want is Ralph! Ahh fuck! No, I can't push him. It's not even bloody fair on him, never mind ridiculous! But I'm under pressure. I need to get moving. 'But Jesus!' I sighed, 'I only want Ralph!' Hmm, I thought, because one way or the other, I am bound to him for life. I could never have this kind of love or passion with another man. No, there is only one Ralph, I thought. With or without him, for better or worse, I love him with all my heart. Yeah, I'm really only a one-man woman, I thought, staring down at my glass, seeing it was empty.

Jaysus, I polished the lot off! How did that happen? Where am I putting it these days? Mind you, I didn't have a drop when he was missing. I didn't even think of it. No, I'm not hitting the booze! It's just me enjoying myself. 'Now, where did he put that bottle?' I muttered, deciding to deny meself nothing. I have been cautious far too long in my life. Time to let the hair down and let the devil take care of his own, I grinned, reaching down to pick up the bottle.

'Here we are, sweetie, and I found these,' he said, producing a box of Belgian chocolates. I looked, seeing the box was still wrapped with a ribbon. 'Found those secreted in the kitchen,' he laughed. 'Hope Madame was not planning something useful for them!' he grinned, whipping off the ribbon and opening the box. 'Do take one,' he said, holding it open for me.

'Oooh, I love these, Ralph. They're my favourite,' I said, stuffing a big white one in my mouth, then roaming my eyes and fingers, moving in for the next one, taking up two this time. 'Delicious!' I spluttered, looking up at him with the chocolate dribbling down my mouth.

He stopped chewing and stared at me with a grin on his face. 'No, don't wipe it away,' he whispered, shaking his head, coming closer as he pulled me to him.

'What?' I said, with my head leaning on his arm.

'No, darling, you don't really intend to lick that now, do you? Best leave it to me.'

'Lick what? Leave what?' I said, swallowing and laughing, feeling the thick sweet chocolate sliding down my neck.

'This!' he said, dropping his head without warning, clamping his lips on me. Then he gently kissed me, running his lips and mouth around mine, tasting the chocolate plastered on my mouth. Suddenly he pulled me tighter into his arms and kissed me hard, drawing out my breath, then plunging back in, locking his mouth as our tongues went deeper, searching and drawing on the other's taste.

I could feel myself wanting to open, as the heat of passion started to take a grip. Then he stood back, looking at me with his eyes laughing softly, saying, 'Hmm! That, my darling, is delicious.' Then he dipped into the box and popped another one in his mouth.

'Ooh, I liked that,' I said, breathing hard, staring at him in astonishment with a ripple of delight and excitement running through me. I wanted more, as I wrapped my arms around his neck.

He just grinned back at me as he chewed, letting his brow lift, then he winked, giving me a sexy look, saying, 'I knew there was a way to your heart. Eat up, darling, we might discover something even more delicious!' Then he turned and landed the box on the table and whipped me up, sitting himself down, then sliding along the sofa, taking me with him. 'Now for the chocolates,' he said. 'We really ought to have these with a nice dessert wine. I think there is a bottle in the fridge. Shall I go and fetch it?'

I hesitated, then heard him say, 'Perhaps later. Meanwhile, here are the chocolates,' he said, leaning his arm across me and landing the box on top of my belly.

I picked up my wine, saying, 'You have another one, Ralph, before I eat the whole box. Or take them away. I will be sick if I eat any more.'

'Good idea,' he said. 'Now, I do remember earlier you made me a promise!' he continued, running his hands along my leg then over my skirt and along my hips. 'You do have a wonderful shape, darling,' he murmured, stroking my belly.

'That is very sexy,' I murmured.

'Yes, very,' he sighed, kissing my face and barely whispering over my skin with his mouth. Then he sat up and reached for his drink.

'Do you think we are acting like a couple of teenagers, Ralph? I mean—'

'I know what you mean, darling,' he said, interrupting me with a grin. 'No, I would say they are acting like us!'

'Like us?' I said. 'But we're doing bloody nothing, Ralph!' I snorted. Then I glared at him, saying, 'Where do you get your self-control from, Ralph? You are made of bloody steel.'

'Really?' he said, raising his eyebrows. 'So, pray, what is your secret? From where do you get your self-control?' he said, looking at me with a smile ready to break out on his face.

'Oh, yeah, I suppose you are right,' I said, thinking about it. 'So why are we being so self-controlled?'

He shook his head, saying, 'I don't know, why are we being so self-controlled?'

Suddenly I pulled away from him and jumped up, going to the centre of the room. 'Well, I can tell you this now,' I said. 'I promised myself earlier, when I got dressed for dinner, you were not going to see these!' I said, pulling up the hem on one side of my skirt and lifting my leg, letting him get a glimpse.

His shock at my suddenly moving slowly dissipated as his eyes lit up, taking in the sight of the stocking with the bare leg showing above. Then his mouth opened in a wide grin, saying, 'Oh, you sexy little wench! Come here, you!'

'No, forget it,' I said. 'You are not peeling your eyes on these again.'

'Really?' he said, letting his hands fall each side of him on the couch, getting ready to spring at me.

'NO! Get stuffed. Don't even think about it,' I said, making for the door with a laugh fighting to erupt out of me.

'I shall stuff you!' he muttered. Then he sprang, and I whipped open the door, making straight for the hall, leppin outa me high heels. The next instant he was sprinting past me, flying onto the stairs and stopping with his arms held wide open, blocking my path. I nearly ran into him and stopped dead, saying, 'Oh, bloody hell,' spinning my head for a way to escape.

'Now I have you, my beauty!' he growled, making a leap and grabbing me up in two long strides. He held me out wide in his extended arms, shouting, 'TO THE VICTOR THE SPOILS! You may keep the gold! But the wench is mine! All mine,' he said, dropping me close into his arms and nuzzling my face and neck. 'Yes, I have found my treasure,' he murmured, walking back into the sitting room and dropping me on the sofa. 'Move, woman, or I may be forced to titillate you with a feather. You may not like it,' he said, lifting his jumper over his head, then opening the buttons on his shirt. Now,' he said, whipping me up and sitting himself down, sliding along the sofa as he cuddled me to him. 'Off with the skirt,' he murmured, flipping me over and moving himself alongside me. 'I demand satisfaction! Show me your treasures!'

'No, I never break a promise,' I said.

'What?' he said, grabbing my arms above my head and throwing his leg over me. 'Do you intend resisting me, my little wench?' he said, breathing close to my lips.

'Yes, I do! I'm not afraid of you!'

'Well, then, may the Lord have mercy on your head,' he said. 'I intend to plunder you! Sorry, darling,' then he lifted my jumper and ran his hands along my stomach and under my breasts. 'Shall you or I?'

'No, you first!'

'What! But I am a man, darling, I call the shots here! You are my booty! You are supposed to say—'

'What?' I said, suddenly moving and sending him flying off the sofa. He twirled, landing on his hands, and I was flying over him, making for the door.

'Oh, it's fun and games, is it? The lady runs to protect her virtue,' he said, haring out the door after me.

'No, stop, Ralph!' I shouted, making for the stairs and into his bathroom. I just got a foot in the door when I was yanked back.

'Oh, we intend fighting to the death!' he said, whipping me over his shoulder and marching me into his bedroom. Then he landed us both on his bed, saying, 'Now I have you in my lair there is no escape. Do you wish to pray first? Because I have not eaten in a long time.'

'Fuck off, Ralph! Get stuffed!' I shouted, rolling away from him. Then I screeched laughing as he grabbed hold of my foot and yanked me back as he dived after me, giving me a slap on the arse.

'Got you!' he said, twisting me around and lying on top of me.

I was breathing heavily, wanting but not wanting.

'Now,' he said, holding my arms out and putting his full weight on me. 'Shall I love thee, my comely maiden?'

I laughed with nerves and the excitement setting my insides on fire. I looked into his eyes, seeing them shining with the want. He wants to take me, and I want to open to him. I could feel the weight of him sinking into me, with the powerful strength of his muscles and the heat of his body as he stretched along me, responding to me as my body turned to melting liquid as our bodies touched. I could feel him growing very hard between his legs and I wanted to open mine and wrap them around him. He was breathing heavily and my chest was rising to meet his as our breath got faster.

But then a feeling of fear hit me. I could feel it locking tight, shutting me down inside, cooling me very rapidly. Somehow I just knew it was not appropriate right this minute. We are both soaring with very powerful emotions. I am ecstatic he loves and wants me; he feels the same relief we are still together. But he is not yet ready to make a clear commitment to me. It would put him under a burden, make him feel forced now to make a decision. He is too honourable, and it would probably destroy our relationship because he did not arrive at it freely.

I could see him reading my face, seeing my fear as we stared at each other. I watched as the intensity slipped away from him, letting his face settle into a more calm softness.

'That was great fun,' I breathed, letting my own face settle, becoming more placid.

'Darling,' he whispered, looking into my eyes as he spoke softly. 'Whatever brought our paths to cross once more, I am so very grateful it has happened. You have made me very happy, darling. You are so dear to me. I love you very deeply,' he whispered, then slipped his weight off me, pulling me into his arms and letting us lie quietly.

I lay with my head on his chest, enjoying him stroking my hair and running his hand down my back. Then I said quietly, laughing as something occurred to me, 'You didn't get to admire my sexy underwear after all, Ralph. I did warn you I'm not that easy to be had.'

'Yes, darling,' he whispered, shifting to look at me. 'But I have that to look forward to,' he grinned. 'I shall await your pleasure, my precious,' he said, pulling me tighter to him and kissing my head, then running his hands more firmly up and down me, saying, 'You are an extraordinary woman, Martha. You have such insight but you use it in such a loving way.' He sighed, settling me beside him then cuddling me into his arms and staring into the distance.

I rested my eyes on his face with my hand on his chest, seeing him looking very relaxed as he stroked me gently, letting his hand roam around me while the other one held me cradled into his chest. I gave a huge sigh of contentment but wondered, will I ever hear the day when he will say, *Martha, I have made up my mind. I know what it is I truly want. I want to marry you.* It gave me a little shiver of fear, knowing I may never hear that. So I couldn't be truly contented with that nagging fear haunting me. I am not too lucky when it comes to love, I thought, thinking if only I had half the luck in that like I do when it comes to survival. Then I always come up smelling of roses, no matter what. It could be a raging epidemic demolishing half the population but I would still be around to tell the tale. How lucky can you get? But Jaysus, when it comes to love, I'm on the sunny side of the street when the other is raining bleedin pennies! Jaysus, I thought, pinning my eyes on his face again and stroking his gorgeous soft skin. Hmm, I sniffed, he smells lovely. No, it's too good to be true. I can't see myself being called Martha Fitzgerald, wife of Doctor Ralph Fitzgerald. It's like waiting to see if your sixth number comes up to win the lottery. No chance! I wouldn't win a fucking argument! Still, I couldn't be better off than I am right this minute, I thought, reaching up to kiss him gently on the lips.

'Hmm. Delicious,' he breathed. 'Your kisses are so sweet, my little honeybee. Do you know?' he half-yawned, covering his mouth. 'I do think if we lie here for much more we shall be saying we slept together,' he laughed, sitting up on his elbow and looking down grinning as he gently landed his finger, rubbing it along my face. Then he bent down and kissed my nose, saying, 'Shall we see what is happening downstairs, or . . . ?'

'Or what, Ralph?'

'Come along,' he said, lifting me to my feet and hugging me, then he was heading out the door, saying, 'I need a cigar and we must check to see if the fire is still burning. Don't you think, darling, that will keep us out of mischief?'

'No, what's the mischief option? Mind you, I got very little sleep last night because of you and your bloody rowdy party and your floozy girlfriend!' I snorted, thinking of that again.

Then he stopped suddenly, looking very annoyed. 'Now wait one minute, I say. You must not speak about my "girlfriend" in that manner! I will fight to the death to protect her honour!'

'WHO?' I screamed, pulling away, feeling my face turn all colours! 'Madame Butterfly? The man-eater? Fucking fuck-face with the matching red talons? She uses them, ye know, to scrap and suck the marrow out of a man's bones! She would eat you alive!' I hissed, seeing him look so serious.

'Don't be silly, I only have one woman in my life and that's enough for me, you silly goose!'

'Who?'

He shook his head, saying, 'Darling, don't toy with me. You know very well about whom I am speaking! Now behave, or I shall be forced to take stiff measures to reassure you of my love. You must try to trust me. I do know my own mind, you know, but thank you for that kind piece of advice. I did wonder about those talons, as you call them,' he said, giving a pretend shiver, then grabbing and squeezing me to him. 'Now, let us have no more silly bickering, darling.'

'Then give us a kiss,' I said, not getting enough of him.

We stood outside the sitting room while I wrapped my arms around him, kissing him on the lips as he responded, pulling me to him and running his hands down my back, resting them lightly on my arse.

I pulled away, muttering, 'OK, that's your ration of passion. Now, let's do something more interesting,' I said, feeling myself getting out of breath as he pulled away grinning.

'I think, darling, you are a slow fuse to burn,' he suddenly said, bending down and whispering into my ear.

'Tut-tut, dirty aul man,' I muttered, giving him a filthy look.

'Sweetheart, you know how to trigger me off. I shall not let you get away with that remark, take it back at once,' he said, grabbing and pinning me against the wall.

I roared laughing, feeling him press me up against the hard wall. 'Stop, you are going to bore a hole in me,' I screamed, feeling him press the life out of me as he used his full weight to trap me. 'Ralph, stop, what are you trying to do to me?' I laughed, feeling him sink his mouth into my neck, sucking me. 'STOP!' I screamed. 'It's killing me with the tickles. Stop! I'm dying! I can't take it!'

'Do you admit you were wrong?'

'Yes, no! Get off! Stop, Ralph, I will grab your what-nots!'

'You will?' he suddenly said, stopping to look at me, pretending to be serious! 'I think you say that to tease, darling. Now I shall really make you suffer. So now I know your weakness, where else should we explore?' he said, muttering and sucking his way around my neck then breathing down my back.

'It's too ticklish. Stop, I give in, now stop,' I said, wrestling to get free. Then he had his knee between my legs. 'Ralph, stop, we'll end up on the floor,' I said, getting hysterical with the laugh and him getting carried away with his game and ending up making himself go crazy. 'Aaah!' I screamed, laughing and crying as he nuzzled behind my neck, swinging to plant me in front of him, holding me in an iron grip.

'Do stop screeching, darling. You are disturbing my supper,' he muttered, stopping to tell me, then suddenly landing his hand gently on my face and the side of my mouth, saying, 'Do turn that way and screech at the wall. Now, I say, this is rather good,' and he went mad, sucking and moaning, driving me hysterical with the tickles.

'I give up! I give up! Stop, stop! Enough,' I said, getting my head and back bent as he held me over, nearly toppling the pair of us headlong onto the floor.

'Are you sure?' he said, stopping and looking at me all red-faced with the laugh and excitement in him.

I nodded, moaning, 'No more, yeah, yes!' I said, nearly bent in half.

'Oh, damn pity. I was just getting into that meal,' he moaned, looking at my neck and sliding his eyes down the rest of me with a mad glint in his eye.

'No, you're not getting your hands on me again,' I said, sloping away from him with my eyes watching him sideways. 'You're a bloody maniac!'

'But you loved it, darling! All that screeching, I thought you wanted more and more! I was simply obeying your orders, darling! Now the lady protests! Did I not please you, my love?' he said, looking pained. Then he grinned. 'Perhaps we should try again,' he said, making a move for me.

'Get away from me!' I screamed, laughing my head off with my heart suddenly flying as I dived into the room, stopping in the middle, looking for a way out!

I slowly took off my high heels as he crept towards me with his arms out, saying, 'I have lots of innovative ways of torturing you, my love. Good idea, do start with taking off the shoes,' he said, throwing his head at them then pinning his glittering eyes on me.

I started to feel weak with the laugh. He was getting the better of me. 'No, you have to give me a chance to defend myself,' I said, trying to think my way out. 'Fair is fair, Ralph, you are bigger than me! Look at the bloody size of you!' I moaned, throwing my hand at his bulk.

He lifted his brow and flashed his eyes, giving a little nod with his arm spread towards the door. 'You may try, fair lady. Go, sweep past me, but I shall catch you! Then you will weep!' he cautioned, lowering his voice to a whisper and pointing his finger.

I started to cry and moan, staring at the distance between him and the door. 'You have to count to three,' I said, rocking inside myself to get up the power of speed.

'Indeed yes!' he said crisply, nodding his head, looking like he was very much in control.

'You won't best me, you bloody caveman Neanderthal!' I snorted, trying to rattle him. Get him to make a false move.

'Oh! The lady gives fair warning, good! I shall enjoy hunting you down even more!' he said, speaking in the same tone.

'Good idea, let me go, shut the door, then see if you can find me?' I said, looking at him, giving him a wheedling little grin out of myself. I was beginning to enjoy this no end, thinking, he hates to lose!

'There will have to be a forfeit for the loser,' he said.

'Yeah, good idea. What will you give up?' I said.

'ME! Darling, I grew up on these house-party games! Goodness, we played sardines as children . . .'

'What is that?'

'Never you mind, I see your delaying tactics. You are trying to tire out "an old man", as you wickedly called me! Well, darling, I think I shall have to prove you wrong in the most fundamental way,' he said, raising his eyebrows and flashing his eyes at me, then wriggling his body.

Then it hit me what he meant. 'You dirty old man!' I shouted, screeching past him, slamming the door shut as I stopped so suddenly with my head flying around I caused a draught, making my head spin.

'Where?' I breathed, feeling my heart racing and my body flying without moving. Jaysus! Think, Martha! Study! I lunged for the passage just as the door plunged open.

'Ah-ha!' he shouted, taking a step back with his head thrown in the air, then he sprang as my hand was gripping the door handle.

'NO! You're cheating!' I screamed, getting swung through the air as his hand landed on my waist, swooping me into his arms and nosing his way past my ear down through my hair. 'No, stop, play fair, Ralph. I'm not happy!' I shouted, bucking and wrestling myself out of his arms.

He held me in front of him with one hand on my arse and the other one on my back, looking into my face, saying, 'Methinks the lady doth protest too much! Enough, I have won fair lady's hand in a just and lawful manner. Now, what was that you said about me being a caveman?' he muttered, trying to carry me back to the sitting room as his eyes roved over me.

'No, put me down. I am not caught, Ralph. You didn't lay down the ground rules, not even saying how much time I should have! No!' I said, pushing him with my fists.

'Yes!' he grunted, marching off with me locked in his arms, heading for the sitting room and kicking the door shut with his foot. Then he dropped me on the sofa and held me down, saying, 'Yes, now for the forfeit. I think we should have off the—'

'What forfeit? You didn't say what it would be!' I shouted, trying to lift my head but getting it pushed back down, with him saying, 'Yes, top or bottom, darling?'

'What?'

'This or this?' he said, flicking my jumper and rubbing my skirt.

'You must be joking! You are not getting my skirt! What would you have given up if you had lost? Which you have!' I snorted, feeling myself in a rage.

'My top or bottom, darling, preferably my shirt!' he said, shaking his head and looking very reasonable.

'No, let's start again! That was only a practice run, Ralph! Anyway, I might ruin my stockings. They are the only pair I have,' I said, seeing him whip his head down and run his hands along my leg, right up to the top of the stocking.

'Oh, darling, that is the least of your problems,' he moaned, making himself comfortable, sliding down next to me.

'No, I am not a happy woman,' I said. 'This is a terrible injustice. I intend taking my protest to the highest authority!'

'Oh, good, that would be me, darling. Pray tell, what is your complaint?'

'I'm thirsty . . . And hungry! And . . . I need a cigarette!' I said, staring at him as he ran his hands down and around my belly.

'Hmm,' he said, thinking about this. Then he lifted his head to look over at the clock. 'Five minutes to eleven. Yes, good, the night is still young and so are we, my beauty,' he said, giving me a soft kiss on the lips, then pulling me to my feet.

'Thank you,' I said, looking up at him, seeing him looking at me so soft and kind and loving. 'I love you so very much, Ralph,' I suddenly said, wrapping my arms around his neck.

'Oh, darling, you make me so wonderfully happy. I love and cherish you very deeply,' he said, stroking my face and holding me to him.

We stayed that way, quietly listening to my heart flying then slowing down and hearing his do the same. I am so happy, I thought, thinking, if nothing else but bad happens to me in the future, I will always have the memories of these times when I felt safe and warm and loved and protected by Ralph. Now I know what it feels like to be truly loved. It was worth waiting a lifetime for. Dear God, Ralph is such a wonderful man, how could I settle for less? I thought, feeling the cold little knot of fear raising a warning voice in me. I gave a shiver, feeling like someone had just walked over my grave. That is the second time lately I have had that terrible premonition, I thought, thinking, I am very seldom wrong. My sixth sense is rising, suddenly putting the fear of God into me. Maybe it is just me being afraid of such happiness. I have learned not to trust it; it never lasts. But just maybe this time . . .

'Are you OK?' I heard Ralph whisper as he lifted my face, staring at me with a worried look in his eyes.

'Yes,' I whispered. 'I was just thinking how happy I am being with you again, Ralph.'

'Oh, darling, I have carried you with me always,' he said softly, stroking my cheek. 'Sometimes when I would sit and watch the sun set after a long gruelling day, I would wonder about back home, then you would enter into my thoughts. I hoped and prayed you were happy. I know we had not parted as I would have wished. A particularly poignant moment I always remembered is when you and I said goodbye for the last time.'

'Do you remember that time, Ralph?' I said slowly, realising he had kept that in his mind. He had been thinking about me after all.

'Yes, I do. Of course I do, darling,' he said, staring into my face, looking pained. 'It was bloody awful,' he said quietly, lifting his head and looking into the distance, thinking about it. Then he slowly nodded his head, saying, 'We drove back to Dublin. I had taken you out to lunch. It was intended as a farewell. I wanted to prepare you.

It was necessary for you to break all ties with me.'

No, I didn't know that until it was too late, I thought, getting the terrible memory of that time again.

I stared at him, listening, realising I must have meant something to him after all.

'Yes, I do remember. I saw you to your door then I sat and watched you. I felt so wretched, then when I saw how devastatingly tragic you looked I was tempted to stop the car and take you away with me. I loved you,' he whispered. 'But I thought it best you should be free to live your life, darling.'

I looked up at him and suddenly I burst into tears.

'Darling, what is it? What have I said that has upset you so?'

I buried my head in his chest, feeling the pain of the terrible loneliness of those years without him suddenly hitting me. 'What made you think of that, Ralph?' I sniffed.

'Well, darling, it was one of the hardest things I had to do. Yes,' he smiled, thinking about it. 'You were a young lady then, just on the threshold of becoming a woman, though you were rather too attached to me.' He shook his head slowly, thinking about it. 'I was not good for you. It was not healthy. No, I felt it absolutely necessary,' he said, shaking his head.

'Well, the wheel has turned full circle, Ralph. I still love you. Nothing has changed except I am now almost a middle-aged woman, in my thirties, and you and I are now mature adults. We are now equal,' I said, looking into his face, seeing him staring at me like he was thinking about the wonder of that.

'Oh, darling, I never want to lose you again,' he said, kissing me very hard on the lips, pulling me tighter against him as his hands moved up and down me, stroking my back.

I responded to him, wanting to cry with the happiness. But all I could hear was our breathing and the moans of pleasure.

'Food, drink, smoke,' I gasped, coming up for air.

'Heavens!' he moaned. 'Darling, I was just getting started. Must we interrupt? I should think what you have in mind is a very poor substitute!'

I laughed, seeing his hair standing up in all directions. He took no notice, saying, 'Seriously, darling, may I not eat you?'

'Wow, I never realised how randy you are, Ralph Fitzgerald!'

'What? Sweetheart, you have not lived! It all awaits you, my precious!' he said, making a grab for me, nearly catching my skirt.

I ducked, screaming laughing, and lifted my skirt, giving him an eyeful, saying, 'Rubbish, you wouldn't have a clue what to do with this.' Then I flew for all I was worth, with him screaming like a red injun behind me!

'Oh, good heavens, woman! You have a death wish,' he gasped, tearing into the kitchen then stopping when he saw me holding on to the table, getting ready to make a run for it.

'I shall clear that table and jump it,' he said, raising his eyebrow and sounding very treacherous.

'What? Then what's the number for an ambulance? Because you will need it for the heart attack'! I screamed, roaring with the laugh, not able to get myself moving with the hysterics.

He made a run, catching me because I was standing still, rocking with the laugh. 'No, darling, change of plan,' he said, hoisting me towards the table. 'It is not for jumping,' he said, lifting his elbow and pretending to clear the table. 'I am going to undo you,' he said, slapping the table. 'On this you will be undone! On this very table.'

'Yeah? Well, you won't be able to climb up without getting yourself a hernia,' I snorted, trying to get it out with the laugh on me.

'Oh, darling, you have too many misdemeanours now listed against you. I think we should call a recess for supper, then I shall consider your punishment!' Then he slapped his hands, saying, 'Good, settled then. Now! What has our Madame left out for us? Or rather, what has she stashed, hidden away?' he said, nosing around the cooker and looking into pantry presses.

'Here we are. Cold meats,' he said, 'bread, pickles, salad, cheese there, darling if you wish,' he said pointing to the dish on the table.

I sat down and he produced a bottle of Chablis from the fridge, opening it. 'Now, let us begin,' he said, slapping my thigh and ladling meat onto my plate.

'Hmm, delicious, I really am starving with the hunger.'

'Darling! Hunger is redundant in that sentence!' he said, whipping his head to look at me then attacking his food.

I paused with the meat to my mouth. 'Well, if you were a Dubliner like me, you would understand that sentence perfectly well!' I snapped, talking a big gulp of wine.

'My dear one,' he said, 'it is not intended as a criticism, it is merely an observation! Frankly I find your turn of phrase quite appealing! Now, we shall not bicker. Cheers, darling!' he said, raising his glass and tipping it gently towards me.

'Oh, I feel better. Thank you, Ralph, I enjoyed that. Honestly, I don't know what I would do if you weren't here to feed me!'

'You would help yourself,' he grinned.

'Well, I love the idea of you minding me,' I said. 'It's a novelty for me. I usually get to mind other people. Come to think about it, I doubt I would have it any other way. I'm too independent. Except I love you taking care of me. It makes me feel very warm and special and feminine,' I said, feeling myself melting at the sight of him sitting listening to me. He is so gorgeous, I thought, looking at his sexy green eyes with that sleepy, come-to-bed look he was resting on me now. His hair was all mussed and I grinned at him, seeing him giving me a sexy smile back, showing his dimples with the white teeth flashing.

Then he sighed, saying, 'Darling, I have travelled far and wide, but no one I have met compares with you,' he said. 'You are an enigmatic woman of many hidden qualities. One cannot pin you down, really. It is one of the aspects I find most interesting about you. You never fail to surprise me, darling,' he said, taking my hand and kissing it.

18

I woke seeing the morning light streaming into the bedroom. Oh, I yawned, stretching, feeling a ripple of excitement and delight running through me. Ralph loves me, he really does, I thought. I can't believe that only this time yesterday morning I was preparing to go home today or get the tickets for tomorrow!

'Oh, life is a bowl of cherries!' I sang, diving out of the bed and grabbing for my dressing gown. I picked up my washbag and flew down to brush my teeth and wash my face. Then I was back, throwing down the bag, and was out the door, rushing for the kitchen, still in my dressing gown.

'*Bonjour, Madame,*' I gushed, rushing in and sitting myself down.

'*Bonjour, Madame,*' she said, nodding slowly, letting her eyes light up in a smile.

I knew she was wondering what has me in good humour. But she could take one guess. 'Lovely,' I said, as she put a basket of hot rolls in front of me and a lovely plate of fried eggs with tomatoes. I told her I like eggs and she always checks with Ralph to find out what I would like. Or at least she did! Until he disappeared. Which, come to think about it, I wonder where he is?

Just then I heard the front door slamming and my heart leapt with the sudden excitement. Ahh, he's coming. Gawd, I must have died and gone to heaven because, Jaysus, here I am now, still here! But I wonder for how long more? No! Don't think about that, let the time come when it does, I thought, nearly losing my appetite at that sudden worry.

The door opened and I turned my head slowly, holding my breath, waiting to see if there was a change in him. You never know, it could be all a flash in the pan. He could get fed up with me, maybe think I'm crowding his space.

I watched as he paused, taking me in, seeing me digging into the big breakfast. Then he turned and shut the door.

'Good morning, my lovely. Did you sleep well?' he said, rushing to make his way over with a big smile lighting up his face.

'Yes, great,' I said, hearing meself croak with the nerves.

Then he bent down to kiss my cheek and hesitated, giving me a kiss full on the mouth instead, saying quietly, 'It is lovely to see you, darling. How are you this morning?'

'I'm feeling great, Ralph. I had a lovely deep sleep. I'm fresh as a daisy. What about you?' I gasped, losing the run of myself with the excitement of seeing he loves me and getting that kiss.

'Oh, very well, thank you, but I dare say I was rather tired. One very late night followed by a particularly energetic and most enjoyable night spent with you, darling, had me sleeping like a log.'

'Oh, it's like I said, Ralph, you are going to need stamina if you intend keeping up with me!' I droned, then stared at him, keeping my face straight.

He stared back, letting a slow smile light up his eyes, then he bent close, whispering in my ear, 'You will eat those words!' Then he straightened, lifting his chin, saying, 'I shall see you later, meanwhile . . .'

'What have you got there, Ralph?' I said, seeing him handing me something.

'For you, darling,' he said, grinning as he handed me a gorgeous bouquet of flowers.

'For me! You bought those flowers for me?'

'Yes, of course!' he said, wondering why I should think twice about that idea.

I looked at them, staring at how lovely they are. Then I looked to see Madame smiling, looking at me and the flowers, giving a sideways glance to Ralph, seeing him with his hand resting on my shoulder. Then she turned back to her business, looking like she had a secret smile on her face, with her taking it all in. Uh-huh, she definitely sees what's going on, I thought, looking over to Ralph, seeing him leaning and down writing something in a notebook. Then he was gone out the door, leaving me to point the flowers at Madame, wanting to get myself a vase.

Gawd, he really is romantic, I thought, making myself a lovely display. Then I put them on the table and myself and Madame stood back, smiling and admiring them, nodding our heads as she said one thing and I said the other. But it sounded like we were agreeing with each other. Then I gave her an extra big smile, feeling the happiness should be shared.

I sighed, letting out a big breath with all me contentment. Then I waved, heading out of the kitchen, seeing her shake her head in a grin. Jaysus, she's probably asking herself now how long we will last this time!

No sign of Ralph, I thought, looking around for sight of him. OK, get your bath and get dressed, then head off for a walk, it will do you good. I put on my coat and looked down at my jeans and boots. I'm grand, I won't bother putting any make-up on. I can do that later when I change for dinner. I need to let the fresh air at my skin and get a good airing into my lungs, I thought, making my way down the stairs and out along the side passage. I heard a noise in Ralph's study and stopped. Will I go in? He might be busy. I don't want to get in his way and annoy him. Ah, go on, just let him know you're going for a walk. Then get yourself a quick kiss. Lovely!

I knocked on the door gently then put my head in. 'Ralph!' I said, seeing he was sitting at his desk writing with papers streamed around him. 'Sorry, I won't disturb you, I'm on my way out,' I said, seeing him lift his head.

'Oh, good, excellent idea. Incidentally, darling, we shall be having some—' Then the phone rang and he picked it up, saying to me, 'Sorry, one moment!'

I waited, seeing him get bogged down in a conversation. 'I'll see you later,' I said, seeing him raise his hand to me, then I shut the door quietly, heading off out for my walk.

I walked for miles along country roads, taking in the odd house here and there that could only be seen in the distance through fields and woods. Then I turned back and headed off in the opposite direction, making for the village. I wanted to take a good look around. I never really gave it much time, so now I can enjoy myself doing a bit of exploring. I have plenty of time and maybe the less Ralph sees of me the better. It doesn't do to be hanging out of each other. He needs to get on and do what he wants to do. Yeah, sure, we have all the time in the evening. Oh, this is marvellous. Never but never have I ever been so happy and contented. Imagine if it was like this all the time! You never know, Martha, you could end up married to him . . . Hmm, bit too good to be true. If nothing, I'm a realist! Yeah, keep it that way, Martha. Hope for the best but expect the worst. Then you won't be disappointed. Grand! I sighed, humming, 'Oh, I do like to be beside the seaside!' On second thoughts, it's too bleedin cold! I grinned, feeling God is in his heaven and the world is put to rights.

I stamped up the drive, dragging my, boots, feeling all the puff blowing out of me as I rounded the last bend, bringing the house into sight. Then I stopped dead, taking in all the cars parked outside. What's going on? Oh, he must have people over. I could feel my heart begin to start drumming. Wonder what's happening? I better get in and make myself look decent! Jaysus, the one day I didn't put make-up on, I thought, flying around the corner heading for the side door. I could hear voices coming from the sitting room and people laughing, then I turned into the main hall, hearing a familiar voice. I stopped. It was coming from the kitchen. 'It's that fucking one!' I muttered, making straight for the kitchen, forgetting all about the state of me.

When I got to the door, I slowed down and sidled in, trying to look casual. But no, my heart dropped, there she is, looking large as life and ugly as sin! The fucking vamp trying to wrap herself around my Ralph. And he's not exactly trying to fight her off. I couldn't believe what I was seeing. I stopped dead, taking in the scene with my heart flying and blinking like mad to clear me eyesight because it fogged up from the shock.

Ralph was leaning over her with his hand resting on the back of her head, while she held his waist as he searched her eye with a white handkerchief. They were talking in French and she was moaning, '*Ohhh, blah blah,* pain, cry, moan, *blah blah!*'

I said nothing, wanting to take it in and keep my mouth shut. But I heard myself shout as soon as he stroked her face, smiled and let go, admiring his doctoring of her left eye. She blinked, then leaned into him, giving him a kiss on the cheek close to his lips. He tweaked his left eyebrow, smiled and shrugged, then put the hankie back in his pocket. That's when I said, 'Well, hello, Ralph! How nice to see yourself be so terribly helpful.' I grinned, seeing his face whip to the door, looking a bit confused for a minute.

Then he said, 'Oh, I did wonder where you got to, Martha.'

'Well, here I am! I've turned up like a bad penny, Ralph,' I grinned, making no move to go near him. I saw Madame Butterfly turn with a curious look to take me in, then she turned away, looking bored. I was definitely nothing of interest.

'Oh, Martha! Do come and meet my friends, we are preparing to have a bridge party. Soviah,' he said, taking her arm and walking her down to me, 'may I introduce my dear friend Martha Long. Martha, this is Soviah de Montfort!'

'How charming,' she said, handing me a limp white hand with a long pair of red talons dangling at the end.

'Oh, how lovely to meet you,' I said, whispering in my sexiest voice, digging up the best manners I could scrape. I have no intention of letting this trollop think she has a clear field to my Ralphie! Then she dismissed me and turned to Ralph, saying something with lots of ouf-ing and pouffff-ing, and lifting the shoulder with the eyebrows raising and the eyes closing, fluttering the bleedin eyelashes. Jaysus, I hate her, I thought, smouldering with the rage at how lovely she looked. A soft, warm, dusty dark bluey-grey frock sat on her hips and breasts, and snuggled her legs and arse, to just hang on the knees. It was low cut in a V showing her lovely milky-white breasts large as life, looking like a man would kill to get his hands on them.

The frock had long sleeves and came to a V at the hands. Fuck, she's disgustingly lovely! I wanted to slither out of the kitchen and nurse me wounds, having a marvellous time feeling terribly sorry for meself and sulk like mad. I hate that kind of competition when I'm not prepared for it. Ah, Jaysus, I bet them two are having a fucking affair. She can't keep her maulers offa him, I fumed, watching her lean into him as he put his hand on her back, drawing her out of the kitchen.

'Come along, Martha. Do let me introduce you to some friends of mine,' he said, putting his hand around my waist while keeping his hand lightly on your woman's back as the cow leant into him.

I could hear my heavy breathing, with the rage threatening to get the better of me. No, Jaysus, get the fuck out of here before you let rip and do something you will regret for the rest of your life.

'Ralph! I just need to pop upstairs for a minute,' I said, wanting to lean up and give him a kiss. But the tight feeling of fear and insecurity, and the madness of thinking he was enjoying himself with the fucker, wouldn't let me. 'I will be down in a minute,' I smiled.

'Yes, that is all right. We shall be in the sitting room,' he smiled, waving me off then leading the bleedin Mona Lisa down the hall, heading for the sitting room.

I dashed up the stairs and into my room, closing the door and landing myself into the chair by the window. I grabbed my tobacco out of my pocket and lit up a cigarette. Then I took a deep drag, trying to get my senses back. Now, sit here and think quietly. No, lie back and sit on the bed. Jaysus, am I glad to be away from that. I could feel myself shaking from the shock and the rage thundering through me, knocking all the sense out of me. Jesus, Martha, what came over you? That kind of thing has never really bothered you before. That was always the least of my problems. Jealousy? No, Jaysus, no, I am never bothered by that. But now, I could easily mash that bleedin cow to mush! Then a thought hit me. I'm even in the right place to do that. What is it they say about murder in France? Oh, yeah, *It voss a krime of passhione! I did it out ov lauve! It voss a ménage à trois! One of oze ad to go! It vas not go-ink to be meee! Non! So I keel her! She voz try-ink to take my luv-ver. Vell! I voz plan-ing eee shuld be my luv-er!*

I sighed, looking around the room, thinking it would be lovely to have the comfort of a hot sup of tea to go with my cigarette. Or better still, a glass of wine. Then I heard a knock on the door.

'Martha! May I come in?'

I listened, hearing Ralph's voice. 'It's open,' I sighed, lifting my shoulders, not wanting him to see the state of me.

'Darling, are you OK? Why do you not come down?'

'Oh, I am Ralph, just give me a minute! I just wanted to have a smoke and relax for a minute. It was a long walk. I didn't realise how long until I got back. It only hit me then,' I rushed, trying to smile but keeping my eyes rambling from the floor to the cigarette, looking anywhere but at him.

'Darling, what is it?' he said, sagging down on the mattress, landing me nearly on his lap as he sat down beside me, putting his arm around me.

'Honestly, I am fine, grand, Ralph! Why would you think there's something wrong?' I said, flicking my eyes at him then turning away, feeling very foolish and very out of my depth suddenly. It was like I didn't belong. I was punching above my weight with him and his friends. I knew this never bothered me before. I could always hold my own. But it was the terror of losing Ralph.

He sighed and took in a slow, deep breath. 'Martha, look at me,' he said, taking my face in his hands.

I couldn't lift my eyes. Somehow I felt shamed by my awkwardness around him and his friends.

'Listen to me. I know you are upset by meeting Soviah, and particularly my giving her what seems to be rather intimate attention. But, darling, please, I do know you very well. I understand your difficulty in dealing with this sort of thing. I know you are feeling terribly insecure and threatened by this lady. It is so sad, really, you do not see how worthy you are. Listen to me, darling!' he whispered, taking me in his arms and cradling me. 'You are no longer the waif made to feel unworthy, bedraggled and abandoned. You have endured and grown to become a very wonderful woman, darling. As a young girl, you had the courage of a lion, now you have grown to become a very formidable lady. Do not underestimate your worth, Martha. Goodness! Why do you think I love you, darling? I admire you greatly. It would be nonsense if one dared to compare you and Soviah. Simply ludicrous. She is a mewling, drooling infant, a pussycat compared with you, my love!' he said, pulling me tighter into his arms and talking softly into my face.

'I understand where this comes from. Our relationship is terribly important to you, as it is to me. I do not play games, darling. I would not hurt you in that way. Listen to me, Martha. Soviah is the wife of a friend of mine, Jacques de Montfort. He is a doctor, a heart surgeon. He has his mistress,' Ralph said, grinning at me. 'She takes her lovers! In France, within certain circles, this is quite acceptable,' he said, shrugging his shoulders, dropping his mouth and lifting his eyebrows. 'But we won't busy ourselves in the politics of their domestic arrangements. But, yes, I think perhaps you are right. She is making it rather obvious she would like to add my name to her bedpost,' he laughed.

'Feck off!' I muttered. 'I see nothing funny about that, Ralph. You are really enjoying it!'

'Oh, darling, please. Do you really think I would have difficulty in handling Soviah? Look at me, Martha!' he said, taking my face and forcing me to look at him.

'I don't know,' I muttered, still wondering just how much he was enjoying himself with all this grovelling and drooling your woman was giving him.

'Darling, I am a man. I live in a world populated by you divine creatures. I am not immune to you all but I do know how to conduct myself. Certainly as a doctor, and indeed a priest, I have had experience with women showing a rather strong interest, sometimes more than I would consider healthy. I keep an emotional distance, darling. I have had years of practice. So you must not allow yourself to feel under threat. I would never betray you. You are the only one with whom I have succumbed,' he laughed, grabbing me in a tight hug. 'Now, come along, let us go downstairs. I cannot neglect these people. It is very bad form to abandon one's guests.'

'Yeah, OK, but who does your woman think she is anyway?' I snorted.

'Oh, she is really rather unhappy, darling. Do try to be kind to her. Just think, you could have been her! A thoroughbred who has learned the art of using her wiles to feed her wants but not her needs, poor girl,' he said, looking very sorrowful.

'What do you mean, thoroughbred?'

'Oh, her lineage!' he said, thinking. 'Her mother's line comes through a royal house. She is a countess! Soviah within her own social circle, well, they are two a penny, darling. Unlike you! You are a rarity. A colossus among these mere mortals,' he laughed, trying to make his face look sorrowful.

I stared, then lost the rag. 'Stop, Ralph, cut that out. I thought for a minute there you were serious. I was beginning to believe you. Now you are just making an eejit outa me. Colossus, me arse, I just want to know you are not really interested in her, that's all. Because if I think you are not serious about me, then I'm not wasting my time, Ralph!'

'Oh, darling,' he puffed, looking at me then wandering his head to the door, getting pulled with me up here and them down there.

'I mean it,' I puffed, snorting air in and out through me nose, letting him see I mean business. I can't compete with a bleedin house of royalty, I thought, thinking the only house me and the ma had was under the fuckin stars!

'Oh, yes! But you are, darling. To me, you are the morning sun that rises from the dawn, the moon that settles—'

'Fuck off, Ralph!' I shouted, seeing him with the hands looking like poetry in motion. 'There's no need to wax lyrical! I just wanted you to tell me in plain language. OK, I will ignore her,' I said, feeling mollified, letting him look happy as he gave me a quick squeeze then went to grab my hand.

'Yes, darling, you are wonderful. Forget all this silliness. Now, trust me, leave poor Soviah alone! Let her have the occasional nibble at me!' he laughed, throwing back his head, thinking that was hilarious.

I didn't laugh. 'Fuck off, Ralph, you are not funny.'

'Oh, Martha, do give me a smile,' he said, leaning into me, staring.

I just stared then said, 'OK, you go on, I need to change.'

'Nonsense, come as you are. You look wonderful.'

'Lying sod!' I muttered, raging as I wasn't looking lovely.

'No!' he said slowly, looking down at my boots and jeans and big woolly jumper, with the face looking like a ghost and me hair knotted in a plait, pinned on the back of my head.

I stared, waiting to see what he thought.

'You look . . .' he said, trying to think. 'Beautiful,' he said, dragging the word out then grabbing my hand and marching me out the door.

We walked into the sitting room with Ralph going ahead. I slowed down. Immediately my eyes lit on the vamp propping herself up at the mantelpiece, holding out a long black cigarillo. I looked again. I hope they're not fucking my ones! I left them sitting there in a box!

She suddenly shifted herself, losing the half-dead, bored look and slowly made to stand herself up straight, letting her eyes home in on Ralph as she took in a slow deep breath, making her chest heave in and out. Then she stood, bringing the cigarillo slowly to her mouth, taking in a long drag while she studied us, flicking her eyes over me, seeing that I was with him. Then she dismissed me, pinning her eyes back on him, blowing out her smoke in a long, slow, sexy puff, looking like she was blowing a kiss.

I stood watching the smoke blow out then waft around her, making it look like she needed the fire extinguisher. Then she sighed, lifting her face, and oozed her way over with the hips slowly rocking and her left arm held lazily in the air, saying, '*Ralph! Blah ohhhh poufff!*' like she was nearly crying. He answered in French, letting her keep her hand lightly on his arm as she tried to lead him away. He muttered something to her, giving her a smile, then took my arm, saying, 'Please may I introduce my dear friend, Martha Long!'

They all stood up, looking me over, waiting politely with enquiring looks and ready smiles.

'Martha! May I introduce my good friend Jacques de Montfort.'

'I am charmed, Madame, most delighted,' he said, bowing and kissing my hand when I held it out for a shake.

So that's Ralph's friend. Gawd, he's nearly as handsome as Ralph, I thought, seeing the impeccable cut of his clothes, with the dark wool jacket and matching trousers, the white-linen shirt and gold cufflinks. He had thick, dark-brown wavy hair brushed back off his head, and sapphire-blue eyes that looked deep into you. They looked like he was smiling at seeing something inside you that interested him.

Yeah, they are about the same age. I can see why they would be friends. He is a real gentleman and very charming. They would have a lot in common.

'This is Heinrich von Leiberstrum.'

My eyes peeled on him, looking into the face of a blond man about the same age. He had dead-straight silky hair combed back with not a strand out of place. He stood very erect then bowed, taking my hand gently but firmly, saying, 'Madame, it is an honour to meet you,' then he bowed from the waist.

'And his good lady wife Isolda,' Ralph said.

'How do you do?' I gushed, looking at Isolda with the shiny blue eyes flashing a lovely white smile, with the lovely white teeth and the matching face. My eyes lifted to the mop of curly blonde hair and the rosy-red lips. Then I looked down at the snow-white hand, looking weighted down with the dazzling diamond ring and the diamond-and-white-gold watch. I could smell the whiff of exotically delicious and expensive perfume as it wafted up me nose when she leaned in to shake my hand.

Jaysus, I forgot to even put a squirt of perfume on meself, I nearly cried, wanting to run off and nurse me sorrow. If only I was sitting here now, dressed up to the nines in my lovely new frock and the diamond earrings Ralph bought me. The curse a Jaysus on him for not warning me!

Then we all sat down and drinks were poured. They got their glasses refilled, with the men helping themselves after taking care of the women.

'Darling, your drink,' Ralph said, coming over and handing me a big glass of white wine.

I sipped, watching him and Jacques talking while he busied himself opening new packs of cards, taking them out of the cellophane then putting them down on the two little card tables covered in heavy green felt that were set standing in the middle of the room.

'Are you German?' I said, turning to Isolda, trying to make myself look polite.

'Oh, yes, I am from Switzerland, and vere are you vrom?' she said, sounding very German.

'I am from Ireland,' I said, leaving out the 'vrom', nearly getting carried away with copying her, I was that busy listening to her lovely accent.

'Oh, how very lovely. I have vished myself to visit your lovely country! But you see ve are so very busy. It is the seasons, you see. Now ve are in the snow season it is time vor the skiing! Ve go next veek! You vill be coming also? It vould be so nice if you vere to join us! You like to ski, of course?'

'Of course! That sounds wonderful!' I said, throwing an eye over at Ralph to see did he catch that one. I hardly know what snow looks like, never mind how to slide in it.

'Please, do tell me a little about your country. I have heard so many vonderful things about it! I believe it is vonderfully charming and, of course, your history is so terribly tragic,' she said, looking like the mother of all sorrows. 'My husband Heinrich, he knows so much. These things are all so very interesting vor him. He is a diplomat, you see. So I must listen ven he speaks. Because it is good vor me also. Then I vill be informed. So please, do tell me vat you can!' she said, all glittering eyes and teeth, sitting forward to hear every word as I took in a sharp breath.

'Oh, it is very charming,' I said, smiling and nodding slowly with her as she listened, making it look like I am absolutely fascinating with the things I have to tell her. 'Well, it is a small island out in the middle of the Atlantic Ocean,' I said then stopped, wondering about that. Is it really? Jaysus, I should have kept me mouth shut about that one. I don't know much about geography. She waited while I paused.

'Now, our main industry is agriculture. You see, we have a lot of land and very few people, because our main industry is in the export! We have to export the population. Emigrate! We've been doing it since the famine! Since the British starved us out of it,' I said, wondering where all me information was coming from.

I saw her smile, beginning to get a bit tired. This wasn't very interesting. So then I said, 'Now, we were a very primitive people. Not like yourselves, you Continentals. No, we were stuck on an island with only our nearest neighbours, the British, for company. But we didn't like them! So we were very much on our own. You see, we are the furthest point west. Once you get to our little island, you can't go any further. Next stop is America. Yes, we are the last outpost of Western Europe. It is very remote.

'It brings out the best in people and it can bring out the worst. We're very passionate. We can be very raw, primitive, but that's mostly a good thing. It stirs us to great passions. We are fiercely independent. We make great soldiers. The British wouldn't have won their wars without us fighting Irish. We won their wars for them. We even fought the wars for the Americans, right back to some of their finest generals during the war of independence, under George Washington. Oh, yes, they were the Irish. The passion stirs us to other things as well. For such a tiny island, we have produced some of the most powerful people on the earth. Kennedy in the White House for one. There was a lot more before him. We have produced some of the greatest writers known to man. Beckett, Joyce, Yeats, Sean O'Casey. I can name them all. All this from such a tiny island. What kind of place can produce that, you probably ask yourself. Well, it's the culture, it's our history and, more importantly, it's our weather. During the winters, we have nothing to do but sit indoors and think! So let me tell you a little about it.

'Now, about our nearest neighbours the English. Well, I do have to say, we have made great progress since we managed to run them out of the country.'

'Oh, yes,' she breathed, seeing how serious this all was, nodding and agreeing with me.

I felt delighted I had something to talk about. 'Well,' I said, 'now we don't keep pigs in the kitchen any more.'

'No?' she said, shaking her head.

'No,' I said, 'and not just that, but we gave up the donkeys and carts. They're swapped now for motor cars!'

'Really?' she breathed. 'Yes, I have seen this postcards vit the donkey and carts you are speaking of!'

'Yes, they used them for carrying the turf,' I said, 'but not any more. Especially since the lottery came in. Now we have farmers winning the million and buying themselves Maseratis. They use them to carry the hay!'

'Really?' she said.

'Oh, yes!' I said. 'They throw it up on the roof rack and it's away with them, flying around the country roads with the hay blowing off the top and not a bother on them,' I puffed. 'Oh, yes, we are getting very modern now, we even have colour televisions. But the only problem now is, in the country they can only get the one television station. RTÉ, that's the national TV station.'

'But this land, you say it is not many people . . . So it must be very lonely!'

'Oh, very,' I said, shaking my head. 'The poor farmers never see a woman from one end of the day to the next, especially along the west. You see, the women won't marry a farmer. The life is too hard! They prefer the bright lights of England or America. There, the living is easier for them.'

'Most fascinating,' she said, shaking her head slowly, looking at me like I was the next best thing to Einstein himself. 'And vot else can you tell me about your vonderful country?'

'Oh, let me see,' I said, thinking. 'Well, we have the highest rate of madness in Europe!'

'Really?' she gasped.

'Oh, yes, you see it comes from all the inbreeding! We only have a little population, only under three million! We had eight million during the famine!'

'Really?'

'Oh, yes, so you get the picture, Isolda, very lonely for the poor people isolated on their farms. So they go mad, especially all the dark nights sitting on your own with only the dog for company! Sure, who wouldn't go mad? And knowing at the end of it you are going to die a virgin. A very . . . eh, have no family! Nothing to show for your life's work. Sure, what kind of life is that?'

'Yes, so true!' she said, jumping in to agree with me.

Then, the woman with the coiffeured brown hair moved closer to nod and agree as she had turned to listen in.

'Françoise, ve are talking, Martha and I, about her beautiful island! I must visit, soon, very soon. As soon as the season ends!'

Françoise followed Isolda's nods with her own nods, listening and then looking to nod at me as we all leaned into each other, nodding.

'Ladies, may we please take our seats?' the men called, looking over with drinks in their hands, waiting, smiling and holding out a hand to the chairs.

I noticed the vamp was sitting opposite Ralph, so she must be his partner! 'Fuck, that one never gives up,' I snorted, muttering to meself, then looked to see her husband Jacques take a place on the next table. There were four to a table, with everyone having a partner. They played with each other against the rest of the players.

'It was so lovely to talk vit you, we must talk again,' Isolda said, laying her hand on my shoulder. Then I watched them all sitting down while Ralph organised the Madame's nibbles on little tables close to hand.

I sat watching and sipping and nibbling and dozing, then I got up and wandered over to bend down close to Ralph, getting a look at his hand. I didn't know what I was supposed to be looking for but I stared, trying to make myself look very intelligent. Anyway, I didn't get too close, because it wouldn't look right. They were all looking very civilised and sitting up straight, giving all their attention to the cards held out in their hands. Someone would put a card down and their partner would watch very closely, then put one down too. Otherwise there was dead silence except for the occasional lifting of the hand to take up a drink and sip while keeping their eyes on their cards and watching to see what their partner was doing.

Ralph managed to take his eyes off his cards and the vamp long enough to give me a wink, then settled his attention back on the game. Then someone called, or whatever it was they did, and people started putting their cards down, counting them. Suddenly Ralph let a roar at Madame Butterfly, pointing and showing his own cards as he put them down. She waved her hands and puffed and pooh-ed, then shook her shoulders, taking a delicate sip of her wine, looking tragic and pitiful as she pleaded at him, talking rapidly, showing her own cards. But it was lost on him. He was too busy stabbing her cards, waving at his own, then people stood up, making for the drinks and taking a stretch.

19

I moved over to the mantelpiece, looking for me cigarillos. They were gone! I looked, seeing the vamp take one out of a box that looked suspiciously like mine. Then she lit it up and lifted her neck, blowing smoke into the air before blowing Ralph a kiss, leaning across saying something that sounded like, 'Oh, do not be cross with me, you will break my heart!'

I snorted and raged, feeling my heart flying and my blood boiling, watching him shake his head at her, then lean forward, puffing out a mock annoyance. Then I was marching over and whipping up the box, saying, '*Merci, Madame!* Do you mind if I take one? I do not mind in the least, sharing them with you,' I said, keeping my face neutral.

'Poouuf,' she breathed with a little wave of the hand, dismissing me. I saw Ralph stare, looking like he was astonished, then waiting to laugh as his eyes followed me sashaying in me boots over to the fireplace and doing a 'vamp', lighting up my cigarillo then leaning back and blowing smoke into the air, giving him a big smile plastered on my face. But he could see my eyes were smouldering with the rage and boring holes into the vamp as I turned to look at her. She sighed and leant forward, holding out her glass then putting it on the table, looking to him to get her a drink.

He stood up, saying, 'Martha, would you like another drink, darling?'

Darling he called me in front of her! I beamed. 'Yes, please, that would be lovely,' I purred, dropping my pursed lips in her direction.

She took that in – it was very quick – but then she feasted her eyes on him, letting a smile light them up. Then she stood and made her way over slowly to the drinks and leaned in beside him, brushing her right breast against him. He turned and handed her a drink, then she put her hand on his shoulder and let it drop down his chest, looking up very intently to his face, saying something. He smiled and shrugged, standing talking with my drink in his hand while I waited. Then I marched over, saying, 'Thank you, Ralph, you are very kind,' and pushed in gently, getting in her way.

'Do be kind, darling,' Ralph whispered, giving me a quick kiss on the cheek.

I moved off, wandering over to see what the others were up to. Jacques was huddled over by the window talking to Heinrich and Françoise. They looked like they were having an argument, with lots of shrugs and huffing and puffing and waving arms and raising eyebrows. Then they all seemed to agree, with the nodding of heads at each other.

Ah, fuck this! I suddenly thought, making my way out and heading into the kitchen. Madame was slaving over the cooker, getting all red-faced from steaming pots and stuff getting lifted out of the oven. I felt like asking did she need a hand, it felt more real somehow. I couldn't be easy in myself in that room with those people. I haven't a clue what they are saying and it's bloody hard going being so polite all the time. So leave them to it, Martha. Take a break. Jaysus! I need to try and get my bearings. I'm not used to feeling so out of control. It's the nerves worrying about Ralph; the emotions are flying too high. I have never been in love like this before. Now I know why it can drive people mad, even wanting to commit murder. Jaysus, I was always so easy-going around people, especially men! I never had a problem, now I feel like I'm from outer space. I'm off kilter. It feels like I am reeling from one powerful emotion to the next. It's that bleedin Madame Butterfly. She's determined to get Ralph. But if you were calm and thinking, Martha, you would look at it like this. She was around before you came here and she is still here but not with him. You are, so, as he said, trust him and act your age, woman. Stop behaving like a bleedin halfwit! Right, I sighed. Just give him space and simply ignore her, let her get on with her fun and games. If you were thinking clearly, you would sit back and enjoy it.

Right! Take it easy, sit back and enjoy her making a fool of herself. Mind you, no one else seems to take notice. It looks like they think this is all normal, hanging out of Ralph with her husband right within eyeball distance. Yeah, he doesn't seem to care. Hmm. Never mind, enjoy yourself, give up the nonsense, Martha. You will be a long time dead. These are very much the good times rolled around again. Only this is beyond your wildest dreams. You have Ralph back in your life. Not just that but now you are a woman on equal terms, living with him in his very own home. Jaysus! Be grateful, Martha, he loves you! He is all the time proving that. Oh, thank you, God, for looking after me. I survived the massive suicide attempt and now here I am reaching for the moon and hitting the stars. My God, he must be in his heaven, because all is well with my world, I sighed happily, giving a big smile to Madame as she turned around to look at me, brushing a stray bit of damp grey hair out of her eyes.

Then she said something to someone walking in the door. A girl came in and picked up the covered dishes Madame had just landed on the table and wheeled over a trolley, putting them on the trays and making out the door. Oh! We must be having dinner in the dining room with that lot. They must be guests staying for dinner.

My heart flew. Jaysus, the state of me! I took out the door and flew up the stairs, making straight for my room. Right, change, get ready! What will I wear? Bleedin hell, wouldn't I just love now to have had a long soak in a bubble bath. 'Ah, Jaysus, Ralph, did it not occur to you to tell me what was going on?' I moaned, creasing my face into a crying look. I will never get ready in time. It will be very bad manners if I suddenly disappeared, leaving them all waiting. Ralph would not start the dinner until everyone is seated. No, Martha, leave it. Much better to go as you are and not cause trouble. He would only lose face over being involved with someone as hick-country as me. Anyway, I would be only letting myself down as well. No chance! Get moving. The dinner is already heading in.

I took off back down the stairs, hearing voices already coming from the dining room. I walked in to see them all sitting themselves down and looked to see where I would sit. There was an empty place at the end next to Françoise. I made my way down there and sat looking back up the table to see the vamp sitting on the left of Ralph, with him sitting at the top of the table. Heinrich was trying to say something to her, he was sitting on her left, but she was too busy sulking at Ralph, who was talking to Pierre, the man with the moustache and slicked-back blond hair that reminded me of the fellow from James Bond, Simon whatever his name was, with the lovely-looking looks.

Jaysus, they really are very polished looking, with their plumy, dulcet-tone speaking voices, and their air of having nothing ever lacking in their lives because it is just there for the taking.

Suddenly Jacques turned to me, saying with a smile on his face, 'Is this your first visit to France, Martha?'

I looked at him, seeing his eyes laughing, looking very interested.

'No, Jacques, I think now I have been the length and breadth of France. I have travelled here many times before. But only as a pauper!'

'Pardon me?' he smiled, not looking sure as he leaned in towards me, wondering was he hearing right.

'You know, arriving on a wing and a prayer! Determined to have fun without the mon!' I grinned, feeling the devil in me kick in again.

'Oh, I see,' he said slowly, not seeing at all, though his eyes were staring, trying to work me out.

'Oh, yes, I have seen your *Mona Lisa* in the Louvre! I studied it quite intently. Frankly, I think she had just been well fed by Leonardo and he had just promised her another helping if she sat still. A genius like him could work miracles with a woman. She was certainly looking forward to round two with him, or maybe it was even round three!' I said, staring him straight in the eye.

He listened very politely, nodding with every word, then thought about it for a second as I sat back grinning at him. Then it hit him and he suddenly burst out laughing. 'You think he was her lover?'

'But of course,' I said. 'That man must have had an insatiable appetite for women. He had a ferocious appetite for everything else; nothing that moved escaped his attention. He needed to understand and explore everything! He sketched the skeleton of the human form right down to the minutest detail of bone and muscle. Can you imagine how a woman would feel with his attentions singled on her? Hence the secret smile! Those are the eyes of a woman who has just been loved, made to feel a goddess by a man who is an Adonis and well trained in the art of love and seduction. He probably planned it, groomed her, to capture the essence of a woman in love. His need was to understand, to dig deep and capture the essence, searching for the soul. He did that through the face of Mona Lisa, showing her inner passion. Then through Christ, showing the agony of his grief and suffering,' I said, thinking of the *Pieta*, then thinking, or was that Michelangelo? Never mind, keep waxing lyrical. 'Oh, yes!' I continued, 'he was searching for the soul, needing to capture a glimpse, then immortalise it in a painting. He knew we were mere mortals; he wanted to live on. Now he does, through his great works of art.'

'Yes,' he said slowly, 'I do see what you mean,' then he clapped his hands, laughing and saying, 'Bravo! I love it! A very acute observation, Martha. Yes, I do like it,' he said, raising his glass in a toast.

I grinned at him, lifting my glass, and inclined my head, saying, 'My pleasure, sir!' Then I looked down the table to see Ralph staring down at me with a surprised and thoughtful look in his eyes, as if they were smiling. He slowly raised his glass, inclining his head, then bowed, saluting me. I stared back and slowly raised my glass, returning the salute, then grinned, letting him know I was out for mischief. I noticed Madame Butterfly was suddenly taking notice, as if someone had told her I was a wasp that stings. I raised my glass to her without smiling, saying quietly, '*Madame!*'

She lifted her glass politely, returning the gesture, then snapped her attention on Ralph, saying something in rapid French, sounding like she was completely fed up and wanted him to do something. I laughed inside myself, thinking, yeah, two can play your game, Soviah darling! For now, you have the looks, so I have to dig for other resources.

I sipped on my delicious liquor, feeling it coat my tongue as it slid down the back of my throat, making its way to my full belly. It warmed me, filling my head with a rosy glow, letting me think I must be back with the ancient Romans when they enjoyed great grandeur while devouring their fabulous feasts. Oh, Mammy, this is the way to live, I thought, letting my eyes wander down the table, seeing everyone looking relaxed and sated after this lovely dinner. I could still taste the creamy soup and the mouth-watering pieces of lobster that came floating in a gorgeous sauce. Not to mention all the lovely vegetables – the farmers must have just dug them straight out of the ground.

Then my eyes lit on Ralph, who looking very contented and happy with himself. He was sprawled back in his chair with his arm resting over the chair of Madame Butterfly. She had her hand on his arm and the other one lying on his chest, leaning right into him. He was giving her his full attention. The hairs on the back of me neck bristled and I could feel a fire coming into my belly. I sat up straight, then looked around, seeing Jacques turn to rest his eyes on me. He had been deep in conversation with Françoise. I had been lost in me own world, letting it all run over my head. But now I was wide awake.

'Jacques,' I said, staring at him as I leaned across smiling. 'I am curious about French men.'

'Yes?' he said, raising his eyebrows, letting his eyes flash in a smile.

'Oh, yes, is it true what they say about them being wonderful lovers?'

He laughed, thinking about this, then said, 'But of course! We speak the language of love!'

'Ohhh la la!' I said. 'Then it is all ahead of me. I had intended saving myself for the worms but you have just persuaded me otherwise.'

'For the worms! Pouf! What a waste,' he said, giving his hands a swiping clap and running his eyes up and down me. 'No, this would be a tragedy! You must live today as if tomorrow does not exist.'

'That sounds to me like the language of a philanderer!' I said, taking a sip of my drink.

'Of course it is, my dear! We French are great lovers of life.'

'Yes, but some prefer a foreign dish,' I said, letting him follow my head down the table to land on the pair of lovebirds.

'Pouf,' he said, lifting his face up and back to me, then waving his hand. 'Each must have his own taste,' he said, dismissing the vamp. Then he looked back and caught Ralph's eye, giving him a shrug with a smile on his face, much as to say, *She is desperate, my friend, but it is your problem!* Ralph then landed his eye on me, giving a grin and shaking his head, much as to say, *You are up to your mischief again.* I winked at him, giving him a big grin, thinking, if that's all he does, I have nothing to worry myself about.

'*Au revoir! Bonne nuit,*' Ralph said, as we stood at the door waving off the last of the guests, seeing them motor down the drive, heading themselves off for home.

'Well,' Ralph sighed, shutting the door to keep out the cold, dark, windy night. 'I think that went quite well. It was a pleasant evening,' he smiled, putting his arm around my waist and heading us back into the sitting room. He started to fold away the card tables and I collected the glasses, putting them on the drinks trolley and weaving it out

the door, heading for the kitchen. Ralph followed me in and started
to stack them on the draining board and around the sink, then went
back to tidy up the sitting room. When he'd finished there, I followed
him into the dining room, watching him as he looked around. He
blew out the candles sitting in the silver candlesticks and collected
up all the ashtrays. I started to stack the dessert dishes, picking up
stuff and loading the trolley for taking away.

'No, darling, leave all that. In the morning Madame will have the
girls in from the village to help. Come along,' he said, holding out
his arm, waiting for me. 'Let us sit and relax.'

'Great idea,' I smiled, grabbing hold of him around the waist and
walking out with him, then waiting as he stopped to close the door
behind us.

'Here we are,' he said, going over to switch on the radio. 'Let us
have some music to soothe the savage beast,' he said, grinning at me
as he made to sit down beside me on the couch, while some soft
music by Brahms filled the room with a lovely sense of peace.

I looked, seeing him sit down and stretch his legs before flopping
his arm around me and pulling me closer to him. I turned quickly
and sat up on his lap, letting my arms wrap around his neck while
he rested his hands around my waist. We sat staring at each other,
saying nothing, just taking the other in.

'I love you, Ralph. With you I feel complete. It is like I have
arrived after a long and hard journey. I am not talking, either, about
the trek it took to get here,' I said, smiling at him. 'I mean it is as if
every step I have taken in my life has been leading me to you. I think
the time when we first met was intended as a preparation for you
to post me in the right direction. You have been the most powerful
person in my life. I told you there was only one other, but he showed
me the dark side of life. I followed you because you lit up my heart
with goodness and light, and showed me there truly was a God in
his heaven. So now you know, Ralph. I could never love another man
the way I love you!'

He just stared at me, searching my face, looking deep into my
eyes like he could see into my soul. Then he kissed my face and my
eyes, murmuring, 'Darling, you are the only woman I have loved as a
man should love a woman. As we were born to do. I want you with

my soul and with my body. Darling, I too could never love another woman as I love you. I feel very privileged you have been saved for me, because you are most precious. Your heart is pure. You have such great gifts, my darling. I believe you have yet to even touch on them. But you will. Yes, darling, one day you will.' Then he lowered me off his lap and whipped me around, lying me on the sofa, and stretched down beside me, stroking my hair and face.

I stared at him, seeing how soft his eyes were as he stared back, giving me a look of infinite tenderness, letting his love for me pour out through his eyes. I could hear the words, 'I want you with my body and with my soul.' That means he truly loves me. So is he going to ask me then to marry him? Is he now ready to make that decision? I could feel myself getting very shy. The blood was pumping through me, making my heart go like the clappers. Does that mean he is going to sleep with me? I want to ask him . . . but I couldn't bring myself to get it out. That's what makes me feel shy. I am afraid he might reject me because I am jumping the gun. No, if he was ready, he would come straight out and ask me. Let it be. I know what I want. But he still has to arrive at what he wants.

I sighed and put my lips close to his then gently kissed him. He let me linger as I gently tasted his lips, barely moving them. Then he pressed his down onto mine, kissing me harder as he slowly opened my mouth then searched, finding my tongue and drawing me into him. He pulled me into him, turning me on my back, then put his hand under my head as the other one went around my back, drawing us together.

20

Suddenly we heard the rushing tyres as a car screeched to a stop, dragging the ground from under it, making a crunching sound. Then the engine stopped and we could hear the slamming of a car door. Ralph pulled away from me, muttering as he stood up. He looked at me to say something but before he could get a word out there was an unmerciful banging of the knocker on the door.

'Good heavens! What is going on?' he said. 'Who in damnation would make a house call at this time of night?' he snorted, looking back at the mantle clock as he marched for the door, whipping it open then slamming it shut.

I listened with my eyes on stalks as I stood up, but I didn't make for the door. I felt this was his business, I have to keep my place. No matter what, I am still the guest here.

I could hear the front door being whipped open, then muted voices through the sitting-room door, but they were raised in what sounded like trouble. I listened but could hear nothing to make head nor tail of. It sounded like they were confused, with people rushing questions, then someone rushing an answer. Jaysus! What's happening? Has someone had an accident? One of the guests on the way home from here? Is that the police?

I moved to the door, letting my hand drop on the handle, then hesitated. No, don't go out there! He might get annoyed if he thinks you are interfering in his business. I hate to be in the way when I am in someone else's house. I'm never sure where I stand. I went over to the mantelpiece and grabbed up my tobacco. Jaysus! I hope this is not trouble.

I watched the door push open and saw Ralph stand back as Soviah glided in with him following at her heels. Her face looked like it was cut from stone but the eyes glittered with malice, looking like she was out for vengeance. Someone has crossed her, I thought, watching as she slowly took in the room, glancing past me but not really seeing anything. Then she dug her hands into the pockets of her long fur coat, letting it swing open. She was wearing black-leather thigh-high boots and the frock she had on earlier. She looked at Ralph, saying something, then stretched her arm, dangling car keys in her hand. He said something and she waved her head towards the outside, shaking the keys at him. Then he nodded and took the keys, disappearing out the door. I stood gaping, seeing her move over to the window and stare out into the night. My heart was dropping, looking at the style of her. Jesus! I have no chance against her. She really is incredibly gorgeous looking, very beautiful, chic and classy. What is she up to? I could feel a red-hot anger beginning to rise but I knew that would only play into her hands.

I heard the front door bang shut and looked out into the hall, seeing Ralph set down two medium-sized leather suitcases. I shut the door behind me and walked down, saying, 'Ralph, what is happening?' Then I looked down at the suitcases, saying, 'Is she going to stay here?'

'Oh, perhaps for tonight. It would appear she and Jacques have had rather a heated row. She certainly seems very upset,' he said, running his hands through his hair then taking in a big breath. 'She needs to talk,' he said, opening the door then closing it behind me after I followed him in.

'*Ralph, oohhh!*' she snorted. '*Mon dieu!*' she said, pacing up and down, letting the coat swing around her as she puffed out smoke from her cigarillo, leaving it to trail out behind her.

He said something, waving her to a seat, and she paused long enough to say, '*Cognac.*'

'Would you like a drink, Martha, a brandy?'

'No,' I said, feeling my heart sink down into my chest.

She sat down on the sofa where he usually sat and let the coat slide off her. Then he handed her a drink, taking one for himself, and pointed at her coat. She put out a limp hand and he took it while she lifted herself. Then he bent down and swooped it up, aiming it across to land on an armchair.

I watched as he picked up his glass and stood against the fireplace, taking a sip of his drink then turning his attention to her. She stretched and crossed her legs, letting her frock ride up, then lifted her head, seeing him take this in. He took another sip, letting his eyes follow the length of her, right up to rest on her face, then he said something, speaking very softly.

She lifted her face, pursing her lips, looking like she was going to cry, and started moaning. Then her voice lifted and she hissed, speaking slowly while her eyes narrowed, looking at Ralph. Then she snorted, speaking very fast, shouting. '*MON DIEU! Blah blah, snort! Jacques, yak yak, MERDE!*' she roared.

Ralph nodded slowly, never taking his eyes off her, then I interrupted, saying, 'Ralph!'

He looked over for a second, then whipped his eyes back, wanting to catch what she was saying.

'Right,' I said to the fresh air, walking over to pick up my tobacco. 'I am going to get changed for bed.'

He nodded, saying nothing, then focused back on Madame Butterfly.

I walked out of the room and headed up the stairs, feeling my whole world had just collapsed around me. Then I undressed and put on my dressing gown, heading for the bathroom. 'A long soak in a hot bath will do me good,' I sighed, trying to cheer myself up.

I brushed out my hair, plaiting it, then pinned it at the back of my head and put on a fresh pair of pyjamas and the dressing gown. Then I slipped on my leather slippers and sat down by the window. My eyes lit on the tobacco and I rolled one up, taking a long pull of the smoke, dragging it deep down into my lungs. Then I stretched out my legs, feeling the softness of the silk soothing against my warm dry skin. 'That's better,' I sighed. It's grand being lovely and clean, now I feel much more relaxed.

I let my eyes wander around the room, resting them on the shadows of the trees, watching as they danced up and down the walls after finding their way into the darkest corners of the room. So, Martha, it looks like there's trouble ahead. She might have been around before me but suddenly she is making an all-out effort to get her hands on him. Row, my arse! She knew what she was doing. Maybe she was certainly interested in Ralph before but she was playing for time. Now she sees he's suddenly involved with someone and she's straight in for the kill. Where better, then, to get him than right under his own roof. She sees him as a serious challenge now, particularly as he's shown he's actually interested in a woman. Up until now he was just a priest on sabbatical. Yeah, and she doesn't see me as much competition. I would be a joke to her. We may be around the same age but I am a country hick by comparison. So what an evil bitch, she takes what she wants and lives a life of self-indulgence. Sex and men are her forte. They fill the emptiness in her. She will dump Ralph for a better proposition after she grows bored with him.

I know he's not interested. He sees her for what she is. As he said, she's shallow. She's got very little going for her, so she has to get by on her looks. But nonetheless, that woman has seduction down to a fine art. She could, and will, find a way to bring him to heel. So the question is what to do about it, Martha? This woman is a very serious threat.

Hmm, I will have to play it by ear. Meanwhile, keep a very low profile, say nothing and just keep smiling. Don't put pressure on him; he's already under that, with his head wondering how I am taking this. So keep the head, Martha. Play this as pure and simple business, so there's no emotion coming into it. Yes, use the clinical approach. You are good at that, you have been doing it all your life, woman. Business is business, and this woman is interfering in my fucking business.

I took in a deep breath, letting it out slowly, feeling all the fears and worries and confusion slowly ebbing away with that breath. 'Yes, I do know about business. That I can handle,' I muttered, looking beyond the window out into the cold dark night, hearing the lonely mournful keen of the banshee as her cries carried on the wind to come screaming through the trees. She comes to warn of death, I thought, suddenly remembering my childhood days and dark wintry nights when she came crying, then the fear of God in my mother's eyes as she sat wondering who would be next. Why wouldn't she? My mother had most of her family lost to the ravages of disease and poverty in the space of nine months, all when she was only herself a little child. Bloody hell, the ma was tough! Yeah, right, so am I.

Suddenly I gave a little laugh, thinking, Soviah, you are the joke. You are not equipped to take me on.

I stood up to make my way down the stairs and padded along the main hall. I could hear laughing coming from the sitting room. Right, here goes. Best not cause any surprises. I knocked then waited, counting to three before opening the door to see Ralph lying on the sofa. He had his arm behind his head and the other one held a cigar. Then my eyes peeled to Soviah, who was sitting on the floor with her hands resting on his belly, gently stroking him. He looked very relaxed, like he was enjoying himself.

'Oh, hello! Everything OK?' I said, breezing into the room and leaning down to kiss him on top of his head.

He jumped, looking around with his eyes staring in shock. 'Goodness! I did not hear you come in,' he said, with his eyes suddenly taking in the picture of her stroking his belly while he lay clapped out. 'Are you OK, darling?' he said, trying to sit up and get his feet past the vamp. 'Sorry, Soviah, may I just move you, please?' he said, moving her out of the way. She looked confused, getting rocked out of her little seduction act, then ended up on her arse, looking up at me like I was a smelly dog wanting to crawl all over her.

'Darling! May I get you something?' he said, sounding out of breath as he moved to kiss my cheek, saying, 'You look good, darling. Have you had a relaxing bath?'

'Yes, it was lovely, thank you.' Then I whispered, reaching up to land my lips close to his ear, giving him a little kiss, 'How is poor Soviah? Is she over her trauma?'

'What, darling?' he said, looking to see if I was serious.

I ignored this, saying, 'She seems much better. Well done, Ralph, you are a magician. You have managed to calm the poor girl down.'

He sighed, looking relieved, then put his arm around me, saying, 'What would you like to drink, darling?'

I grinned, looking up at him and saying, 'How about you making me a nice hot chocolate? I feel like something comforting after seeing how distressed that poor woman was. Are you OK?'

'Yes, darling, I am fine,' he said, squeezing me then smiling at Soviah, saying, 'Shall I get you another drink?'

She sat herself up on the sofa, looking very sour as she handed

him her empty glass. Then she gave me a dirty look as her eyes slid
up and down me, definitely finding me wanting in my chaste silky
pyjamas, looking comfortable, clean and very ordinary.

I curled into the corner of the sofa, resting my arm over the back
with my legs under me, then sipped my drink. Ralph sat next to
me, sitting back but not too close. He was all business, giving his
attention to Soviah while she sat nursing her brandy, sitting on her
own on the opposite sofa.

Ralph stood up, helping himself to another cigar from the
mantelpiece, then sat down and stretched his legs, sitting even further
away from me. Soviah watched him with a greedy look in her eyes.
They stayed focused while she devoured him with a hungry look,
feasting on his legs, his chest, his hands, missing not the slightest
movement he made.

I listened to the rapid speech, hearing the intonations, the dropping
low key and the rise, hearing the musical lilting tones of the language.
I imagined it help me understand what they were talking about. I
picked up on the odd word, trying to piece what they were about. It
made me feel very much the outsider, which suited Soviah.

'Ralph,' I sighed, when there was a lull in the talk.

'Yes, Martha?' he said, looking around at me like he suddenly
remembered I was actually there.

'Does Soviah speak English? I mean, are you discussing something
very personal and private? Otherwise, maybe you could speak English.
It would be easier for me,' I said, smiling and giving a little shrug.

'What? Oh, no, we are not saying anything too personal, but of
course, forgive me, darling,' he said, giving my foot a rub and shaking
it. 'Soviah, you do speak English? We ought not to leave Martha out
of our little tête-à-tête,' he smiled, letting it break into a wide grin,
flashing his teeth as his eyes lit up.

She barely flicked an eye over me as she shrugged, saying, 'Yes,'
as she slowly moved her hands, looking the essence of grace and
femininity. Then she sighed and lifted her body, letting her chest
and neck go rigid while she held out her hands, saying, 'Darling, you
know, I cannot believe I am to be treated in this fashion! The man
is a brute! What . . . What does he do to me? He delivers me home

like a package, I have time to almost not breathe when he picks up the telephone, because it rings, I hear him speak, it is all so fast, then pouffff! He is gone! To be with that woman! That half-child! I will have him arrested!' she exploded. 'He has done this to me! ME! I cannot believe! I have been with him for six years! I am his wife! Pouf! It is impossible! To think I divorce my first husband to marry this pig! It is unthinkable. My first husband was divine; he was so kind to me. Nothing for him was impossible, he adored me. He would do almost anything to please me. Whatever he think may please, he would buy for me! Then, to think I was so *stupide* . . . I divorce him. I am such a fool, now look at me!' she snapped, giving her lap a slap. 'Men have always pampered me, I am used to nothing but the best! Ohhh,' she cried, moaning and dropping her voice, looking at the floor. Then she straightened herself, looking determined. 'I will divorce him . . .'

'But you and he have discussed this, Soviah. You say you do not wish to divorce him,' Ralph said, reminding her about part of the problem.

She pinned her eyes on him, listening, taking this in. 'Yes, you are right. I will not divorce the pig. I will kill him! No, I will go to meet with my advocate, Pierre Jan de Frei! Ohhhh! He will slice him to millions of little pieces. I will take everything. I will bring him to his knees. I will strip him naked! He will cry! I will crush him under my foot!' she said, lifting and stamping her boot, squashing the rug underneath.

Ralph looked shocked at the venom pouring out of Soviah. I never enjoyed myself so much. I listened nodding, saying, 'Tut, tut, shame, so brutal!'

She ignored me. Ralph listened intently, saying nothing, waiting for her to calm down. Then there was silence. Ralph sighed. I clucked. Then she said, 'Ohh! This is all so hopeless. I was to believe Jacques was so tender, such a wonderful lover, he was so kind . . . Just like you, Ralph!'

'Me?' Ralph said, sounding shocked as he took in the 'wonderful lover' bit.

I stared, looking very accusing at Ralph. He snapped his head to me then pinned his eyes on her, saying, 'But, Soviah . . .'

'Ohhh,' she suddenly said, letting her face crease into a cry, waiting for the tears to come. They didn't but she snapped her bag open anyway, muttering, keening and sobbing, tearing the hand around for a missing hankie.

Ralph stood up, whipping out his snow-white freshly ironed hankie, rushing to hand it to her, whispering, 'Soviah, my dear . . .'

'Ohhh, Ralph! What am I to do? I am a woman alone! Ohhh, I am so alone! I am distraught! My life is at an end! I am all alone! I have no man to protect me! What will become of me? Oooh, Ralph, I come to you! Now you are the only person in the whole world who cares if I live or die. You must help me! Please!'

'But what would you like me to do, Soviah?' he said, lowering himself onto the sofa beside her.

'Please, I need you!' she said, plunging herself into his arms, wrapping herself around him, with her head dragging along his chest, looking like a dying swan.

The shock hit me. Immediately I bristled and my heart leapt! I started breathing heavily, heaving for the want of air. I took in a sharp breath then sighed it out. Yes, Martha, let that go. Take it nice and slowly, breathe easy.

I closed my eyes, lowering my head and feeling myself get calm again. Then I began to feel the tension slipping slowly away and sat back, watching.

She moaned and slithered all over him, while he was killed between letting his hand drop on her head and holding it in the air, looking like he had suddenly been scalded. Somehow it all looked very comical. Then I felt like laughing and giving her a huge applause, shouting, *Bravo! Encore! What a wonderful performance!* But I stayed quiet, watching Ralph now sit still, looking down at her as if he was thinking.

Right, enough is enough, I thought, then let a roar out of me. 'Oh, dear,' I said. 'Ralph! Quick!' I screamed, shouting and laughing, looking agonised. 'My foot, my toe, it's cramped! Help!' I laughed, trying to lift my toe as I curled it around, letting it lock. 'Hurry!' I screamed, trying to stretch out the leg.

'Darling,' he said, gently letting Soviah's head slide all the way off his lap to the sofa. That was where it had been heading anyway, but Ralph's lap was in the way because she was burying herself so deep it must have been putting a hole in him. He sat down beside me, carefully taking my foot in his hand, looking at it and then gently massaging it, rubbing his hand along the muscle of my leg.

'Ohh,' I cried, thinking I was giving an even better performance than Soviah. 'I was sitting on it, Ralph,' I moaned, looking crucified, with my pitiful face looking up at him. 'Ohhh, that feels better,' I moaned, hearing him say, 'Give me your other foot, darling.'

I opened my eyes, trying to gracefully lift the other leg, wanting to copy Soviah. She does it lovely. Then I lay back, watching him massage my legs and feet, letting them sit in his lap. Then his eyes went to Soviah, and mine followed.

She was lying with the hankie pressed to her head, moaning she had a headache.

'Tut, tut,' I muttered, 'the poor thing is really going through the mill.'

Ralph looked at me, saying, 'Yes, these two play some awful bloody games.' Then he flicked his eyes, lifting the eyebrows at Soviah, then turned back to me. 'Now . . .' he said, pausing, 'this is the consequence.' He sighed, looking very sad, then sat back and concentrated his attention on my feet.

I sighed, whispering, 'Ralph! I do love you so.'

He looked at me, saying, 'Darling, I love you too. You are a wonderful woman, yes, wonderful,' he muttered, examining my feet, saying, 'I must cut your toenails!'

'I don't have nail scissors!' I said, wanting him to know I don't usually neglect my nails.

'Yes, darling, we will see to it,' he said. Then he sighed and stood up, saying, 'Soviah, we must organise a room for you. I shall take your bags up. Please do follow when you are ready.'

She sat up, suddenly looking very alert. 'Ohh, *oui!* I must change,' she said, looking down at herself, then lifting her legs, giving a flash of dark knickers!

Ralph marched out and I followed. 'Is the bed ready?' I said, as he picked up the cases then stopped to think.

'Yes, good question,' he sighed, running his hand through his lovely thick hair. It was still silky and flopped over his right eye like it used to do. My heart gave a jolt, with me wanting to wrap my arms around him and bury myself inside him.

He breathed in, thinking about it, then said, 'You know, I think next door to my study . . . that is probably the most suitable. The bathroom is just one floor up. She may use that. Yes, I shall go and prepare that.'

I looked from the side passage hall to the floor just above. Ralph's bathroom and Ralph's bedroom! Hmm, I think this may need careful watching. This looks like a case of 'the Night of the Long Talons' meets 'the Night of the Long Knives'! Yes, dear lady, you have the long talons out for Ralph but I have the long knives out for you!

Soviah suddenly appeared with her fur thrown over her shoulder, clutching it with her fingers while the other hand gripped her expensive Italian handbag. She lifted her head, indicating she wanted to know where we were going.

'Ahh, Soviah my dear, we shall put you in here,' he said, opening the door to the passage as the pair of us filed after him. Then he swung open a door and snapped on the overhead light. We all walked in, looking around as Ralph made for the bed.

Oh, this is nice, I thought, letting my eyes take in the size of the room. It was huge, bigger than mine. Down the end of the room was a big king-size bed with matching double walnut wardrobes and mirrors. They took up the alcoves each side of the bed, with two bedside tables and lamps standing beside it. Ralph switched on the lamps, making the room look very bright and warm. A matching double dressing table stood against the wall inside the door, with a lovely white ornate wooden chair with an embroidered padded seat left sitting in front. Then on the right wall was an old-fashioned washstand with a basin and a flowery antique jug that stood on the marble top. Next to that was a very cosy armchair and an antique oak horse for holding a man's trousers.

It was lovely. I sighed, getting the smell of lavender furniture polish and years of living coming from everything that was put into it, and sensing the ghosts of people who would have lived in this room at one time. They all left something of themselves behind. Then I noticed the bookcase with the shelves of dusty books. Some looked very old but others were quite recent. Gawd, wouldn't I just love a room like this? I thought. Then whipped my eyes down, seeing Ralph take off the blankets and quilts. They were left folded at the end of the bed. That was done to air the covered mattress. I noticed there was no window, so it wouldn't get much light, but it is still lovely, I thought. Not able to get over how much character it had.

Ralph took off out of the room, saying, 'I need to get some bed linen.'

I lit up a smoke, waiting for him to come back, thinking Soviah may not be pleased. Then she walked past, dismissing me as if I was invisible. I watched as she hung up her fur coat in the wardrobe then humped her case up on the bed and opened the straps, taking out her stuff. She lifted a long silk dressing gown and a cream silk short nightdress, with the top covered in lace and long thin straps. That came with matching knickers. My breath caught, seeing how it flowed like liquid as she lifted it up. Then she took out a huge washbag and a small vanity case from the other bag and dumped the lot on the bed. She left it there and went to the wardrobe, taking down a wooden hanger and throwing it on the bed. Then she slipped off her frock, hanging it up in the wardrobe, and sidled over in nothing but long boots snuggling her thighs and a very brief pair of dark-brown silk knickers with lace round the edges, and a matching bra that lifted her big breasts, with the colour making them look very creamy. Then she sat at the dressing-table chair and tried to pull off the boots. 'Pouf,' she snorted, giving up after a few seconds and stamping her foot, staring at them.

Ralph came rushing in with white embroidered bed linen and his eyes flew to her.

'Ralph!' she moaned, saying something in French.

He dropped the stuff on the bed and went back to bend down and pull the boots off one by one. Then he stood up, brushing the hair out of his eye, and made for the bed again.

I picked up the sheet and shook it out to him, saying, 'Ralph!' I whispered, with a laugh lighting up my eyes. 'It is just as well we are in a windowless room, or you would be in trouble.'

He smiled then looked confused, leaving the sheet hanging in his hand.

'Well, if there was a window, you would more than likely pole vault out through it, seeing as you must have grown an extra leg,' I sniffed, throwing my head over to the vamp, seeing her lift the eyes up, taking in what I just said.

He threw his head back and roared laughing. 'Oh, Martha, you are naughty but very funny,' he said, then laughed again, looking at me. 'No, darling,' he said, shaking his head. 'It is no mystery to me! I have seen more of this than you have had hot dinners.'

'WHAT?' I roared, trying to take that one in.

He grinned, then started laughing again. 'Darling, you only know the priest. Of course that is forbidden to me. But you seem to forget I am a doctor.'

'Yeah, but still,' I said, thinking about that. Then I leaned forward, whispering, 'Come off it, Ralph, you do not fool me. Are you telling me you did not find that stunningly attractive?'

'Attractive? Yes, of course! But it is you, darling, who needs to be careful. You are the one in danger,' he said, flicking his brows up and down, giving me a dirty grin.

'You dirty old man,' I whispered, throwing the sheet at him.

He ducked, laughing as it caught him on the side of the head. 'I warn you, my lady!' he said, pointing a finger and pinning his eyes on me as he slowly nodded his head.

'Oh, Ralph, one of these days you might just strike lucky. I may decide to slow down and let you catch me,' I said, blowing him a kiss.

He grinned then took in a deep breath. 'Come on, let us get this over with. This night is beginning to drag on and I would like to see the end of it,' he said, letting the light out of his eyes as his jaws worked, showing the muscles grinding up and down as the long heavy night began to get to him.

21

Soviah had disappeared out the door by the time we finally finished making the bed and turned the ends of the quilt down, pulling back the covers for her. Ralph looked around to see if anything needed doing, then put his arm around my waist. 'Darling, you have been very kind. I do appreciate your patience. I am sorry I had to neglect you,' he said, stopping to take my face in his hands then gently kiss me. Soviah came softly back into the room then dumped her huge washbag and big vanity case on the dressing table. We both turned to take her in as she bent into the mirror, examining her eyes then taking up a silver hairbrush to do her hair. Then she turned to look at us and walked over to the bed, letting the dressing gown slip off and land on the bed then slither to the floor, where she just ignored it.it.

I watched as she moved slowly over to Ralph, wagging her arse and showing the little silk knickers with the lace trim and the short top that stopped just above the knickers, showing off her milky white breasts that stood up under the top. You could quite clearly see the nipples standing out and see the breasts from the low-cut negligee. She looked incredibly sexy, with the long cream legs and the toenails manicured with a clear, pink, shiny hue. Her face looked snow-white and her grey-blue eyes stood out like huge saucers. She looked even better now than she did when she was dressed. Younger and even more feminine!

She moved into him, gently dropping her hand on his chest, looking into his face, saying something, acting as if I was not there. Ralph dropped his hands by his side, clenching them into fists, making it look like he had to control them, as if trying to stop himself from grabbing her.

'*Non, non,*' he said, shaking his head and pulling down the sheets, feeling the bed.

'Ohhh!' she moaned, dropping her head to the side, making herself look like a little girl.

'*Bonne nuit, Soviah,*' he said, taking me and marching me out of the room. Then he shut the door behind him, saying, 'I think we ought to retire now, darling. I do think it is quite late.'

'OK, Ralph,' I said, letting myself fall into his arms as he pulled me to him, kissing me hard on the lips.

'Do get some rest, darling, you need your sleep.'

'But tell me, Ralph, what was she saying about the bed?'

'Oh,' he breathed, sounding fed up. 'She was concerned it was not properly aired. She may become ill. I reassured her it was perfectly fine, she would be quite all right,' he said, giving another big sigh, sounding very tired. 'Goodnight, darling, sleep well,' he said, blowing me a kiss. Then he was gone.

'Yeah,' I sighed, seeing him go into his room as I made me way up the rest of the stairs, heading for my bed.

I woke up to see the grey early-morning light trying to creep through the dark and into the room. Something had woken me up. I listened, hearing the dull noise of what sounded like voices.

What time is it? I squinted, trying to get one eye open to look over at the clock sitting on the dressing table. Five-thirty in the morning. Then I heard a door banging. I listened; it sounded like it was coming from downstairs. I wanted to turn over and doze back to sleep but my mind was becoming alert. Is your woman on the move? Is she in with Ralph? No, never!

But my hand was already throwing back the bedclothes and my legs were swinging out of the bed. I groped for my dressing gown at the end of the bed and squinted with one eye open, seeing my slippers and digging my feet into them. Then I opened the door quietly and went downstairs, hearing Ralph's voice coming through the half-open door of his room. My heart started thudding like mad as my legs turned to jelly. I hope and pray this is not what it looks like, I thought, silently arriving on the landing then making for the door.

I turned in, saying, 'Is everything OK?'

Soviah was standing with her arms folded looking out the window into the still, dark early morning. Ralph was pacing up and down in his dressing gown, looking very grim. His head lifted as I walked in, and he came hurrying over to me, saying, 'I am sorry, darling. Did we disturb you?'

I looked from him to her as she turned, giving me a vicious look like she wanted to stick a knife straight through my ribs, ripping the heart out of me.

'What's happening, Ralph? Why is she in your room?' I said, deciding enough was enough.

'Look, darling,' he said, then watched as she walked towards the bed and stretched out, letting her gown hang wide open as she curled up one leg, leaving her exposing everything to be seen between her legs because the knickers were see-through. I turned away in disgust just as he made towards Soviah on the bed.

'*Non, non!*' he was saying. Then his voice rose and I heard him saying, 'Martha! Wait, I must speak with you.'

Soviah murmured something in French and I took off walking fast, making for my room. I could feel the shock leaving me icy cold. The blood had drained out of me completely. I lifted the covers of the bed, throwing them over the pillows, and walked to the wardrobe. Then I humped out all the hangers with my clothes and landed them on the bed. Right, Martha, if you are fast, you might be lucky to catch a train somewhere heading in the direction of Paris. Fuck this, home sweet home.

I lifted the clothes off the hangers and started to fold them one by one, piling them on top of each other. Then I heard running on the stairs. The door flew open and Ralph came tearing in, stopping with his hand on the doorknob, taking everything in at once.

'No, for goodness' sake! This is not what you think, Martha. Please, you must listen to me,' he said, rushing to grab hold of me, taking the stuff out of my hands and swinging me around.

I felt like a rag doll as he whipped me over to the chair, sitting me down, letting himself sit in the other chair. He shook his head, staring at me, trying to find his voice to speak. I stared, wanting to hear nothing. In this life there is no such thing as happiness lasting for more than a short time. I was expecting it to end sooner or later. Of course it was too good to be true. But let him talk. It will cost me nothing, then he will go and I can get on about my business.

But I heard myself speaking. 'Ralph,' I whispered, feeling stone-cold numb. 'Whatever you have to say, please say it quickly. I want to catch the train back to Paris. It is over. We have nothing to say. No more games, please. I am very tired of it.'

'Martha,' he whispered, trying to take my hands.

I gently slapped his away, leaving my eyes looking hard as pebbles with no life in them and my face like marble.

'Martha, if I am to be punished for anything it is that I did not lock my door. I woke up finding she had crawled into my bed and was trying to seduce me. What you must have perhaps heard was my voice ordering her out of my room. The rest you saw. I give you my solemn word I am speaking the truth. I may add also, I have been very foolish in allowing her to stay, but hindsight is a wonderful thing. Unfortunately, I underestimated the woman. It would never have crossed my mind, I did not have the remotest idea, she would take it this far. Up until this time she was always simply flirtatious. I saw it as being quite harmless. Now I see she is very disturbed. I must speak with Jacques. Meanwhile, she will leave my house. I want her presence removed immediately,' he said, staring into the distance, looking very grim and very determined.

I could see how all the colour was gone from his face. His pupils were nearly black. Then he looked at me, seeing some life coming back into my eyes as I softened. 'I believe you,' I whispered.

'Oh, Martha, my poor, poor Martha! Oh, how bloody stupid of me to cause you this sort of misery. I do love you so very much. I promise you I have never, and would never, love another woman as I love you,' he said, grabbing me to him and sinking himself into me.

We stayed quiet as he rocked me, then he looked at me saying, 'Darling, you look so pale. Come along quickly. I am going to get you a hot drink with a little brandy. You look terribly shocked.' Then he took me in both his arms and walked me out the door. I was glad to hold on to him because I felt terribly weak. All the good had drained right out of me.

We arrived on his landing and went straight past his room. The door was wide open but Ralph didn't look in. 'I will deal with her later,' he muttered. 'First we must take care of you. You have gone into shock, my darling. I must get some brandy into you quickly.'

We walked into the kitchen and he switched on the kettle, getting out two mugs, then reached into Madame's press and took out a big bottle of Courvoisier brandy. He poured it into the two mugs then made the tea and sat down at the table. 'Now, darling, drink that quickly, it will warm you up,' he said, putting the mug to my mouth.

It was then I saw my hands shaking. I still couldn't speak. The shock was still working its way through me. I had nearly lost Ralph, and in the most brutal way for me. To be used, then made a fool of, then thrown away. That is how I had read it. My immediate way was to go into action. Do something, have a back-up plan, then move on. It doesn't matter what it is, just do something. Walk away keeping your head up. This was not going to bring me down. But the shock had been hard. I am not as physically strong as I was. Things do take it out of me. My spirit may rise but the bleedin body can let me down, like now. I can't stop fuckin shaking.

'Darling, I am such a bloody fool. Who would think one has to lock one's room on guests?' he half-laughed, sounding in shock himself. Then he shook his head, staring at me, saying, 'For a time, I thought I had lost you, my darling. It would certainly not have taxed the brain to figure out one plus one equals three in this situation. Please, darling, you do forgive me, I mean for putting you through this?' he said, moving close and wrapping me to him.

'Yes,' I said. 'I do love you, Ralph, and I trust you. But it is what I saw that shook me, particularly when she draped herself like that in your bed. What was she doing?' I said, looking into his face, seeing how exhausted he was.

He sighed, dropping his eyes, thinking about it. 'She was being perverse, my love. She was trying to drive you away from me, and . . . I presume, in her sick mind, showing me what she had to offer. Please, darling, we must not dwell on this. There is no rationale for madness. The woman is quite clearly out of her mind. I am afraid this whole business with Jacques has driven her over the edge. I shall telephone him this morning and he and I must speak. I do not want that woman to set foot in my house again. She is not my problem to deal with. But my concern is, she may not let go of me so easily. This obsession of hers could very quickly spin out of control if Jacques does not help her.'

I sipped at the tea and brandy, and Ralph gently held it to my lips, saying, 'No, darling, do not sip, drink it down quickly, then I think we must get you into a hot bath. Meanwhile, I must see what is happening with Soviah.'

'Will you get me another drink first, Ralph?' I said, holding up the empty mug as he stood up.

He went to make another drink and I walked out of the kitchen. 'Not in Ralph's room,' I muttered, coming back down the stairs. I opened the door to the passage and marched straight down to Soviah's room. I stopped just inside the door and stood staring at her, taking her in. She was lying on the bed with her legs crossed, covered by her dressing gown, with her hands folded across her belly. Her eyes lit up with interest for a second then narrowed with a vicious, malevolent look of spite and anger as she realised it was only me.

'So, here you are,' I whispered, closing the door quietly behind me and walking down slowly, making my way to the bed. I could feel a cold anger rising gently to the surface. I kept my breathing easy and a half-smile on my face. 'Do you really want Ralph?' I said, making conversation as I moved closer to the bed.

Her mouth curled into a sneer and she made a soft phew sound with her lips, then flicked her eyes away, saying quietly, like she was sparing her energy, 'What business is it of yours, peasant?'

'You are quite right. That does not concern me,' I said. 'You may want him all you want, it is up to him whether he wants you or not. BUT, BITCH, YOU DO NOT TRY TO RUB MY NOSE IN IT. YOU DO NOT INSULT ME, LYING WITH YOUR LEGS SPLAYED LIKE THE WHORE YOU ARE! TAKE THIS!' Then I lunged, grabbing a handful of her hair in the front of her head with my left hand and whipping up her face, then I lifted my right hand, throwing it back in a fist, and brought it smack down, straight into her face. Then I let her head drop.

Immediately her nose spurted blood and she screamed. Ralph came running, shouting, 'What is happening? Martha, where are you?'

I walked out of the room just as he came spinning in. 'I think she needs you, doctor,' I said quietly, pointing my head at her.

He took one look at me calmly walking out the door then down at her, spurting blood all over her gown, face and sheets, and screaming like the banshee for all she was worth. He ran to grab a towel from the horse rail and raced to stop the flow of blood.

I walked along the passage, heading back to the kitchen. My hot drink was waiting for me and I sat down calmly, then got up again, walking into the sitting room. 'Ah, here we are!' I said, reaching up to the mantelpiece to take down down what was left of my box of cigarillos.

I was back in the kitchen smoking and drinking when Ralph came in, looking even more shocked. He was snow-white and looked shattered, like he had never seen the like of this in all his born days.

'Martha, what did you do to her? She says you attacked her. For heaven's sake, why add fuel to the fire?'

'Ralph, is she gone?' I said, speaking quietly as if I was talking about the weather.

'No, not yet, but I have managed to stem the flow of blood. I must get her a hot drink,' he said, rushing to whip up the kettle again.

I got up, taking my tea and smoke, and made my way into the sitting room, then sat down, thinking, poor Ralph. That will teach him to wake up. Otherwise he could spend the rest of his life making hot drinks for all the bodies lying splattered around the place. Then I laughed, feeling the life coming back into me.

I looked at my drink, seeing the mug was nearly empty, and drained the last of it, feeling it warm its way down into my belly, heating me up. 'Oh, that's better,' I sighed, feeling a lot more relaxed as the brandy made its way through my bloodstream, doing its work. I stubbed out the end of the cigarillo in the ashtray and stood up, making my way back into the kitchen. Ralph was gone. Suddenly the side hall passage door shot open, then Soviah appeared, carrying two suitcases, with the fur coat hanging off one shoulder and the handbag dangling off the other. She stopped dead when she saw me. I stared, looking at her red nose with the hair standing up and the clothes sticking out of one of the suitcases.

'MERDE!' she suddenly screamed, losing the rag at the sight of me.

I felt lovely and calm with the brandy floating inside me, and I just grinned, saying quietly, 'Whore! Would you like a second helping? Perhaps the teeth this time, or even the hair?'

Then she took up the suitcases again and went flying for the front door just as Ralph came rushing down the stairs, still in his pyjamas. His hair was wet and it looked like he was just out of the bath. 'What is happening now?' he croaked, looking like he wasn't able for any more.

'Don't know,' I said, looking from him racing down the stairs to her, with the front door left open wide, looking battered and in threadbare order. She didn't wait to put on the make-up or even brush the hair.

Then she saw him coming and started screaming in French. Ralph got very annoyed and came racing into the hall, then slowed down, marching to the door just as she turned on me, pointing and saying, 'You are a crazy peasant!'

'Out! Please leave my house at once! You have caused enough trouble. I will not tolerate this outrageous behaviour!'

She turned her face to the door then looked back at me, seeing me waving her out the door.

Then Ralph let a roar out of him. 'GET OUT OF MY HOUSE! I DEMAND YOU LEAVE AT ONCE!' he bellowed, pointing his finger out the door.

She took off in a hurry and he slammed the door shut, muttering, 'Good gracious, what a debacle!'

I took off back into the kitchen, putting the kettle on for myself just as he came back in, saying, 'Darling! Are you OK? Come along, get ready. I shall run a hot bath for you. Was that bloody awful woman trying to upset you again?'

'No, I think she might have come out of it a bit of a casualty herself. As you said, there's no cure for madness. But, Ralph, that woman is mad in the right way. Don't you fret about her. She knows exactly what she is doing.' Then I thought, yeah, there's only one cure for her, hit her where it hurts, in the looks department. Kindness and soft words are lost on that one. She is a rotten spoilt bitch. But she sure has a great sense of self-preservation!

'Yeah,' I said, 'I don't think you should worry about her coming back, Ralph!'

'No, darling, I should think not,' he said, raising his eyebrow, looking disgusted at even the thought. 'But if I may,' he said, bending down and talking softly into my ear. 'I do not condone violence. That was rather naughty, my love!'

I sniffed, looking at him, saying, 'Ralph, I would do it again. She asked for it. The woman understands no other language. She bloody insulted me once too often. Besides, you were right what you said about her coming back to torment you. I saw that. I knew she would never have given up. The madness was on her. Now I knocked it out of her. So it was pretty effective. You should know me, Ralph! I am still an alley cat by nature. Cross me and you do it at your peril. Besides, I was gentle with her. I could have knocked her teeth out.'

'Oh, darling,' he said, grabbing me. 'You are not an alley cat. You are simply a fiery little thing who will fight to the death when threatened.'

'Yeah, well, anyway, Ralph. You were too kind to her. It doesn't always work! She is totally amoral.'

'Yes, you are quite right, my darling,' he said, letting his face drop at that thought. Then he sighed, saying, 'I want you in that bath now. Come along, you are procrastinating.'

'What? You want me in the bath?' I said, giving him a shocked look.

'Yes, I do!' he said slowly. 'You have been through a . . .' Then it hit him. 'Oh, I see,' he said softly, grinning at me. 'Come here, you!' he said, moving towards me and taking me in his arms, then resting my head as he bent to kiss me, bearing his mouth down, kissing me long and hard.

I wrapped my arms around his neck, pulling tighter into him. Our breathing was getting faster and louder as he stroked my back and ran his hands over my bottom, pulling me into him. I could feel him pressing into me as he started becoming more aroused. Then he slowly pulled away and stared at me. 'Darling, you are so beautiful, I do love you so very, very much,' he said, shaking his head slowly, staring into my eyes.

My heart soared with the sudden thought of not losing him and having him look at me with such tenderness and love. Oh, dear God, I am so happy. What did I ever do without him? I thought, wanting to stay this way and never let go. To just feel his body so close to me made me feel safe. 'Yes, Ralph,' I whispered, stroking his face and staring back at him. 'I love you with all my heart,' I said, wrapping my arms around him, feeling so warm and loved and lucky to have him.

'Come on, sweetie,' he said, walking me up the stairs. Then he stopped outside the bathroom, saying, 'You go along to your room. I shall prepare your bath then we ought to get dressed. Madame will be arriving in approximately one hour. We can breakfast together. Perhaps we can do something later.'

'Like what, Ralph?'

'Well, I am not sure yet. I do have some things I must attend to. But we shall see.'

22

I put on a blue shirt and black flared skirt that went below my knee, with black wool tights and flat slip-on shoes, then pulled on a heavy, navy-blue wool jumper. Then I stood in front of the mirror and combed out my wet hair. I think I will let it hang down; it needs to dry out. That will do, I thought, fixing the gold-stud earrings into my ears. Now for a bit of make-up. I just need a little; it's too early in the morning, for anything more. I put on a little eyeshadow, then mascara and some pale-pink lipstick. 'Ready,' I muttered, standing back to see how I looked. Fine, you look grand and fresh. Now, is everything nice and tidy? I let my eyes fly around the room, seeing everything was back in its place. I had hung up all the clothes left scattered on the bed when I thought, in the early hours of this morning, that I was going to make a quick and permanent exit.

Jesus! Imagine that, Martha? I would never have seen Ralph, or even this place, ever again! Suddenly I shivered, getting the memory of that terrible shock. It was so bad I didn't even let half of it sink in. No, I went deadly calm, just working on automatic pilot. But now I could see just how devastating it would have been. No, Ralph really does love me. I have been right all along about him. He has no hidden motives or agenda. He behaves as he believes, his word is his bond. He is completely honourable and very highly principled. To top it all, he is so bloody incredibly handsome, even more so now than when he was younger. Yeah, he is distinguished, self-assured and very polished. People take him seriously. Even the waiters, who are nobody's fool, they recognise an eejit when they meet one. The clicking-finger brigade, flashing the money and tripping over the tongue with the false accent.

Good God! How did I ever get so lucky meeting him? Not just

that but, yes, it has to be true, he loved me from the beginning. The raw sixteen year old scraped off the streets. My God, Martha, just think, he could have had Soviah for the taking. Why not? He owed me nothing! Verily, it must be love.

Listen, God! You can have me now. I will die a happy woman . . . but give us a chance to enjoy it first. I want to die knowing happiness does last more than just a short while. Right, have we a deal, God? You have been good to me up to now! So I trust you. 'Oh, life's a bowl of cherries,' I sang, grinning my way out the door. Then I was flying back in. 'A little dab of Chanel perfume,' I gasped, feeling out of breath from the hurry. I can't wait to get to Ralph. Lovely! When I waft in, I'm hoping he'll see instant beauty, and all from just the smell of me.

Ralph was sitting at the kitchen table writing in his notebook when I pushed open the door. 'Hello!' he said, turning to look at me, then snapped the book shut, slapping it down beside him on the kitchen table. 'You are here! I waited to have breakfast with you, darling,' he whispered, as he folded me into his arms, kissing me on the mouth. 'You do look much better,' he said, standing back to look into my face. 'Hmm, and you smell nice too,' he said, letting his nose and mouth brush my neck.

I shivered and laughed, saying, 'You look very nice too, Ralph!', looking him up and down admiringly, taking in the dark-cream trousers with the brown-leather shoes and the black polo-neck sweater.

He lifted his eyebrow and flashed his green eyes, giving a little nod with his head, saying, 'Hmm, you like, darling?'

'Yes,' I breathed. 'You could wear a sack and I would still think you gorgeous! Isn't it terrible how love can blind you?'

'You are so naughty,' he whispered, grabbing me and giving me a quick squeeze, pulling me tight into him. Then he turned to Madame, who was making her way to the table. She put down a hot plate of rashers and tomatoes and eggs for me, and a boiled egg for Ralph, with hot rolls and croissants.

'*Bonjour, Madame,*' I said quickly, giving her a slight bow of my head, then saying, '*Merci!*' Then I dug into the breakfast, while Ralph took his time, carefully breaking and buttering a little piece of his bread.

'Oh, the bloody upper classes and their little nibbles at the table would put years on you,' I moaned, stopping to watch him. Then I gave a huge grin, seeing him lift his head, giving me a questioning look. 'Ahh, wait till you hear this, Ralph, then you'll understand,' I said, bending into him. Then I told him about this posh nun I met in a very posh boarding school in England. 'Mind, I was only there for the few hours,' I said. 'They had to fumigate the place when I left,' I snorted then laughed.

He roared laughing, listening as I told him how the pair of them, her and the schoolgirl, spent the afternoon tea chewing on the one and only tiny finger sandwich they managed to eat. 'Oh, you are funny,' he said, pulling me to him to kiss the top of my head.

'I shall see you later,' Ralph said, standing up after we finished the breakfast, then kissing me quickly and heading off out the door.

I sighed, looking around wondering what I was going to do with myself. I went into the sitting room and looked out the window, thinking, I will go for a walk. I'm still feeling a bit dozy after being up half the night. Yeah, we got to bed late, then up before the dawn barely broke. I stared out, looking over the lawns, seeing the mist on the grass and the trees looking miserable as they stood waving in the breeze with the rain dripping off them. 'No, forget that,' I said, swinging my head around the room, looking for something to catch my attention. My eyes peeled on the bookcase. Read? Watch television? What? This hour of the morning? Never! I'm not that far gone. Right, book it is.

I lay back on the sofa, trying to get into the book but it was hard going with the eyes half closing. George Orwell's *Animal Farm*. 'Oh, I'm not in the mood,' I sighed, dropping the book beside me, feeling myself wanting to doze off. Then I heard footsteps and the door suddenly pushed in. I whipped my eyes open, looking with interest at the sight of Ralph dressed in his coat and wearing a scarf around his neck.

'Darling, good idea, you take some rest. I have to go out for a while. There are some things I must attend to. I shall see you later.' Then he made to shut the door.

'No wait, Ralph! Surely I can come with you?' I said, throwing my legs onto the floor and getting to my feet.

'No, sweetheart, you have some rest, you look tired. Do, please!' he grinned, then gave me a pleading look. 'I shall bring you back a little surprise!' he said, getting even more persuasive as he rushed over, giving me a quick kiss on the lips, then made his way out the door, shutting it firmly behind him.

'Oh, what kind of surprise?' I asked the empty space, then listened, hearing the front door slammed shut with a bang. 'Wonder why he won't take me with him?' I muttered, sighing me way back to plaster myself on the sofa.

I was just waking up from a lovely sleep. Gawd, I really was tired. That was great, now I feel fresh as a daisy, I thought, taking a stretch and getting ready to move. Then I heard the car tyres whirring past the house, heading around the back. Ralph! He's home! I leapt up then thought, no, let him get in the door and get his breath. I have to remember he is not used to having people hanging out of his neck. He expects a certain type of behaviour from a woman my age. Decorum, he would call it.

Right, you better start trotting out your best behaviour, Martha. Come to think about it, sure, you have always lived on your own. I suppose this is why it is such a novelty for me, having a man in my life. Someone who does things for me. I'm not used to that. Now it has brought out the scattered me. I'm all over the place. It's all these new emotions rushing through me. I'm not used to being loved, or even feeling dependent on someone. It sort of makes me feel a bit childish, brings out the silliness in me because I haven't grown into these feelings. I didn't grow up with them. I bypassed all that kind of thing and now it's hit me all at once. So I get shy when he looks at me with tenderness or shows he feels I'm desirable to him as a woman. No, I end up feeling foolish, going all bleedin girlie! Like a bloody schoolgirl. Now, if he was an ordinary man! No problem, I could teach the vamp a few things on driving the aul fellas mad, with them only barely getting a sniff of me. Yeah, but now it's like I'm eighteen again and feeling foolish with it. Well, who gives a damn? He loves me the way I am. Yeah, oh my God, if only I knew how happy a human could be! I would have gone demented searching for it. Jaysus, no wonder people top themselves. Imagine losing happiness like this.

What are you talking about? You tried to bloody top yourself! Yeah, that was different. I was grieving the loss of . . . Who cares? This is me now. I have arrived at nirvana. Oh, yeah! I know what I was grieving. It was not just the loss of health, the death of Harry, or the loss of Sarah. It was the loss of hope. Yes, it was the loss of God after Harry died. I was left bereft, believing I was completely alone and had always been alone. There was no God; there was no nothing. We are just hatched, batched, matched and fucking dispatched. I had been fooling myself all along. But now, I do believe he had been there all the time. Yes, when I couldn't find him in the dark, it was because he was right next to me. I only heard the sound of one lonely pair of footsteps. I thought they were mine. But, no, they were his. Because God was carrying me! I couldn't understand why I didn't die. Now I know he had plans for me; he was sparing me for better things to come.

So once again, Ralph, with his goodness, has been brought back into my life. That has to be for a very special reason. The first time was to prepare me for what was to come. I understand now that I needed to have experienced that glimpse of love from him. It was what kept me going. I then knew there was such a thing called love. So now what is he being used to prepare me for this time, if it's destined I am not to spend the rest of my life with Ralph? What will be ahead of me that I need him again? I don't know, but I am sure of one thing. The good Lord is with me and he works in mysterious ways. I feel his love for me through Ralph. He is, and will always be, taking care of me. That makes me feel very special and is giving me an inner sense of peace. It is the knowledge I can come to no harm because he will protect me, just like he has always done. Yes, thank you, Heavenly Father, for bringing me this inner sense of peace, a feeling of being at one with life. I am sure that is your way of showing me you are close by.

Then a thought hit me. First time round when I met Ralph, he took me off the streets. Then, when we broke up, it hurt him too. He had given up medicine, he saw no call for it in his life. He wanted to work as a priest. But soon after we split, he took up medicine again and went off to the Congo, working with people suffering from leprosy, people who really needed him. He obviously thought he was more useful there. So maybe that was my purpose in his life then. Now he is thinking of giving up the priesthood. He has even stopped working as a missionary doctor. So maybe that is not intended for him. I am probably here to serve a purpose for him. Anyway, whatever the reason, we were meant to meet and serve a very special purpose for each other. Hmm! No wonder the vamp didn't get a look in!

I walked over to the mantelpiece and took down my tobacco, lighting up a cigarette. Then I heard the passage door open and Ralph's footsteps walking into the hall. I waited, but he went past. Then he was back and the door opened. My eyes lit on him coming in carrying parcels.

'Hello, darling,' he smiled, making over to me then dropping the stuff down on the sofa. 'A little gift for you, my love,' he said, taking in a slow deep breath as he took me into his arms.

'Oh, I missed you,' I said, feeling his cold wet face after getting hit by the rain.

He kissed me, then gently rubbed his cheek against mine as he sighed, saying softly, 'Oh, darling, it is wonderful having you in my arms. Do you know, I miss your presence when you are not with me? I would love to have taken you this morning but I wanted you to have rest. Notwithstanding,' he grinned, pulling away from me and lowering his head to the packages, 'I wanted to surprise you! Try to make up for the awful difficulties we, you, have had to endure recently.'

'Me! Presents?' I said astonished. 'Oh! What did you get?' I said slowly, looking up at him whispering, then making for the bags.

'Take a look! I hope it is suitable. Believe me,' he said laughing, 'I had no idea what I was doing. Shopping is not something I do. I leave that to others but, my love, I made a special effort for you,' he said, collapsing himself onto the sofa and crossing his legs, watching me open the parcels.

I took out a gorgeous white-linen blouse with a high-necked pure-lace collar buttoned at the back of the neck with pearl buttons. 'Oh, that is lovely,' I breathed, holding it up, stroking the soft linen, running my hands over the exquisite lace neck. Then I picked up a long black-velvet skirt that swung out when you walked. It had a matching hunting jacket with the high collar of an Austrian army officer. The collar, edging and under the cloth buttons were embroidered with dark-green stitching. 'Oh, Ralph, you bought me a hunting skirt with a beautiful matching jacket,' I whispered. Then I opened the box sitting in the bag and lifted out a pair of flat black-and-wine-leather hunting boots. 'Oh, the lace blouse goes with this, the whole lot go together. This outfit is modelled on the old-fashioned ladies' riding habit they used to wear when riding side-saddle. Oh, they are all the fashion now,' I gasped, 'but you won't see anything as authentic-looking as this. They are beautiful, Ralph, very classy!' I said, looking at him.

He nodded with a smile and lowered his head, delighted I liked them.

'How did you manage this? How did you know what to get me, Ralph?'

'I imagined they would be perfect for you,' he murmured. 'I think they should suit very well,' he said, making it look like he knew what he was doing.

'You have great taste,' I puffed, feeling out of breath. I could barely speak as I dipped into the bags, pulling out more stuff.

'A frock as well!' I said, lifting it up. It was a clinging, light-brown, cashmere frock that would hug my curves. 'Another one!' I shouted, seeing a cream-silk dress nestled in a box. I picked it up and it flowed down weighing about as much as a hankie.

'It is beautiful,' I whispered, holding it up to myself. 'How did you know my size?' I said, looking to see, and, yes, it was my size!

'I simply looked at what you had in your wardrobe, darling,' he said, grinning at me like he had done something very secret. 'Martha, perhaps you may want to wear something tonight. We are invited by Jacques for dinner this evening. I was speaking with him this morning on the telephone.'

My heart dropped. 'But, Ralph, what about your woman?' I said, thinking that is really looking for trouble.

'Oh, that is not a difficulty. Jacques tells me she came storming home, packed and has simply taken flight! She has left him!' Ralph said, grinning at me, waiting to let out a big laugh. Then he said, looking like he just thought of something, 'I say, Martha, I could hire you out as a hit woman! We could do awfully well out of it,' he laughed. 'Needless to say, Jacques is quite chuffed! He is in high spirits. I do believe this is a celebratory dinner!' Then he started laughing his head off.

'Does he know I boxed his wife?' I said, wondering if that would cause a problem. It's one thing getting rid of her but another if you beat her up, I thought!

'I don't know, darling, unless you intend telling him. He mentioned nothing of it to me.'

'Oh, good, let's keep it that way, Ralph,' I said, letting out my breath with the relief.

'Go on, darling, there are one or two things more,' he said, pointing at the bag hidden under the boxes.

'Underwear!' I screamed in a loud whisper.

'Lingerie! I asked the assistant to help out with that. She chose, darling, I had no idea what you would like.'

'These are gorgeous,' I said, lifting up the cami knickers with the matching silk top and bra. 'How did you know the size of this?' I said, holding it out to him.

'Oh, with a lot of difficulty. I spent an age discussing but eventually I judged the cup to be approximately your size,' he said, giving me a big grin as he thought about it.

Then I lifted up a jewellery box and pulled out a short string of pearls. 'Oh, these are beautiful, Ralph,' I gasped.

'Yes, I thought you might like them,' he said, fixing his eyes on me as he stood up, saying, 'Allow me, darling.'

I turned as he lifted my hair and clasped them around my neck. Then he lowered his head, nodding as he stared at me, saying, 'Yes, you look beautiful. They do you justice, my darling. You have the earrings to match, do you not?'

'Yes, they will go great,' I said, feeling like I have died and come back as the Queen of Sheba. 'And a box of Belgian chocolates!' I squealed, and there was more stuff – a pair of black high-heeled shoes and finally two packets of grey-black tights.

I folded the stuff carefully and put it back in the bags. I could hardly open my mouth to tell him how much I appreciated it. Words just wouldn't come to me. I felt shy and tongue-tied, marvelling at the idea he actually went into shops looking for nice things to surprise me. I just can't get over it, I thought, staring at him as I folded the stuff. Seeing him watching me as I tried to find the way, the words, to tell him what it means to me. No, not the stuff. The love he put into it doing it for me.

'Oh, Ralph,' I suddenly said, flinging my arms around him. 'The stuff is beautiful, it takes my breath away. But it is you! I feel like crying with the happiness because you are so loving. I am so lucky to have your love, Ralph,' I said, throwing myself on top of him, landing him flat down on the sofa.

He grabbed me, laughing. 'Oh! Is that all it takes to please you, my love? Goodness, I am the lucky one,' he said, swinging me onto the couch then pulling me on top of him. Then he locked his lips on me and I could feel the ripple of excitement starting to fly through me, but something was bothering me.

'Wait, wait!' I gasped, trying to push away from him.

'What! What is it?' he said, looking startled.

'My stuff! Get your bloody feet off them!' I said, crashing his legs to the floor while I tried to rescue my new, good, expensive clothes from under him. 'You will tear them and dirty them,' I snorted. 'Men have no bloody clue! A woman would never do something like that!' I said, holding up the silk frock to examine it, making sure it hadn't been damaged.

He shook his head at me, saying, 'You started this, darling. You pushed me down, intending to have your wicked way, then, like a bloody woman, you changed your mind!' Then he suddenly dived for me. 'Well, but not this time,' he said, grabbing the stuff out of my hands and swinging me around, landing the pair of us on the floor. 'Now, you can forget the rug, as that is the only thing we can damage,' he said, rolling me under him, then holding his hands out in front of me, making a face like he was going to eat me alive.

I laughed with the sudden shock, seeing the face he was making. Then he made a roar, going for my neck, saying, 'I am going to eat you alive here and now, on this bloody floor.' Then he lunged into my neck, sucking and kissing.

I started screaming with the laugh. 'Stop, wait! You're killing me! No, I mean it, hold on! It's serious!' I said, trying to make myself stop laughing, and I was puffing and huffing trying to get away from him. 'No, no, I mean it, Ralph!'

'What is it now?' he said, letting me up but still keeping hold of me.

'These! My new pearls! You will break them!' I said, putting my hands on my neck to check they were still in one piece.

He looked at the wall, giving a big puff, muttering, 'There is only one way to fix this!' Then he whipped his head on me, staring with a glint in his eye.

'What? What are you looking at?' I said, getting the idea he was up to something.

Suddenly there was a knock on the door. Madame put her head in, seeing the two of us sitting on the floor with my hair standing around my head looking like someone had used me as a mop. Her eyes lit up as she took us in.

Ralph rose immediately to his feet, saying something in French. Then he said, taking my hand and lifting me to my feet, 'Come along, darling, lunch is served.'

'OK, I will just take these things upstairs. I won't be long,' I said, rushing to gather up all my things and make out the door, heading for the stairs.

23

I climbed into the skirt with the wide black band attached and tucked down the linen blouse, fastening up the skirt. Then I sat down in the chair and pulled on my new black boots and eased the jacket on, buttoning it up, leaving only the lace of the high-necked blouse to be seen through the tailor-made cut of the jacket. 'Hmm, lovely,' I said, looking down at myself as I walked over to take a look in the long wardrobe mirror. 'Oh, my God! Is that me? I look so different! Jesus! I look amazing,' I whispered, smiling at my reflection in the mirror. 'I look like something out of a much earlier century!'

I had my hair piled on the back of my head, tied in three knots, then sitting in a soft wave, framing each side of face. My diamond earrings glittered. Bloody hell, I never thought I could look so lovely. Jaysus, pity fuck-face the vamp is not here. I'd give her what-for, calling me a peasant! Bleedin cheek! I'm no bog woman! I hardly ever set foot in the country! Ah, never mind her. Jaysus, would you look at the style of me! Oh, I knew it! That ugly cow wouldn't have looked half as good if it wasn't for the money. Look at me! This is what you can transform yourself into with just a few bob! Right, get going, grab the bag. Oh, I better not forget to take the cigarillos from the mantelpiece in the sitting room. Jaysus, no, I can't sit rolling me own cigarettes in this get-up. Yes, great idea! The cigarillos will go with my outfit.

I headed off out the door, making my way down the stairs, seeing the skirt whip out around me. It felt heavy and substantial, making me feel like I was well covered. There was nothing of me to be seen but my hands and face. Great, a woman of mystery.

I stepped into the hall to see Ralph suddenly appear out of the sitting room. He was dressed for the evening and looked like he had been waiting for me.

'Oh, my! You do look quite lovely,' he said, looking up and down the length of me, smiling all over his face.

'Do you like it?' I said, giving a twirl and letting the skirt fly around me, then stopping on the balls of my feet, holding out my arms.

'Darling, you look quite elegant. It is as I imagined you would look,' he said, kissing me gently, with his arm resting lightly on me. 'Shall we leave?' he said, putting his hand on my back, starting to head for the front door.

'Oh, I have to get my cigarillos, they are on the mantelpiece.'

'No, darling, I have taken them for you,' he said, taking them out of his coat pocket and making to put them in my bag. 'Now, shall we go?'

'Yes,' I nodded, walking with my head held high, getting into the feel of the new me.

The car suddenly slowed down as we drove in through big gates and headed along a drive with huge trees casting dark shadows, making the place look a bit creepy. Then the car turned into a wide opening and I looked up at an enormous granite mansion. I stared, wondering if this was a house or were we meeting in a big swanky old hotel or something. 'Where are we, Ralph?'

'We have arrived, darling,' he said, switching off the engine and looking at me half-smiling and wondering what I was talking about.

'Is this Jacques and Soviah's house?' I whispered.

'Yes,' he said, nodding.

'But it's huge! How could they afford something like this? Didn't you say he was a heart surgeon? How could he afford the like of this on what he would earn?' I said, looking at the big steps up to it, seeing chandeliers throwing out sparkling light from the downstairs rooms. To the right there was a path heading around the side of the house. I could see a big stone fountain with the statue of a Grecian woman upending a basin of water while a cloth hung off her other arm.

'I doubt he is dependent financially on his work,' Ralph said. 'He is heir, both he and his sister, to a substantial inheritance. His grandfather developed a pharmaceutical industry. Now it is quite vast. It is managed by a board of trustees. So, yes, he is quite comfortable,' Ralph said.

'Ahh, no wonder! The philanderer, I called him. So I was right!' I said, grinning at Ralph.

'I shall hold my own counsel on that,' Ralph smiled, looking at me sideways.

I leaned forward, suddenly giving him a big smacking kiss on the lips.

'Hmm, that was nice,' he said. 'I am looking forward to more later,' he suddenly whispered.

'When? We're here now, Ralph!'

'Oh, darling, we do have a home to go to,' he said, looking at me like I was daft as a brush.

'Ah, now, Ralph, an aul fella of your age needs his beauty sleep,' I said, shaking my head, looking at him like it's a very serious matter.

He peeled his head from one side to the other, then landed it back on me, giving a big sigh, saying, 'You are in very serious trouble, my lady. Later, I shall deal with you most severely. But I shall be fair, you may choose your punishment.'

'Like what, Ralph?'

'Later! Now, come along, let us get inside.'

Ralph rang the doorbell while I stood looking around. Jaysus, it looks a bit like the Jardin du Luxembourg, the lovely park I spent many a long day wandering around, right in the centre of Paris.

I whipped around as the door shot open and a voice boomed, '*Mon ami!*'

I found myself looking into the beaming, happy face of Jacques, who held out his arms. 'Come in, come in, my friends!' he said, throwing open the big heavy doors and waving us into a huge entrance hall.

My breath caught at the sudden sight of the grandeur. I walked into a vast marble hall with a sweeping staircase standing right in the middle and big mahogany doors on either side. I looked up to a landing with a big window taking up the centre of the wall; that would throw in coloured light from the bevelled glass when it caught the sun. It had a cut-glass picture of a Grecian woman staring out.

'Madame,' he said, kissing my cheeks then taking my hand. 'You are very welcome, a delight to meet you once again,' he said, bowing to kiss my hand.

I smiled like my face suddenly exploded, with a gush of pleasure rushing its way around me.

'You make a handsome couple,' he said, lifting his face and grinning at Ralph as he greeted him, with the pair of them exchanging kisses on both cheeks.

Ralph beamed at me, moving closer to lay his hand on my waist and draw me to him. Then he was handing over his coat to a woman waiting to take it, and he went to take mine. I hesitated, wondering if I should take it off. 'Allow me, darling,' Ralph whispered, taking the jacket as I unbuttoned it.

I stared down, seeing I looked just as good if not better. Now I was showing off my linen-and-lace blouse and the long velvet skirt. Yeah, I looked great, I thought, lifting my head and feeling all very much like the quality.

'Come along, meet our guests,' he said, waving us to follow him.

We walked to the end of the hall and went in through a door on the left, into a big room. Then through another door into a room the size of half a football field. It had tall, ornate white French windows going down the length of the room onto a long terrace with tables and chairs. That overlooked a huge park laid out in a straight line with trees and statues, and in the centre was a big fountain spurting out water that glittered and sparkled, lit up by lights. More lights lit up the wide paths, leaving areas shaded in dark.

I stared, letting me mouth drop open. No, forget the Jardin du Luxembourg, that's only the front. This sweep of landscape is more like the Palace of Versailles!

'Martha!' Ralph was saying.

I blinked, realising I'd forgotten where I was and that people were being introduced to me.

'You have met Heinrich and Isolda.' They waited while I moved in for the kisses, then I was nodding and shaking, kissing and smiling, and forgetting names, as it all went over my head. I need a cigarette, I thought, dying to whip out me cigarillos. A drink was put into my hand by Ralph as he took one off a tray that was being carried around by a man in a dickie bow wearing a black suit. He must be the waiter, I thought. No, not a waiter, this is not a hotel. Right, this is someone's house! I couldn't take in the massive style and elegance of the place. Jaysus, Mary and Joseph! The things money can do! My imagination never stretched to anything like this. I always thought 'rich' was having a nice house in your own grounds, with the big car sitting outside

the door, wearing a fur coat and popping into Brown Thomas for the
odd bit of shopping. But this! You could go in and buy up the bloody
place. Send the waiter in to collect the stuff! Get it delivered! Brown
Thomas? No, forget that! I have seen the places in Paris where Ralph
took me. Now that makes B and T look like paupers!

Ralph had gone to sit down beside a very handsome-looking man
with a mop of wavy brown hair combed back off his head then
curled just above the collar of his white Charvet shirt with the blue
silk tie and a diamond tiepin. He was wearing a dark-grey suit and
shiny handmade black lace-up shoes. Ralph was in a black suit with
a Charvet linen shirt and a dark-wine silk tie with a gold tiepin.

People were spread out along deep leather sofas going around in a
U-shape, where they sat facing each other. I moved in beside Isolda,
who turned to settle herself, letting her eyes rest on me.

'Oh, how nice it is to see you again,' she beamed, laying her hand
gently on mine then sitting up straight to look around and point out
people to me. 'Now, some of us here are old friends but I am not
sure about some of the others. So I am like you, Martha dear, I too
am looking at the strange faces.'

I nodded slowly, keeping my hands sitting demurely on my lap,
wondering when I could get them on the smokes. Then I sighed quietly
and lifted my drink, taking a sip. There was a roar of laughing from
the men as one of them was in the middle of a story. Jacques called
over the waiter and quietly whispered something, then the waiter
took off and was rapidly back carrying a tray and holding it out to
the men. They dipped in one by one, taking a big fat cigar out of
a box, then the cutting started and they were all ready to be lit up.

Great, I thought, a smoke at last. I grabbed my bag then it hit
me. No, forget that, save your own. If they're getting them free, then
what about us women? I tried to get Ralph's attention but he was
now caught up in conversation with a very excitable-looking woman.
She was waving the hands, shrugging the shoulders, then leaning in
looking like, *So! What was I to do?*

He listened, giving her all his attention, then suddenly his face lit
up and he roared his head laughing. The woman picked up her drink,
taking a sip and looking like whatever the problem had been she had
dispatched it very rapidly!

Ah, forget Ralph, I thought, looking around, wondering how I could get my hands on a few cigarillos! Then the waiter flew past and I tipped his arm.

'*Madame!*' he snapped, bowing the head to hear what I wanted.

'*Cigarillos, s'il vous plaît! For moi!*' I said, pointing the finger at meself.

He kept the head down, waiting for more information. I stared, thinking, not knowing any other words. 'Smoke!' I said, with the finger at the mouth and the other one pointing at me chest.

'*Pardon?*' he said.

Isolda was listening and she understood. So she told him in rapid French.

'*Ah, oh, oui!*' he said, then went rushing to sort me out. He was back with a smaller box this time. I had a choice of big, long, thin black ones or little brown fat ones, grey-looking ones, and there was a silver cigarette holder sitting brand new in another box.

I took in a sharp intake of breath as my eyes lit on them. '*Merci,*' I said, taking one, then he went to whip away the box. '*Non, non, monsieur!*' I said, grabbing hold of his arm. 'More!' I said, pointing and dipping my hand in. I took two of each and one cigarette holder. I would have liked two, in case I needed a back-up, but I didn't want to make a show of myself with Isolda watching.

'*Merci!*' I grinned, whipping the lot into my bag then lighting up the black one after sticking it in the long silver cigarette holder. He lit it up for me and I took in a deep drag and nearly choked. Isolda immediately went into action and started slapping my back.

'It was too bloody strong,' I croaked, losing my decorum with the coughing, spluttering and ending up with the red watery eyes and running mascara. It's probably streaking down my cheeks, I thought. Ah, fuck! Now I could feel my face tighten, knowing it was bright red to match me eyes. People looked around with their smiles still frozen on their faces, waiting to see what all the fuss was about. Ralph looked over, taking in the long black cigar plugged into the long silver cigarette holder, looking a mile long, and grinned.

'I'm grand!' I croaked, waving and trying to get my 'sophisticated quality' look back. 'Excuse me,' I rasped, smiling and standing up, heading for the French windows and the terrace.

'Oh, that's better,' I gasped, breathing in the night air, with the wind blowing the oxygen from the lovely grass and trees. Then I looked down, seeing at the far end a tall blonde girl with her bare arms resting on the balcony. She looked miles away as she sucked hard on a long cigarette in a holder like mine. She pulled the mink jacket sitting on her shoulders, getting it wrapped tighter around her neck, then leaned down, getting herself more comfortable as she stared out into the distance. She was watching the huge spray of water glittering yellow and sparkling white as it soared into the air, where it caught the light and then came crashing down making a thudding sound, like it was determined to beat the marble basin into submission. Showing it who was boss.

There was something lonely about the way she huddled herself, resting on the balcony. Like she wasn't a part of what was going on here, as if she didn't belong. It was the way she looked around like she was afraid somehow, like she didn't know the place and was worried that at any minute someone would tell her to leave. But yet she was waiting for someone, because she had to wait.

I moved down and stopped a few feet away, saying, '*Bonjour!*'

Her head shot around, looking like she got a fright, wondering how I suddenly appeared.

'Sorry, did I give you a fright?'

She put her hand on her chest and smiled, showing a gorgeous set of white teeth and lovely sky-blue eyes.

'*Bonjour!*' I said again.

'*Bonjour,*' she said softly. 'Are you English?'

'No, Ireland! But the same language.'

She nodded then stared at me.

'Do you speak English?'

'A little, not very well, but I spend some time in London! So, yes, a leetle,' she smiled, wriggling her fingers. 'You are on holiday?'

'Yes, I suppose you could call it that,' I said, laughing.

'And who do you stay with?'

'Oh, I stay with Ralph.'

'Ahh! Yes, Jacques would be his friend! *Non? Vous?* You!' she said, pointing at me.

'No, not me, he is Ralph's friend.'

'Ahh,' she said, nodding her head. Then we went silent.

'You, do you come with someone?'

'No, I stay here with Jacques. Today I arrive, maybe one weekend I stay, maybe more. It depends!' she said, shrugging, showing her gorgeous mouth curl into an O-shape as she thought about that.

'Oh, you are his house guest! His friend?'

'Yes! I am his friend,' she said, making it sound like she was not happy with that idea.

'Do you live around here?' I said, wanting to make conversation.

'No, I live in Paris.'

'Do you work?'

'Yes, I am a dancer with the Folies Bergère!'

'In the Moulin Rouge?' I said, looking at her in admiration.

'Yes,' she said, nodding quietly.

'Oh, you must be very good,' I said, thinking, they are very famous. She shrugged, saying, 'Yes, I would like to think!'

I looked down at her long legs in the leopard-skin shoes with the straps wrapped around the ankles. She had on a very short skirt, showing off the length of her gorgeous long legs, and a silk blouse that showed a lovely creamy cleavage. She is gorgeous, I thought, thinking she must be the mistress Soviah was talking about. Then she looked up as the waiter put his head out the door, indicating we should follow as dinner was about to be served.

24

'Pardon, Madame,' the woman whispered, as she leant down to collect up my empty dishes, taking away my drinking glasses. We had a different wine with every course. My belly was bursting from the amount of grub I shovelled into me, then the waiter bent to pour me another liqueur. I had held up my empty little crystal glass, seeing him going around the table, pouring brandy for the men and anyone who wanted it. I wanted another liqueur. I've given up that brandy stuff; it blows me head off. That and champagne. I'm not used to the high living, even though I have had my moments. I did manage to get around a bit and even stand in the private box at the races. But this is different! This is definitely flying with the quality.

I was dozing over me sixteenth glass of liqueur and nibbling on chocolates left sitting in a bowl that had been doing the rounds until it landed at me, so now it stayed. 'Definitely, I absolutely agree,' I said, nodding me head at Isolda, who had managed to sit next to me again. I was hoping to get placed with one of the handsome men, any of them would have done, but no! I got stuck with Isolda and a baldy consultant doctor on my right. He wanted to talk about the effects of a bad diet on the bowel. It causes terrible disease, he was telling me. Even down to the name of the diseases! I wasn't listening, so he got fed up and turned to the woman on his right. She seemed to agree with everything he was saying. I didn't. I told him that can't be true. Otherwise the whole population of paupers would be dead and buried from it. 'Sure, they eat nothing!' I said.

He didn't agree. He pointed out they had excellent diets; they eat the basic food off the land. Good old vegetables and that sort of thing. Where as us, now! We spoilt, rich, decadent lot stuff ourselves with all this rich food! 'Very bad for the digestive system!' he warned, giving me a look that was enough to frighten even the dead back into life.

Now I was stuck agreeing with everything Isolda said because she was too nice to argue with. Anyway, all I had to do was nod and she was happy, I didn't have to listen. Occasionally I would lift the head from the liqueur, or the chocolates, or whatever was going, and look straight into her face, giving a definite nod of agreement. In return, she told me I was a wonderful listener.

I decided she and I could definitely be good friends. Because nobody ever told me that before! The worst someone told me was that I was a pain in the arse because I was definitely very opinionated. Well, why not? I'm entitled to exercise me right to free speech! So long as I'm not doing any damage or harming anyone.

I took in a huge sigh, thinking, I better get up and go outside for an airing. I'm beginning to feel a bit sick. Talk about making a pig of myself. I never tasted the like of that grub in all me born days. Except with Ralph, of course. His Madame is a marvellous cook. But somehow this grub is like something you would get at a big fancy banquet. No, I wasn't going to pass up the opportunity of shifting second and third helpings of whatever was going. Isolda kept looking to see where I was putting it. No wonder that doctor was giving me an earful!

Right, I'm finished, I couldn't look at another bit of food if I got paid for it. OK, Martha, heave yourself up, get moving. Ah, Jaysus, wait! Nobody has moved, I thought, looking around the table, seeing them sitting back relaxing, looking like they were in for the night. I can't get shifting until they all do; it's impossibly bad manners, I can hear Ralph say. No, sit it out, don't let yourself or him down. I sat back, giving a big miserable sigh out of me, and turned to look at Isolda, staring into her face, saying nothing.

She stirred herself, letting her eyes light up. 'Vell! I vas thinking! Do you know it is not yet the season for us to be—'

'Sorry to interrupt you,' I said, laying my hand on hers and looking around me.

Suddenly people were on their feet, looking to move. Jacques was making his way out the door, with everyone taking up their glass and following.

'Ve are moving, Isolda,' I said, hearing myself say that and hoping she didn't catch it. Jaysus, I must be drunk!

Then we were out the door and walking the length of the house, trailing through one open door after another. Finally we were back in the sitting room. Jacques gave orders to the waiter – or maybe he's a butler, I don't know if they have them here in France. We all sat down and I tried to wriggle myself in between two gorgeous handsome men, but suddenly my arm was taken and I was gently but firmly being led to another place.

'Yes, ve will be much more comfortable here!' gasped Isolda, sitting me next to her on the edge of the sofa.

Fuck! How unlucky can you get! I snorted to myself, looking up at her beaming face as she settled herself down to give me more gossip. But it was only about people I didn't know.

The waiter suddenly appeared with a load of dancing girls trailing in behind him. Then I noticed the little band of men in dickie bows and suits. They were sorting out musical instruments and looking at sheets of music propped open on a stand. Suddenly they roared into life, blasting out a very quick lively cancan. Isolda sat back to watch, nodding at me. I nodded back. So this is what she was talking about when she said, 'Ve vill have a better view of the show!'

The musicians got going and the girls let rip. Big frilly skirts flew as boots kicked them out of the way and into the air, giving us an eyeful of long frilly knickers!

I looked for Lulu-Belle, the dancer – that's her name, I discovered – but she was not there. No, she was wrapped around Jacques, nearly sitting on his lap as he cuddled her to him. He kept running his hand up and down the side of her, getting a sneak feel of her rounded bosom. She sat and watched, looking a lot more contented and happy now, seeing as he was giving her a lot more attention. I lit up my cigarillo, trying out a new one. The little fat brown one, it was even stronger. But I tested it carefully and only let a little down me neck. I blew that out fast and just barely sucked. But I knew it made me look good. Very sophisticated.

Suddenly the waiter appeared, looking very worried as he rushed himself over to Jacques, who was dribbling with his face lit up at the sight of all the girls. They were screaming and smiling, and one of them danced over, giving a big kick to fly the skirt, letting it hit him full in the chops. Then, when he got his eyesight back, he was happily looking up the knickers of the laughing dancer as she wriggled and shook it at him, then turned and dropped, giving him an eyeful of her frilly arse.

I watched to see what was going on. Jacques' face dropped while he held his head down listening, taking in what the waiter was telling him in rapid French. Then he lifted his head, staring into the distance, looking like his face had frozen into solid marble. He had turned the colour of a ghost. But then he was suddenly galvanised into action and his eyes came alive as he roared, '*MON DIEU!*'

Then he went to lift himself. But before he could get standing the door at the end of the room flew open and Jacques' face now turned yellow!

I followed his gaze just in time to see Soviah march in with her eyes peeled on him. Then she turned to Lulu-Belle, who still had her hand on his lap and her head resting against his chest. '*MERDE!*' she screamed, pointing the finger at the pair of them, and she still only halfway across the floor.

He leapt up, putting out his arms, saying, '*Ma chère! Ma Soviah! Blah blah! Croon, sigh!*'

She rushed into his arms, giving him an almighty slap on the kisser, then sent him flying backwards as he nearly lost his balance. She kept walking towards him, pushing and slapping, still wearing the big boots and the long fur coat trailing after her. He was now walking backwards, explaining, talking very fast with his hands waving like windmills.

The band stopped playing and the girls stopped dancing. Jacques waved and smiled at them, telling them to carry on. With that, Soviah ran at one of the musicians and grabbed his violin bow, then rushed at Jacques, missing his head as he ducked but still getting an unmerciful blow on the hand. Then she let out a blood-curdling scream as she made a dive for Lulu-Belle, waving the broken bow with the strings twanging in the air.

Lulu-Belle screamed, leapt and made a dive, landing in the lap of Heinrich, who looked shocked then happy as he stared down at her. She wrapped her arms around his neck, yelling in French for him to save her. Or sounding something like that.

He smiled and wrapped his hands around her lower back, pulling her into him. Isolda, his wife, gasped, I coughed, the baldy bowel doctor leapt to his feet, tackling Soviah, who was caught up trying to get past the blonde bombshell from Italia. She lost the front of her frock as Soviah grabbed hold, trying to steady herself. The Italian bombshell screamed when her ample milkers fell out because the front of the frock was now in shreds. It was only a flimsy thing anyway.

The baldy doctor grabbed Soviah's arms, pinning them down by her side, heroically trying to stop her from getting at Lulu-Belle. Meanwhile, some of the band played on, with lovely music wafting over from an accordion player while the rest were too busy discussing what happened to the violinist and his bow. He looked grief-stricken, with the tears looking like they were ready to pour down his cheeks.

Soviah managed to get loose and Baldy was sent flying to land in the laps of Ralph and another fella. The women stared and gasped, then everyone was shouting, mostly the women. The men sat back, looking very calm and smoking their cigars with a grin on their faces, ducking and moving as bodies got landed, with Soviah now after Jacques again.

He was on his feet, shouting at her, trying to lead her out of the room by pointing and waving, but she took no notice. Her eyes were now clapped on me as he marched off, wanting her to follow him. Then he lost the rag and came tearing down the room looking like he was going to annihilate her. Her eyes whipped on him again. Then suddenly she took in a big breath, holding it, then heaved it out as she tore after him, screaming like the banshee. He changed his mind about murdering her and dived for the terrace, then she changed her mind about killing him and went flying out of the room. Then he was back in, wiping his forehead and looking up and down, making sure she really was gone. Then he was making his way back over to see if everyone was OK.

We all sorted ourselves out, because I was taking no chances and had landed meself sitting on the lap of a lovely-looking man wearing an open shirt with the tie left hanging down. Then I slid off and mooched in next to him, afraid Soviah might decide to do me and me new clothes a terrible harm. If I wasn't wearing my best stuff, I wouldn't have been bothered. She would have gotten more than a box if she came near me.

Then, while everyone was talking, the waiter was rushing over to whip open the French windows. Then he was back, shouting and pointing. The music suddenly dropped, then stopped, and it was then we heard the thumping noises coming from outside. Jacques rushed out to see what was happening and the rest of us followed.

I was on me feet, making a rush for the door. We were all just in time to see golf sticks flying through the air, then the bag followed. Soviah was hanging out the window, screaming blue murder. Then his suits started flying through the air, followed by mounds of Charvet shirts caught by the wind, now ballooning towards the fountain, while some headed for the trees.

Jacques shouted, '*Sacré bleu!*' and turned for the door, then looked back, saying something to the men. They hesitated, then took off, following Jacques. The women stared up, gasping with their hands on their chests, muttering and breathing heavily through their noses while we all nodded, agreeing it was shocking!

Then there was further uproar. We could hear the screams coming from Soviah, then men's voices mumbling quietly as Soviah let out a litany of abuse, letting her voice fall and rise, making it sound like she was telling him what she was going to do to him. The women gasped louder as we held our heads in the air, listening with our mouths open. It was all coming out through the open window.

'What did she say? I gasped, grabbing Isolda's arm.

'No no, it is too shocking!'

'Oh, go on! Tell us!' I said, wanting to hear the shocking bits.

'It is not for the ears,' she whispered, looking like she was going to bless herself.

Then we heard a thump and something crashing! Then a terrible moan.

'That is Jacques!' I whispered, prodding Isolda.

'Yes, I am thinking you are right,' she said, staring with her head in the air.

'Shush! *Silenzio!*' the Italian bombshell hissed, staring daggers as she tried to listen, gripping hold of her torn frock.

Then it started to go quiet, with only a few murmurings. We listened, hoping for more, but that was the end of it. Everything had gone quiet except for the gentle murmuring of men's voices. We all started to trail back inside, seeing the dancing girls were now slumped in our seats. They looked a bit miserable, sitting with their hands on their knees and their frocks pulled up around them, showing their long frilly knickers, while others sat with their leg thrown over the other one, consoling themselves with dragging on a cigarette. They looked up when we walked in, and the band started to play a very slow sad song. It was 'Down Mexico Way' or something like that. It's a cowboy song. Oh, yeah, 'South of the Border'!

'Vy must they be upset?' Isolda whispered, looking at me and pointing at the girls.

'I suppose they are worried they might not get paid, Isolda,' I said, 'seeing as their party ended before it could even get started.'

They all pushed up, making room for the rest of us. Then the women started chattering like mad, making clucking noises, sighing out their disgust and nodding, looking stricken at being exposed to the like of this. Then they shook their heads, sniffed and snorted, showing their displeasure. With each making sure the other knew we were most definitely not impressed by this outrageous behaviour.

'No, definitely not civilised,' I said, sniffing at Isolda.

She snorted and agreed vehemently with me. After all, I was thinking, here's me in my new best clothes! God knows what might have happened if she got her hands on me. No, not with the mood she was in. 'A bleedin Moore Street dealer wouldn't be half as common!' I sniffed, looking around me. 'No, we Royal Dubliners are more civilised than that!'

'Vot is this Mure Street meaning you speak of?'

'Vell! It is . . .' I heard meself say.

Suddenly we all perked up as the waiter appeared carrying a full tray of drinks. He bowed, offering the tray to anyone who wanted one. We all helped ourselves, looking like we needed it. He looked like he could do with one himself; he was looking a bit green around the gills but carried on as if nothing happened.

The dancers looked up hopefully but he ignored them, deciding they weren't worth his tender ministrations. Then one of the girls hopped up and spoke rapidly in French, the others all nodding their annoyance and looking very aggrieved, particularly as they gave us dirty looks, sitting and sipping delicately on our drinks. He walked off ignoring them, rushing out the door with his empty tray.

Suddenly it looked like another riot was about to erupt when they upped and starting telling each other they weren't standing for this. At least that's what it sounded like. Then they were shouting and marching off, heading for the door and the waiter. They were back in with him railing at them, waving his tray and telling them to get back in. At least that's what it sounds like. I can't speak bleedin French. The musicians stopped playing and just sat around looking miserable, waiting for someone to tell them what to do. I was just about to get up and go for a wander, see if anything more interesting was happening elsewhere, when the door opened and the men came walking back in, talking and laughing, puffing and blowing. Jacques was being helped by another man and I saw he was injured. He had a bandage wrapped around his left eye and it was bulging!

I stared as he got closer. Something was hanging out of the corner. I leaned in closer for a better look, seeing it was a piece of ice, a huge lump. It was plastered to his eye and held in place by the bandage tied to the back of his head. Something hit me, then I suddenly started howling with the laugh. I never in all me born days saw anything so funny-looking as he stared, trying to see out of the one eye. He looked so pitiful it collapsed me in a heap, screaming my lungs out, roaring with the laugh. Everyone was looking at me, staring like I was demented. They couldn't see anything funny. The women were horrified, now having something new to start them clutching their chests. That made me worse, then Jacques grinned and came over pointing to his eye, saying, 'Yes, Soviah is a wild woman, she gave me a black eye. It is most fortunate I did not lose it. She hit me with the golf ball. Pity she did not manage to throw that out the window along with my golf cart and sticks,' he said, sounding really mournful at how unlucky he was.

I laughed even louder, then saw the musicians were smiling and suddenly the girls gave an almighty cackle as Lulu-Belle started to cry. They were trying to get her to do something but she sat looking frazzled, pulling shreds out of a hankie. They were slapping their heads with their hands, making it look like they thought everyone was crazy. Then I looked back at Jacques and suddenly it felt like a dose of cold water was poured over me.

'A golf ball!' I said quietly, seeing him still staring, looking tired and pitiful, like all the life was gone out of him and now he just didn't want to move or even know what to do next. 'Jacques, I am sorry,' I said, putting out my hand to land it on his arm, not knowing if I should do that. France is very different. People keep their distance.

He put his hand on my shoulder, saying, 'Thank you, I understand. I believe also she was making a nuisance with my good friend Ralph. This was not good. The woman is impossible! But then it was, dare I say . . .' he said, then hesitated, 'a *ménage à trois?*' he said softly, leaning into me and grinning.

I slowly grinned, seeing the look of pleasure that mischief gave him. '*Non, non,* Jacques. Perhaps, but not quite. Ralph can take care of himself. But it was personal, between Soviah and I. Forgive me, please, but I did not like the woman. She showed me nothing but contempt. She behaved as if I did not exist. She was very insulting, dismissive, churlish. I saw no trace of a well-bred woman. Then she took a step too far when she called me a peasant. I showed her what happens when she insults a peasant. But she is lucky I gave her a controlled measure. I did that only for Ralph. Anything more would have hurt him, made difficulties for him. You know, Jacques? When Soviah looks at you, stares into your eyes, she is looking for her own reflection. But if she had looked more deeply into my mine, she would have seen not just a peasant, oh no!' I said, shaking my head slowly. 'She would have known very quickly her aristocratic breeding did not prepare her for someone of my calibre. My breeding prepared me to be a warrior! That lady was punching well above her weight, she was out of her depth. With all due respect, Jacques, the blood of a royal house ran very thin when it produced Soviah. She is a poor imitation of what makes a woman. Not like yourself,' I laughed, 'rambling in here with that thing plastered to your eye.'

'*Pouff! Mon Dieu!* It caused a stir but it amused you, so better than nothing!' he grinned, holding out his hands and shrugging as he dropped his neck, lifting his mouth. Then he flicked his eyebrow, letting me see a twinkle sit in his one eye. I watched, seeing his smile slowly fade as he got serious and started to stare at me.

I saw him look very calculating at me, like he was thinking, searching for a hidden truth, figuring out I was not all I seemed. Then his eye lit up, deciding his discovery was not a bad thing. A smile slowly appeared like he was amused. Then he sighed in a slow deep breath. 'Martha, it is my fortunate pleasure to know you. Ralph is a most lucky man,' he said softly, taking my hand and kissing it.

'Thank you, Jacques,' I smiled, feeling my heart gladden at his kindness. He had just gotten a glimpse of the real me. 'I am sorry for my behaviour. It was very insensitive to have laughed like that. But my intention was not to mock you. Perhaps I had too much of your delicious liqueur! It shut down my brain.'

'No, no, think nothing of this. Of course it is most entertaining, but I hope my other guests will take this evening's unplanned little Italian operetta just as lightly,' he said, moving in closer, whispering as he looked around with the one good eye. 'But you see, it was not quite so dramatic as I have painted. No, Soviah did not succeed in depriving me of my treasured eye,' he said, resting his hand in the air over it. 'Yes, she did fire the golf ball, determined to knock me senseless. But I deflected its progress and in doing so I punched my fist straight into my own eye, bumph!' he said, making a fist and gently bringing it towards himself. 'So, you see, I gave myself the black eye. This ice pack is a good remedy! It will prevent swelling, so I should be looking at two perfect eyes soon,' he grinned, watching me give another big laugh.

Then he looked up as Heinrich came over saying something, then a few more men who were standing chatting moved in as well. Suddenly the women got restless, waiting for someone to tell them what happened, and they shot up, making over for the men, demanding to know all the gory details. They needed to know if Soviah was dead or alive. They wanted gossip, shocking and all as it was.

I looked around, seeing Lulu-Belle was still in the middle of a fight with the dancers. They wanted her to get moving, sort things out. I could see by the way they were trying to haul her to her feet, pulling and dragging, pointing and prodding her at Jacques. But she was having none of it. She cried even more, wringing the hankie and stabbing them back with her elbow. They waved their arms, puffing and blowing at each other, but it was no good. There was going to be no shifting her. She knew the game was up with Soviah back in the nest and most certainly on the warpath. It was breaking her heart. I could see she was thinking this may be the end now of her and Jacques.

I wandered over to the musicians, who were now getting very relaxed. They were sitting and smoking, drinking and laughing, talking to the waiter. He was having a party, taking a sly sip of the booze while filling in the details for the men, giving them a blow-by-blow account of the goings on of the aristocracy. I watched him talking rapidly, throwing himself backwards and waving the arms, then punching the air with his fists, watching an imaginary someone trying to land a blow. Then lifting his face to give little screams, with the musicians watching and listening with their mouths hanging open, then letting rip with the laughing coming out of them.

Oh, the waiter would be the one to know what went on upstairs, I thought, thinking it's a pity I can't understand a bleedin word. Then I had an idea and I made my way over to them. They all looked up as I moved in, interrupting the middle of the story.

'*Bonjour, messieurs!* Eh! Play!' I said, making a picture with my hands of moving the accordion, then pointing at the musical instruments. '*Non, je ne regrette rien?*'

'*Ahh! Oui, oui!*' they said, looking delighted as they whipped up their instruments and started playing. Suddenly the dancing girls started to sing, hearing the song of their dead national hero, the great Edith Piaf, being blasted out by the musicians.

I stood watching them, seeing how gorgeous-looking they were, and listening to their voices all singing together. It carried around the big room, with the high ceiling sending it to thunder down and crash against the walls. Suddenly we were all sitting and listening. My heart lifted and soared with the power of it. I could feel my guts wrenching with the exquisite tenderness it tore up from me as I listened to the song of a woman who is letting us know in no uncertain terms she has lived and pained, loved and lost, fought and cried, and, NO! She has no regrets! She is Edith Piaf. She is Paris!

Then suddenly the voices of the girls died away as the music stopped. There was a pause while we all listened to the silence, then everyone erupted, shouting and applauding. Shouts of 'Bravo! Encore!' The girls were delighted and beamed, holding their skirts and giving a little bow.

I was feeling a lot better now. The mood had been lifted and everyone was shouting more in relief than anything else. It had been funny but yet there was a lot of tragedy behind it all. Two people living miserable lives, with each dependent on the other to try and make the pain ease if nothing else. But I knew it would be a while yet before these two managed to get out from under each other. She won't let go until she has another man lined up. But it is not going to be my Ralph! Over my dead bleedin body, she will! I will see her in hell first!

25

I looked over, seeing Ralph talking to Jacques. They were both laughing yet there was a hidden pain and worry behind Jacques' laughter. He didn't want to lose any more face than he already lost, having given his impromptu party of wine, women and song and inviting the bloody mistress. If Soviah wasn't getting any, then neither was he.

Jaysus! What a tangle we can get ourselves into, and all in the name of love, money, greed, sex and power. So much for the upper classes. It seems their money gets in the way of their happiness. It blocks them from experiencing the simple pleasures of life that only poorer people get when they are content with what they've got. Oh, well, I sighed, that's the pain of being human.

I made my way over to Ralph, thinking I barely clapped eyes on him this evening, never mind got even two words with him. My heart warmed just seeing the sight of him. I crept up slowly then materialised beside him while he was lost in conversation with Jacques. Then his head whipped to me and suddenly his face lit up in a lovely smile, showing his dimples and flashing the snow-white even teeth.

'Well, hello!' he said softly, putting out his arm to pull me into him.

I sighed as I leaned against him, feeling a great rush of pleasure and joy filling me up. I had still not gotten used to the idea I had a man in my life, and he loved me, and I loved him.

'You must keep tight hold of this lady,' Jacques grinned, putting his hand on my shoulder. 'She is a wonderful find! Where did you get her, Ralph?'

I stared at him, reading something into what he was asking. He was curious to know who I was, where and what I really come from.

'That's a very loaded question, Jacques,' I said quickly, not wanting

Ralph to give any answer. It would just fuel Jacques' curiosity even more. Then I said, letting him know we were on the same wavelength, 'You are a very astute man, Jacques, for a heart surgeon! You keep your eyes wide open,' I said, grinning.

I could see Ralph's eyebrow raising. He was wondering what the hell we were on about. But Jacques said, 'Yes, Martha, it takes a clever lady to see this. I think you are a very clever lady, and also quite an astute one!'

Ralph laughed, saying, 'Goodness, have I been missing something? I am amazed, Jacques, I should have thought your hands were quite full enough with one lady!'

'Two!' I muttered, throwing me eye over at Lulu-Belle, still crying her eyes out huddled in the corner.

'But you have had time to entertain my one also! You had better watch out, old boy, this one is mine!' he laughed, pulling me towards him in a tight hug.

'Nonsense! You are a confirmed celibate, a bachelor! You would not know what to do with this lady! We French, we are the masters of love!' Jacques said, laughing and deliberately drawing Ralph out with veiled insults.

'Bah! Your women come looking to me for succour!' Ralph said, throwing back his head, getting annoyed.

'Nonsense!' shouted Jacques. 'The women, they crowd me! It is no wonder I lose control of the odd one!'

Then we all started roaring laughing, with Ralph saying, 'Well, Jacques, be prepared to die! Because I shall fight you in a duel to the death! This one is mine!'

Then Jacques took my hand, kissing it, saying, 'I bid you goodnight, but if he breaks your heart, come to me. I shall fix it. I am a heart surgeon. I shall be at your service, Martha!' he said, twigging his eyebrow at Ralph.

'*Bonne nuit*, you rogue!' Ralph said, then took my arm, heading for the door so we could make our way home.

I made my way down the stairs, seeing Ralph walk in through the front door then hang up his coat. 'Good morning! Did you sleep well?' I said, rushing down to throw myself into his arms, feeling delighted at seeing him.

He caught me in a hug and swung me around. 'My, you are full of the joys this morning, my love. It is so good to see you,' he said, kissing me long and hard, letting me feel the heat of his mouth tasting juicy and deliciously him.

'How did you sleep, Ralph? The pair of us were squarely banjacksed after that party last night.'

'Yes, absolutely, that is a good way to describe it, darling. I most certainly indeed was fairly tired. But I am fine now, quite rested. I slept very well. Have you eaten breakfast?'

'No, I am just out of the bed. I slept the sleep of the dead, Ralph.'

'Good, we shall breakfast together,' he said, heading us down to the kitchen.

I could smell the delicious fry and hot bread as we walked in. 'Yum! Lovely,' I said, sitting myself down, feeling starving after last night. The amount of grub I polished off had opened up my belly, making me get hungry faster. Mind you, they give you tiny portions, only about a spoonful. No wonder I had to keep asking for more, I thought, feasting my eyes down on the hot plate of cheese and mushroom omelette Madame put in front of me.

'Oh, that was scrumptious,' I said, finally lifting my head after polishing off half of the table.

'Have you eaten enough?' Ralph said, looking at my empty plate and grinning at me.

'Yes, thank you. *Merci, Madame!*' I said, turning to see her nod at me, looking very pleased all her efforts are not in vain. I eat everything she puts in front of me, then go back for more.

'You have put on some weight, darling. You have filled out quite nicely, and in all the right places,' he said, suddenly moving his hands gently up and down my waist, feeling my shape growing. 'But I am surprised you have not gained more. You must have a very vibrant metabolism. It is certainly effective in keeping you looking trim,' he said, letting his eyes rest on my body, taking in my lovely newly acquired curves. 'Yes, you are looking very well,' he said, bending over and giving me a kiss on the lips. 'Now, do you have plans for today? What would you like to do? I suggest we take a walk together, perhaps in an hour or two. When you are prepared. What do you think?'

'Oh, lovely. I would really like that, Ralph. We have never done that together.'

'Good, I shall see you later,' he said, standing up and taking his morning paper with him as he headed off to his study.

'Oh, we are back!' I gasped, catching sight of the entrance gate as I dragged my feet, getting pulled along by Ralph.

'Thank heavens,' he sighed. 'I have almost carried you the last three miles.'

'What? You're lucky you got me that far, Ralph Fitzgerald! When you said "a walk", I didn't know you meant a marathon,' I snorted.

'Oh, darling, it is good for you to stretch yourself!' he said, raising the eyebrow at me and grinning.

'How far did we walk? Was it sixty miles?'

'Oh, Martha, you do exaggerate. Perhaps half of that.'

'No, it was not. We have been gone for at least eight hours,' I snorted, seeing the evening drawing away as the night closed in.

'To be precise, we have been away for . . . seven hours,' he said, looking at his watch. 'Not bad, good guess actually. You do have a sense of time,' he said, grinning at me.

'Well, I'm starved, my feet will never walk again, me arse is creaking and my belly is starting to eat itself alive from the hunger,' I huffed, trying to keep my breath.

'Darling, we have eaten something. You had two pastries and looked like you were settling in to demolish more! Only I felt we should keep moving. We still had quite a distance to cover,' he said, trying to make it all sound so reasonable.

'Well, if there had been a bloody taxi to hail, I would have leapt in, high tailed it back here, Flash Gordon, and left you to get on with your little walk!' I snorted.

'No! WHAT?! You would have abandoned me! Miles from the nearest civilisation! Left me to find my own way home! Is that what you are saying?'

'Yes, of course!' I said, looking astonished he would even question that fact.

He took in a sharp breath, saying, 'I think that deserves a golly good punishing! Be prepared this night, my lovely, I intend taking you to task.'

'Ohh, looka poor little me, I'm quakin in me skin!' I said, rattling me head and shaking my hands.

'You will be!' he laughed. 'Just you wait, my little cherub!'

'Shall we take the back door?' Ralph said, grinning at me as we neared the front door.

'NO! Use your key. I'm collapsed here, you're just trying to torment me, Ralph Fitzgerald! I'm about to lose the rag,' I warned, hanging on to the doorknob.

He put the key in the lock without saying another word, pushing the door wide open. Then suddenly he swooped and lifted me into his arms. 'Come along then, you poor invalid,' he said, kicking out his foot and slamming the door shut with a bang. Then the kitchen door whipped open and Madame put her head out the door, then brought the rest of her as she stopped dead, taking in the pair of us. Her hand went to her chest as she started talking rapidly, sounding worried.

With that, Ralph dumped me on the floor, waving at me and snorting at her. She listened, then looked at me, laughing. Then she disappeared back into the kitchen.

'What did you tell her?' I said, looking at him suspiciously.

'Oh, I simply told her you were a lazy hound, and if we were to eat this night, then I must resort to bloody carrying you!' he said, giving me a slap on the arse, then hanging up his coat.

'I intend taking severe measures against you before this very night is out,' I warned, then headed me way for the stairs, thinking, I might have permanent damage, my body has seized up! Bleedin English public schools and their obsession with sport and exercise! That's where he gets all this carry-on from! I like walking in the countryside, but only at my leisure. That was like a preparation for the army. Come to think about it, they did all that sort of army training at his school, he told me. Naturally he was the commander, or whatever he called it. He would have been! He's very bleedin bossy!

'Darling, dinner will be served in one hour,' he said softly, coming up behind me and pulling me up the stairs.

'Oh, but that means we will be eating early?'

'Yes, does that please you?' he said, bending his head and giving me a kiss.

'Oh, great, that's a good idea, seeing as we missed out on lunch,' I said, continuing up the stairs as he headed into his room.

'Oh, that was heaven,' I said, stubbing out the cigarette in the ashtray and stirring myself, pushing back the kitchen chair.

'Yes, darling, it was good,' Ralph said, standing up and making to clear off the table then tidy up the kitchen.

I picked up the dishes and was landing them in the sink, yawning like mad.

'Listen, darling, leave those to me. Why don't you go upstairs and run a bath? It will help you relax, ease your muscles.'

'Are you sure? I know you must be tired as well, even more than me, seeing as you are an old man!'

He roared laughing, saying, 'Get moving, woman, or you will quickly find out I am not so old as you would have me!'

'What? You mean you can still . . .?'

'Go!' he said, pointing me to the door, not wanting any more guff outa me. 'You tread on very thin ice, dear girl!' he warned my back as I headed myself out the door.

'That still remains to be seen,' I said quietly, looking around at him, giving him a knowing look.

He stopped what he was doing and just stared, keeping a smile on his face but looking like he was thinking. Then I turned and headed for the stairs, leaving that hanging in the air.

Oh, yes, that was a wonderful cure the doctor ordered, I grinned to myself as I made my way out of the bathroom. Now, what will I wear for bed? My eyes lit on the silk negligee and matching top Ralph bought me. I only wore that once. Right, I might as well get the wear out of it. Especially as I am staying here with him. It's no good when I get home. There's nobody to see me in it.

I walked into the sitting room, seeing Ralph leaning against the mantelpiece. He was blowing cigar smoke into the air with his head thrown back watching it billowing up and then fanning out, leaving a lovely scent of sweet air. My eyes lit up at the sight of him. He was wearing pyjamas. I very seldom see him to do that. He looked so elegantly casual with his wine-silk dressing gown and a cream pair of soft cotton pyjamas. I looked down, seeing his feet looking lovely and white, with his toenails cut evenly across.

'Did you have a soak in the bath too, Ralph?' I said, sweeping over to give him a kiss.

'Yes, I followed my own advice,' he said, wrapping one arm around me and giving me a smoky kiss.

Hmm, he tastes so manly, I thought, feeling his skin through the softness of his nightclothes.

'You look very alluring,' he whispered, looking down the length of me. Then he lifted his eyes, letting them linger on mine, showing a softness that spoke of a deep sensual longing.

'Hmm, and I find you very sexy in those pyjamas,' I murmured, running my hand down his back, resting it just above his bottom. It felt strong and firm yet yielded to my touch as I felt the softness of his skin.

'I have poured you a drink,' he said, reaching to the table and handing me a glass of wine. 'Cheers!' he said, clinking my glass. 'What would you like to do?' he said, taking a sip of his wine as I sat myself down on the sofa.

'Oh, like do what?' I said, wondering what he was talking about.

'Well, we could watch a little television, we could listen to some music, or perhaps you would prefer an early night?'

'What, go to bed now?'

'Not quite, but I am simply making some suggestions. It is up to you, my darling. I shall follow your wishes,' he said, grinning at me.

'OK then, what if we do both? Let us lie down on the bed and I can read aloud to you. We can listen to music, then doze off if we want to! That way we can do the lot,' I grinned. 'Oh, and bring up the wine and smokes! Someone, though, is going to have a smoke-polluted room, but it's not going to be me. So that leaves you getting the short straw, seeing as I got in first!' I said, giving him a big smile with my lips clamped tight.

He sighed and shook his head.

'You said you'd do whatever I wished, Ralph! Now you are changing your mind,' I said, getting in before he even had a chance to open his mouth.

'No, darling, if that is what you wish, so then let us do it,' he said, picking up the bottle of wine and heading us out of the sitting room. 'Poor Jane,' I sighed, closing the book on Charlotte Bronte's *Jane Eyre*. 'In love with a man who can't return her love.'

'Oh, he loves her very much, but he is not free to marry, his wife still lives,' said Ralph, speaking very softly as he stared into my face.

I stared back, hearing something in his voice, seeing a multitude written into that stare. It sounded like he was talking about himself. My eyes locked on him, seeing him looking at me like he had a deep and protective love for me. I could see a longing, like he wanted to smother me in that love. Yet there was regret there, too. He looked different, like he had suddenly moved away from me and closed down a very deep and intimate part of himself. He looked sad, like he was saying goodbye to something he craved but could never have. I felt a cold band of steel wrapping itself around my chest. I shook my head. A part of me didn't want to let go. Maybe I'm wrong, I hoped, as I dropped my eyes to get away from that fear.

'What is it, darling?' Ralph said, taking my chin in his hand and bringing my face up to look at him.

I stared into his eyes, saying nothing. I had learned my lesson when I tried to push too hard.

'Does it make you sad?' he said quietly, looking into my face like it was just really hitting him for the first time that he had actually reached a decision. Yet he thought he was talking about the book.

I nodded, saying nothing. We both understood now what the other was really saying.

'I love you very deeply,' he whispered. 'I treasure you so very much, Martha.'

'I know,' I murmured, knowing that to be true, yet he was not prepared to take it any further.

'It makes me miserable if you are unhappy,' he whispered. 'I would do almost anything to make you happy,' he murmured, looking away with a far away distant look in his eyes.

'Almost?' I said, giving a ghost of a smile.

'No, darling, I will qualify that. I would do anything to make you happy,' he said, turning to rest his arm behind my head and slide over to lie down alongside me.

'Yes, except one thing, Ralph. You are not going to give up the priesthood, are you?' I said, hearing myself saying the words that were coming from my guts. There was no more denying it now. I suddenly knew without a shadow of a doubt, as the truth fully hit me. Yes, he is going to go back. His sabbatical is nearly at an end, I thought, feeling I was sinking, going all the way down into the bowels of hell.

A primitive scream tore up through me as a plaintive little voice roared in my head. I'm lost again. I'm going to get smothered up in a big black hole and there'll be nobody there but me and the dark and the cold. I'm lost. I'm all alone. I wanted to run. Get off the bed, don't let him see that part of me. It hurts too much. He has rejected me, I don't belong to him, he only causes pain. Don't let him see how he's hurt you, do not show him any more of yourself.

But I couldn't move. I was frozen solid from the shock. I could feel him stroking my hair, my face, as I closed my eyes with the pain. Then he lifted my head, looking into my eyes. I stared back with one last hope, seeing him shake his head. It was so slight I could only see the truth of it as he closed his eyes, nodding his agreement.

'So it's over,' I muttered, feeling my gut twist as the pain dug deep, knifing itself through me. Then I went dead, feeling nothing.

27

I opened Ralph's wardrobe, staring, seeing something of him in the clothes he wears, all hanging beautifully pressed and everything in its place. The suits covered in dust jackets, the shirts pressed and sitting in their shelves. A separate mahogany hand-carved shelf for everything, including little drawers for his socks and underwear. I opened one at the far bottom, seeing nothing but white Roman collars. He wears those as a priest. I stared at them, thinking of the years I saw him wearing nothing else, that and everything else black. The black suit, black shoes and the long black-wool coat. The only thing offered over to the ways of the world was his different-coloured scarf. He would wrap that around his collar when he was going out, just so he would not stand out as a man of God.

I slowly shut the drawer and closed the wardrobe. It was a man's wardrobe, specially built for a gentleman in a century now long past. It would hold a man's clothes, hang them the way they should be treated. Clothes were handmade then, they cost a fortune and were intended to last a lifetime, so they must be taken care of. Then a thought hit me: yes, clothes could last longer than a life, especially a marriage. They could outlive it all.

I turned away as I heard the sound of a car drawing up outside the front entrance. My heart started to jump then sink. Yet my mind was accepting. I knew what was to come. I knew what the next steps would be. Ralph did not have my experience; he felt it necessary to go through the motions. Discuss his now-ended sabbatical with his superiors and hope for a miracle. He may suddenly find he can walk away from his sacred vows, his commitment. No, Ralph, I sighed wearily, I know when something has defeated me. There is no point in flogging a dead horse. No, you cut your losses and move on. The clock keeps ticking and the world keeps turning, even though yours may have come to an end. I know at the end of it you have to get back on your feet and put one foot in front of the other then stagger on. Keep going until you find your feet again. I couldn't even feel a tear waiting to be shed. My heart had closed down. It has played this old tune for too many a long day now. It long ago learned not to waste time crying in the wind.

I heard his footsteps on the stairs, then waited for the bedroom door to open. He walked in then stopped to look at me standing in his bedroom. We stared at each other. He was wearing a long black coat and his priest suit, but no Roman collar. He had pulled that off when it had served its purpose.

I looked into his eyes, seeing all the sorrow in the world staring out at me. He looks exhausted; it's showing in how pale he is. Neither of us have been sleeping too well. He would wake, or I would wake, finding one or the other of us sitting in the kitchen or slumped on the settee in the sitting room. Then he would pull me into his arms, just resting until we both fell back to sleep again.

'Ralph,' I whispered, going to him. 'I missed you, Ralph!'

'Oh, darling, I felt a part of me missing without you,' he breathed into my hair, kissing and holding me to him.

'Here, let me take your coat,' I said, seeing him drop his leather bags and remove his scarf. He walked over to the wardrobe and hung up the coat, then started to strip out of his suit. I watched as he hung it up, putting it inside a dust sheet, then removed a pair of tan corduroy trousers and a wine jumper and white shirt. Then he slipped his feet into a pair of brown lace-up shoes and stood up, saying, 'Come along, darling, we will take a drink and talk downstairs.'

'How did the flight go?'

'Yes, pleasant, we departed on time. I took a taxi from the airport to the Shelburne Hotel, then prepared for my meetings. In the afternoon I went to my order house and met with my superior. We talked. It was quite informal, all that had needed to be discussed was now done. The decision was simply a formality. Then I had the prearranged meeting the next morning with my provincial, and he confirmed everything was now in order.'

We stayed unmoving for a long time, me sitting on his lap with my arms wrapped around his neck and my head resting on his shoulder. We were so still that we could have been mistaken for two statues locked in an embrace, carved by the tool of a master stonemason. I blinked, then whispered, 'So, are you now organised? Have they given you your papers for the African missions? Do you have your orders from the provincial?'

He nodded then said quietly, 'I leave from London in ten days. Yes, my darling Martha, I shall be back working as a medical missionary. A priest doctor,' he said, musing on the words, thinking about it. 'The family will be arriving on Saturday to organise and take charge of the house. I must prepare myself. I shall need inoculations. All sorts of things must be done. I have a long list of things that need to be done before I take my leave,' he said, looking into my eyes, staring, haunted with regret of what might have been, yet sounding so resigned.

I couldn't feel anything. Just a dead weight knowing I could never entertain any idea of the real loss and pain going through me. I kept it buried and stayed still under the dead weight.

'I fly out from Paris, Charles De Gaulle airport, three days from today, Ralph. Tomorrow I will pack, and we will leave on Thursday morning, early.'

'Yes, Martha, I have already made all the arrangements. I have booked rooms at the Hotel Raphael, close to the Champs-Elysées.'

'Yes,' I said, beginning to feel a stir inside me, an ache. Without warning, it exploded into a sudden shot of pain shooting up through me, heading to send me into a panic. It threatened to burst me into tears. But I hammered it back down inside. I let a deep breath come and an anger. No, damn you, life, this won't break me, it can't even break my heart, because that's turned into a swinging brick. I can't even poxy cry, the pain is too deep for that. Anyway, there will be no one to see or hear, no one will come when he is gone. So don't let go, Martha. It's only life. You've had your share of happiness. You know it never lasts for long. Right, this pain will ease in time. It might even help when I get back home.

'Ralph,' I said, hearing a tightness in my voice as I steeled myself. 'We won't ever make contact. It will serve no purpose. We will just cause ourselves more harm than good. So when we say goodbye at the airport, that will be the last time we will ever see each other.'

'Yes, Martha, I do understand we must make a clean break. But,' he said, taking in a deep breath, 'I want you to take my address at the mission. You must promise me that if you ever need me you will contact me immediately.'

'Yes, if it is a matter of life and death, Ralph, I will contact you, or . . . you will contact me.'

'Yes,' he said quietly, giving a nod of his head as he stared very hard into my eyes, letting me know this is first and foremost of paramount importance. 'You can make contact with me very quickly if you go through my order. They have the means to do that, darling. So please promise me you will not hesitate if you need me?' he said, taking my face in his hands, looking at me like he had gathered all the love to be had in the world and now he had it and wanted to give it to me.

'Yes,' I whispered, almost shattering into a million pieces from the loss of him. 'Oh, Ralph,' I sighed wearily. 'I never thought it would end like this when we were so happy,' I whispered, stroking his face and running my hands through his thick hair, feeling it soft and silky and so familiar to my touch. Then I gently kissed him, stroking his face, getting the smell of his soap and the faint scent of his aftershave. It mixed with his very own manly scent that is unique to him. A scent that means Ralph, someone that makes me feel safe and warm. It brings me peace and makes the world seem less threatening, not so big, like when I have been lost in a world of strangers. One where I am known only by a name but it means nothing to anybody. With Ralph, I could walk up to his door in the middle of the night and knock. He let me in because to him I was somebody. I was Martha, someone he loved. For a while I had found what I have been searching for all my life.

But fuckin typical! I was robbed. Life is a robbin bitch! There I had been, spending my life living like a haunted and hunted Carmelite nun. Being Mother Earth to Sarah, then, when that job is done, what do I do? Gobshite! I pop me head over the parapet and go searching for love. Where else but to Ralph? The one man who loves me and I would give my life for. Only problem is, he loves Mother Church more! You knew this! You may be a fool but you're not that much of an eejit! Ah, fuck ye, Martha! You walked yourself into this. Jaysus,

I must have been on the sunny side of the street when they were over on the rainy side giving out brains, I sniffed, lifting my head to stare at Ralph, wanting to scream like a lunatic with the frustration! Choke him for running off on me, better that than attempt murder on myself. But there must be something I can do! I can't stand sitting here steaming with the stupidity of myself.

Suddenly an ear-splitting shriek from the phone ringing shattered the silence, knocking us back into life. Our heads spun to it, reminding us that the world still carries on.

'Sorry, Martha, let me take that,' he said, standing up and walking over to the bedside table to pick it up.

I looked over at him, listening as he spoke in French. I heard him mention Jacques and me ears pricked up, seeing Ralph's face drop. Then he finished and put the phone back in the hook, looking thoughtful. He looked at me, seeing I was wondering what that was about.

'Martha,' he sighed, sounding tired. 'That was Jacques. He would like to host a farewell dinner party for us both tomorrow evening. How do you feel? Seven-ish, his house for dinner?'

'Would you like to go?' I said, seeing he wasn't all that interested.

'Darling, if you wish, of course we shall go.'

'No, thank you, Ralph. I want to spend all the time left to us without any interference from the outside world.'

'Thank you, my sentiments exactly,' he grinned, looking more cheerful. 'I shall make our excuses to him and take pleasure in it.'

'Why, Ralph?' I said, seeing him look vengeful.

'Ohh, that blighter! Do you know what he said to me when we discussed my departure from France soon for the missions?'

'No! What did he say?' I said, beginning to get annoyed without knowing why, but because Ralph looked upset.

'Quote verbatim! "I wish for you, my good friend Ralph, bon voyage! But now you must allow me to take care of Martha. Tragically, you have abandoned her to open season! I shall take her under my wing and introduce her to some of my finely honed French charms!" Can you believe the cheek of the bloody devil? Confound the dammed rascal! I told him I would knock his bloody block off if he dared throw his cap at you!'

I roared laughing. 'No, Ralph, he is just joking, you don't take that seriously! He is always trying to get one up on you. You pair are very macho around each other. Tsk, men are so bloody childish!' I snorted, giving him a dirty look with a half-smile.

'No, Martha, he was serious. I do believe Jacques is quite taken with you, my love,' Ralph said quietly, looking at me very seriously.

'Well, then, Ralph, he has two hopes, Bob Hope and no hope at all. Even if I was interested, I would have no intention of allowing him to add me to his little harem. Besides, Lulu-Belle would scratch my eyes out if Soviah didn't get me first,' I laughed, getting the picture of the pair of them out for my guts. 'Sounds to me like he wanted a bit of wife swapping! I told you that fella was a philanderer, Ralph!' I said, looking at him. 'But of course, he knows you well, Ralph. He sees how close we are but he knows what you are like. You will never marry, not even break your vow of celibacy, no matter how tempted. He is just being perverse, getting a laugh at your expense. He was right, look how steamed up you are! Only pity for him is he's not here to see it,' I said, seeing him look pained at me.

'No, no, no, darling! He is not quite the rake he would have you believe. He is actually quite an honourable fellow! Oh, no, I do think he would want you for more than a little romp in the hay! I believe he would take you seriously. Jacques is a man of good taste, he is very discerning. I think he finds you rather interesting, an enigma. You are a challenge to him, my love. On that note, I intend keeping that chappie well away from you, my sweet,' Ralph sniffed, lifting his chin and looking very determined.

'Bloody men,' I said, giving him a dirty look. 'Ah, sure, Ralph! The poor thing is unhappy, he may need a bit of comforting,' I said, looking at him while trying to keep a straight face.

'WHAT?' Ralph said, spinning on his heel, looking shocked at me.

'Well! Remember you and Mona Lisa, Madame bleedin Butterfly, the Soviah one! Did you not say the same thing to me when I was upset about her trying to get her claws into you?'

'Touché, darling!' he said, coming towards me as the penny dropped.

'Oh, well! I will be far away and well out of his reach,' I said, sobering up at the reality of what was happening to Ralph and me as he took me in his arms, making it look like he had proprietorial rights. Hmm, I thought. Pity about Jacques! But I wouldn't fancy being part of a squeeze in the middle between him and Soviah. One of us would end up hanged for murder. Anyway! He is Ralph's friend. I would not hurt Ralph for the world. I would rather go back to living as a professional virgin, haunted and hunted like a Carmelite nun. Fuck! Life might still have that mapped out for me. I could curl up inside myself, still hoping and waiting for Ralph to change his mind and marry me. I even read it in a book somewhere! Oh, yeah, Miss Havisham, out of your man Dickens, left sitting at the breakfast table in her wedding frock forty years later and he still never turned up! That's fucking me! I'll die of a broken heart, I sniffed, me eyes crossed in disgust getting that picture. Never! You just tried and failed! That's all, now it's over. Time to move on, see what's around the next corner.

EPILOGUE

'Yes, I reached for the moon and hit the stars, but a star shines its brightest just before it fades and dies. I found my Ralph, then lost him again,' I whispered sadly, looking back into the distance, getting the picture of my last sight of him at the airport. I went through passport control then stopped to look back at him. We both just stared. He looked haunted, mirroring what I felt inside. Neither of us waved. I lowered my head then saw him step on his heel, turn and march away with his back stiff and his head held high. I stared after him, seeing my whole world being taken away with him, leaving me once again with that old familiar haunted feeling of being cold, lost and lonely. I stood on, watching him fade away until I could see him no more. He was now swallowed up, lost in among the heavy crowd of airport strangers. Then I turned to look straight ahead, taking the loneliest walk of my life as I headed off to board that plane taking me back to Dublin and a life without Ralph.

Even now I could feel the terrible ache hitting me all over again. I will never get over him; there will never be another Ralph in my life. No, but I know now what the future holds, because I am sure of one thing. It is time for me to take another risk. So it is once more into the breach for me, yes, just once more. Because this is my last chance at making something real and positive of my life. The first time round was a shotgun wedding. That is one mistake I definitely won't be repeating. Sergei is going to find me a hard bargain. He won't get everything he wants – that is if he is still interested! Russian men are very dominant. They are powerful with it. It is deeply engrained in their psyche. In his society, men have their brute force and women have their subservient place behind the man. He alluded to that when he said he would not try to tame me. Hmm, that sends out a warning bell to be prepared for battle. Fine, I'll be ready. Sergei will have to be roped in straight from the beginning. There will be no ruling me!

It will be partners or the fastest banana boat back to Russia! I have now had a taste of the best. I know what life has to offer and I will keep going until I get it!

Jesus, Martha, you can be cold as a bloody fish. Yes! Why not? Life goes on. I can wear a business hat; men do it all the time. They fragment, put parts of themselves in boxes and move on to the business at hand. We women carry it all with us on a wave of emotion. That is why we miss nothing; we are more in tune than men. But I have gone through life without much love and it has made me very pragmatic. I too can batten down the hatches and move on in the interest of survival. Ralph will do that when he goes to the mission. He will switch off and all his energy will go into his work. Mine will go into building a life for my family. Making Sergei happy and hopefully our children. He will have my loyalty and commitment to that end. I won't be looking for hearts and flowers. I will settle for a solid man who will be a good father and a strong, reliable partner. That will be enough for me. Sergei, too, should have nothing to complain about.

'Taxi, miss?'

'Yes,' I said, coming through the airport doors and stepping back into the old familiar air of grey, dirty aul Dublin! I looked up at the sky, seeing heavily pregnant black clouds look treacherously close to dumping a bellyfull of rain down on my head, threatening to ruin my new look of chic sophistication.

'I'm home, Gawd help me,' I sighed, letting the taxi man hold the car door open as I fixed myself into the back seat. Then I nodded at my bags waiting for him on the footpath.

'Certainly, miss,' he said, looking very respectful as he picked up my fancy Gucci suitcases, with me giving off an air of moneyed respectability. At least I brought back something from France. A bit of French polish! I sniffed, as I looked back, trying to see out through the rain starting to pour down the window of the taxi as it pulled away from the kerb.

I had a sense of leaving something of myself behind. A woman who had reached for the moon and indeed hit the stars. For a brief time she had been deeply loved and cherished, basked in being adored as a woman. It had been a dream life of material plenty. Now that part of me is left forever in France. So, '*C'est la vie,*' I sighed sadly, turning my head back and taking in a deep breath, then looking straight ahead as I tightened my jaw.

Right, that was French living, now for a bit of Russian, I thought, feeling a smile lift my heart as I thought of Sergei. He's got one thing going for him: he's worked in the loony bin. That should come in handy when he rattles my cage and I lose the head. Good! I'll have my own private counsellor! He should be able to handle me. I need the kid-glove treatment. Lots of understanding and tender loving care. Then I'll be putty in his hands. Grand! Things are looking up. Oh, yes, life can definitely be a bowl of cherries!

could not be all things to all people anymore. She was not perfect. She just had to be Phyl Forster, a woman doing the best job she could. And getting on with her own life.

Mahoney leaned over and whispered in her ear, "Guess what?"

She leaned back and looked at him. "What?"

"I've made a reservation tonight at the Moulin de Mougins. Remember, I promised one day I'd take you there—see if their chicken is as good as mine?"

She put her head back and laughed, and then she kissed him. It was a happy kiss. "Mr. Long Shot," she said, remembering.

His eyes crinkled at the corners as he gave her that wide, mocking grin.

"That's me," he agreed, taking her hand and kissing her back.

She nibbled at a salad, and Brad did not seem to be hungry. He sat silently, drinking his whiskey, watching her.

Black clouds appeared over the sea, blocking out the sun, and a sudden strong wind whipped the waves into dark, foam-speckled mountains. She shivered, looking nervously at him in the deepening stormy dusk, wondering why he was so quiet. "Brad, I think I should leave in the morning," she said quickly. "You have been a wonderful host. Thank you for showing me the Kanoi Ranch and Kalani and for your generous offer. But I cannot accept. I just don't want any part of it."

He looked at her expressionlessly. Still, he said nothing, and Marie-Laure felt those warning prickles again. She thought apprehensively that even though Brad was looking at her, he didn't seem to be seeing her.

She got up and walked nervously to the edge of the gazebo. She leaned against the rail, looking out at the ocean, wishing she could think of something to say to break his strange silence. She turned to speak to him, to apologize again for her sudden departure. And then she saw the shotgun, lying on the chair behind him. It was a handsome weapon with a polished wooden stock ornamented with silver.

"That's a beautiful gun," she said, surprised she hadn't noticed it before. "But what do you shoot here?"

"*Predators,*" he said viciously. "Sit down, Marie-Laure Leconte."

There was a sudden whiff of danger in the air, as tangible as the aroma of the whiskey. She froze, staring at him.

"*I said, sit down.*"

There was an edge to his voice that made her obey. Her knees buckled, and she sank into the chair opposite him. "I'm sorry I can't stay any longer," she said, frightened, "but it's better this way. My father was right. I should not have come—"

"Be quiet," he snapped impatiently, "and listen to me, you silly girl." Her brown eyes widened with shock. "Of course you are right," he said in a remote voice. "You should not have come here. And your father should not have come here.

Archer Kane should have killed him at the Villa Mimosa when he killed his mother. It would have been the best thing for all of us." He smiled coldly as he took another gulp of his drink. "And it would have saved me a lot of trouble."

"What do you mean?" Marie-Laure pushed back her chair. She got to her feet and edged nervously away from him. The Doberman gave a low growl and it glowered menacingly.

"You were stupid and silly to think I would give you even the smallest fraction of the Kanoi Ranch. You have seen it. You know that it belongs to the Kane family. That it was our hard work, our intelligence, our dedication, *our superiority* that made this place. All Marie-Antoinette Leconte and her son contributed was money. Not another goddamn thing. They didn't build this house; they didn't create Kalani; they didn't plant the avenue of banyans and build that little ranch house and the medical facility and the church and the houses for the workers. They did nothing, Marie-Laure."

He fell silent again, and she looked appeasingly at him. "I know that, Brad," she said quickly. "You have done wonders—"

"Jack was right," he said, as though she had never spoken. "He said he should have killed the Monkey that night on the island when they had the fight. He should have stuck that knife into his heart and been done with it. He regretted it all his life. He said to me, 'I know in my bones he is still out there somewhere, like a coiled rattlesnake waiting to strike. He will try to take that fortune from us one day, son. He will want to take everything the Kane family has worked for all these years: our sweat and toil, our land, our heritage. *Our name*. Make no mistake, he will come to claim his fortune, and when he does, we must be ready to act. Quickly and without mercy.'"

Marie-Laure drew a sharp frightened breath as Brad slammed down the empty glass. He stood up, towering over her.

"My father is dead," she cried. "He never wanted anything to do with Kalani and the Kanoi Ranch. He never

wanted to come back here. He didn't want anything from the Kane family."

"But *you* are not dead, Marie-Laure. And one day *you* will get to thinking about things. About this rich ranch and this beautiful house and Kalani and all that money. And you will go to a smart attorney with your story and your claim. You'll want more than half then, Marie-Laure. You will want it all. And you see, I cannot let that happen."

"You're crazy," she cried, stepping backward away from him. "I told you I don't want anything from you. I don't want the Leconte name ever to be associated with the Kanes. My father was right about you. You live above the law; you have no morals; your grandfather killed his wife to get his hands on her money, and he would have killed Johnny, too, when he was eighteen. I should never have come here. I should not have listened to you. I should have trusted my father."

Purple lightning zigzagged suddenly across the midnight dark sky. "It's too late now," Brad said. He leaned against the rail with his arms folded, watching her under hooded lids.

"I was going to leave tomorrow," she said, edging toward the steps. "But I think it's better if I go now."

His cold, bitter laugh followed her as she hurried down the steps, freezing the blood in her veins. She started to run. She heard Brad shout a command, and she glanced over her shoulder. "Kill," he cried again. And then she saw the Doberman, a fleet black arrow in the stormy darkness, racing toward her. She screamed and flung up her arms as the powerful dog launched itself at her. She felt a searing pain as its jaws clamped down on her arm. Then she heard Wong shout.

"Down, Makana," he yelled at the dog, and ran toward her. "Drop it. Down, you bastard dog."

The dog let go on command, and Wong flung himself between her and the animal.

"Kill," Brad yelled again, running toward them through the dark and rain with the shotgun in his hands.

The Doberman grabbed the old Chinese man by the throat and sank its teeth deep into him.

"Oh, God, oh, God," Marie-Laure screamed. The old man was on the ground, and the dog was tearing his face to pieces. There was blood everywhere, spurting from the big artery in his neck. A shot rang out, and the dog lifted its bloody mouth from the old man. It stared for a moment at her, then gave a thin, unearthly wail. Its burning red-brown eyes glazed over, its legs crumpled, and it slid in slow motion to the ground, beside Wong's body.

Fear lent wings to Marie-Laure's feet, and she took off down the slippery path, waiting for the shot that she knew would send her into eternity, too. Nothing happened, and she glanced back over her shoulder. Brad was standing in the pouring rain over the two bodies. She saw him throw the shotgun aside and kneel beside them. "Oh, God," she heard his anguished cry, "look what they have done now." He raised his head to the sky, howling his agony.

She fled down the path toward the house. She had to get out of here as fast as she could . . . she would go to the police . . . tell them her story . . . tell them he was a madman. . . . Even as she thought it, she knew it would not work. They would look at Brad Kane, the gentleman rancher who owned a good part of the islands, whose family had lived here for generations. And they would look at her, a hysterical young woman with some wild story about an attack, and she knew whose side they would take.

She started running down the drive to the gates; then she remembered that her money and her credit cards were in her room. She dithered helplessly; she could not get far without them.

She looked back toward the house and saw the servants running, heard their cries of distress and guessed she had a few minutes' grace. She ran to her room, grabbed her pocketbook, and fled back through the gardens down to the gates. The guard had heard the shot. He had run to see what the trouble was, leaving the gates unguarded. She pressed the electronic device that opened them and slid through. Then she

began to run down the hill, jogging steadily in the rain, her heart thudding in her throat.

It seemed ages before she saw a gas station, and she began to slow down. She checked her watch. She had been running for twenty minutes. He wouldn't dare come after her in a public place, she thought, fumbling in her bag for a coin.

She went to the pay phone and called a cab. Then she went into the washroom and cleaned herself up. Her arm was bleeding, and she washed it, then took off her T-shirt and wrapped it around the wound. She put on a light sweater to hold the improvised bandage in place. She rinsed her face with cold water and combed her wet hair and then went back outside to wait for the cab.

Her throat was parched from running, and she got a Coke from the machine and sipped it, still trembling inside. She thought of Brad's grieving face as he looked down at Wong and his wild, agonized howl. And she remembered the dying dog, its eyes glazing over, sliding in slow motion to the ground. She knew that Wong had saved her life, and because of him, Brad would not be coming after her. Not yet.

The cab circled into the court, and she ran toward it. She climbed in thankfully and leaned back against the cushions.

The next United flight left in two hours. Two hours! It stretched in front of her like eternity. She bought a ticket and hurried from the counter, hiding herself in the crowd, watching, waiting. But there was still no sign of Brad Kane when at last her flight was called.

She breathed a sigh of relief when she finally boarded the plane and took her seat. Now she was safe.

And then she arrived in San Francisco. And Brad was there, waiting for her.

Now, sitting on the terrace of her family's beautiful old farm in Provence, Bea wondered how she could have ever thought she would be safe again. Brad Kane was obsessed with the Lecontes. He was crazy. She had not realized how fast he would act. And how silently. She had not known that he was in

the Gulfstream and on his way to San Francisco before she had even boarded her United flight. She could not have known that he was a man who could buy anything he wanted and that he would know where to go to get what he needed—the syringe with the fast-acting anesthetic that would safely put her out for hours, for instance—so he could kill her and make it look like an accident. And then the Kanoi Ranch would finally be only his.

She felt his presence before she saw him. There had been no sound; he was just suddenly there, a deeper shadow against the blackness. She saw the glow of his cigarette as he put it to his lips.

"So, Marie-Laure," he said in that quiet, flat tone, "we meet again."

Poochie bristled and lurched to his feet. He growled and showed his teeth warningly.

Brad laughed. "I hope you haven't brought that mutt here to defend you. Somehow I don't think he's the right breed."

"Where are the children?" Bea asked quickly. She was amazed that her voice sounded so calm. Now that she was seeing her killer face-to-face, she felt a hatred so intense it shocked her. But she had to keep a veneer of calm if she was to win. She had to know he had kept his word and they were all right.

"I kept my promise," he said. "They are in a taxi en route to the Villa Mimosa."

She peered warily into the dark, tracking his hand with the cigarette. "How do I know that's true?"

He shrugged indifferently. "I guess you will just have to trust me, Marie-Laure."

She saw him crush out the cigarette, and then he walked toward her. She put her hand in her pocket, gripping the sharp little kitchen knife. The sweat of fear stuck her hair to her head, and she trembled with hate for him and for Jack and Archer. They had gotten away with their crimes, but she wasn't

going to allow Brad to get away with his. Not again. She would kill him first. She sobbed as she realized what she was thinking. Brad Kane was turning her into a killer, a murderer. No better than all the Kanes.

Then she saw the gun in his hand. Poochie gave another deeper growl. She could see his bared fangs gleaming, and she gripped his collar more tightly.

"We are going for a short ride, Marie-Laure," Brad said, ignoring the dog. "A little sight-seeing. Pity it's so dark, but then you must know these roads like the back of your hand." He took her arm and marched her to her car. He held the door open and indicated with the gun for her to get into the driver's seat. Poochie got in next to her, whining, not understanding.

Brad climbed into the back and said, "Okay, start driving. Make a left at the T junction. You remember, where it begins to climb steeply."

Marie-Laure sensed the gun leveled at her head. She started the car and did as he said. Of course, she knew the place he meant. It was a lookout point where she had spent many a lazy afternoon, scanning the peaceful valley hundreds of feet below, watching the cars crawling like ants up the steep roads to the beautiful *village perché* on the opposite side; listening to the summer sounds of the birds and the crickets; feeling the sun-warmed rocks beneath her as she lay there, admiring the poppy fields spread like a red carpet that changed with the months to acres of lavender or sunflowers, and vines ripening under the hot sun, readying for the fall harvest. The lookout point was an even more precipitous drop than Mitchell's Ravine.

Her hands shook as she drove slowly up the hill, casting around wildly for a way to escape. She still had the knife, but it was no match for his gun. Goddammit, she told herself savagely, she wasn't drugged this time; she would fight for her life. . . . She was not just going to let him push her over the edge again. . . . He would have to shoot her first. . . .

It suddenly occurred to her that Brad could have shot her

just now on the terrace, if he had wanted to. She had been a sitting duck. He could have saved himself all this trouble. But he had not. He didn't want to shoot her. That's why he'd had the Doberman attack her and why he had pushed her over Mitchell's Ravine. Because he didn't want it to look like murder. He still wanted it to look like an accident.

She stopped the car at the top of the road. "Drive to the edge," he commanded. She did as he said, then switched off the engine, waiting. Brad did not make a move, did not say a word. The silence was deafening. She imagined the gun pointing at her head, but now she was sure he did not want to use it. The familiar night sounds began to penetrate her consciousness: the croak of tree frogs; the scurrying of nocturnal animals; the startled whir of disturbed birds. Somewhere, in the valley far below, she saw a car's headlights. She watched hopefully as they flickered, then disappeared. And then nothing. She was alone with Brad Kane.

She heard Poochie whine as Brad got out of the car. In the glimmering darkness she could just make out the outline of the gun, pointed at her.

"Why are you doing this?" she screamed, suddenly needing to understand. "I told you I don't want the ranch. I don't want the money. I don't want anything you've got—"

"You still don't see it, do you?" he said. "All his life Jack was waiting for the Monkey to come back and steal his land, to take his birthright from him. I'm only protecting my interests, keeping Kanoi for the Kanes. I cannot allow you or any future Lecontes to jeopardize that. It is, my dear Marie-Laure, time to redress the balance of things.

"I think this is the best way," he said, and she could see he was smiling at her. "We have to make sure this time, don't we?"

He opened the car door. He reached in and released the hand brake, started the engine, and put it in gear. Brad held her back with one arm as he reached for the accelerator. With a terrified scream Marie-Laure suddenly wrenched herself free. She hurled herself out the other door and Poochie leaped

out after her, barking frantically. She lay stunned on the rough stony grass as the car lurched toward the precipice. It teetered for a few seconds on the edge, then slid over gently. She heard the terrible shattering of glass and the great rending of steel as it bounced from rock to rock down the steep slope—and then the huge explosion as it burst into flames. She would have been in that inferno if Brad had had his way.

Fear brought her to her feet, but Brad grabbed her from behind. He locked his arms around her and forced her toward the edge of the precipice. She screamed, endless throat-tearing screams, digging in her heels, clinging to the thorny branches in their path, scrabbling for a foothold on the loose stones. She had to get the knife, it was her only chance. She had to kill him before he could kill her. She heard Poochie's wild snarl and saw his black silhouette against the red glow of the inferno as the big dog hurled himself at her attacker, taking Brad by surprise and knocking both of them to the ground.

Marie-Laure rolled away and scrambled quickly to her feet. She saw Brad put the gun to the dog's side, and she kicked it out of his hand. She reached down to grab it, but he was too quick for her. He snatched it, then smashed it savagely down on the dog's head. Poochie gave a high-pitched yelp and fell back. Marie-Laure cried out with fear and anger as Brad grabbed her foot and dragged her once more toward the edge.

She kicked out at him and rolled away, but he was on top of her in a second. Then he was banging her head against the stones. The pain was intense, and she knew it was never going to stop. She was slipping away into unconsciousness, and she fought it. She couldn't let him win; she *would not.* . . . Somewhere in the back of her brain, over the noise of her own screams, she became aware of a new sound. Then suddenly there were lights and other people.

Brad was up on his feet in a minute, pulling her with him, holding her in front of him as a shield. Groggily she made out the half circle of gendarmes. Their guns were aimed at them, and dimly she heard Nick's voice shouting to her to "hold on."

And then she slid backward down the familiar black tunnel into unconsciousness.

"Brad," Phyl called softly. "Brad, it's me."

He peered into the lights, puzzled. "Rebecca," he said in a harsh whisper. "What are you doing here? I thought you were waiting for me in San Francisco. We were going to Kalani. Remember?"

Phyl's numb heart felt as though it were no longer part of her body as she looked at him. This was not the charming lover she had known. It was not the urbane man of the world, the rich, handsome rancher, who had it all. She was looking at a stranger.

Taking a deep breath, she walked into the circle of light created by the cars' headlights. Brad was still holding Bea's limp body, and she could not tell if she was dead or alive.

"Let her go, Brad," she said softly, close to him.

His pale eyes searched hers as he said, "I had to do it. You know that, don't you? You, of all people, must understand."

"I do, Brad. I understand. But I think I know a better way."

She was shaking with terror. All it would take was one quick thrust and Bea would be over the edge.

Brad looked at the surrounding gendarmes. He seemed suddenly to come to reality. "It's too late now, isn't it?" he asked, looking at her searchingly.

She nodded, unable to speak. He was changing in front of her eyes, from the cold-blooded, mad hunter with his prey back to the easy, charming man she had known.

"And too late for us," he added softly. "If I hurt you, I'm sorry, Phyl. You were the only woman I might have loved."

He pushed Marie-Laure toward her. Then he put the gun to his head. His wild, mad eyes met Phyl's for a split second. "You traitor, Rebecca," he said viciously as he pulled the trigger.

Her own screams echoed in her ears as Brad's handsome blond head exploded into a thousand bloody fragments and he spun over the edge into the abyss.

fronted the ghosts of her father's life. She believed he would have approved of that.

She went back to her room and found a maid unpacking her bag, and she was forced to smile when she saw her T-shirts, a dress, a skirt, and a couple of shirts, hanging for-lornly in the vast closet. Her simple things were just not up to the grandeur of their surroundings. Rebecca's closet needed haute couture and hatboxes and Vuitton steamer trunks, not an old green canvas duffel from L.L. Bean.

She put on a bathing suit and swam laps in the magnifi-cent pool. Then she lay on a beautiful bamboo chaise under a shady umbrella, sipping iced tea brought by another slippered Chinese servant, and thinking about Brad.

He was behaving very well toward her, she told herself. He couldn't be more hospitable, more sympathetic, more gen-erous, offering her half the Kane ranch. Then why did she still have this sneaking feeling that something was wrong? *Why* was he being so nice? She kept remembering what her father had told her about all the Kanes: that the only thing that mattered in their lives was the Kanoi Ranch and their name. Nothing else counted. They had even killed to keep it.

Then *why* would Brad Kane suddenly offer to give her half the Kane ranch? It was like offering her a half share in his heart.

Suddenly uneasy, she sipped the iced tea. Brad Kane was a hardheaded businessman. He was not a philanthropist or a born-again Christian or a madman. It just wasn't in character. He knew exactly what he was doing. If he wanted to give her back part of the ranch, he must want something in return.

Her father's words of warning repeated themselves end-lessly in her head, she could hear his voice telling her, "Let sleeping dogs lie, in case they turn around and bite you . . . again." Something was wrong. And she suddenly didn't want to stay around and find out what it was. She had to get out of there.

She ran back through the paradise gardens to Rebecca's room. She repacked her bag, took a shower, then put on a

white T-shirt and jeans and her red sandals and went out onto the terrace to wait for Brad.

It was twelve-thirty when he returned. "It's good to see a pretty girl waiting for me when I get home," he said breezily, pouring himself a whiskey.

He offered her one, and she shook her head, wondering if she could be wrong after all. He looked so cool and handsome and suntanned and . . . rich. He looked as though he owned the world. *Then why,* that nagging little voice asked again, *does he want to give half of it to you?*

"You're very quiet, Marie-Laure," he said, watching her.

"I'm tired. I did a lot of swimming . . . laps," she replied evasively.

"I thought we would have lunch at the gazebo," he said. She could see a pretty white wooden folly at the edge of the cliff. He took her hand and pulled her to her feet, sliding a friendly arm around her shoulders as they strolled toward it with the Doberman at their heels.

The gazebo was built like a Hawaiian pavilion, a white wooden octagon, open on all sides, with a curved thatched roof that came to a point at the top. Heavy canvas curtains were swagged back between the posts ready to shut out the wind, and the view was tremendous: straight down the steep black cliffs to the rocks and the great, high-crested Pacific rollers gliding majestically toward them.

Wong was arranging dishes on a buffet, but Brad dismissed him, saying they would serve themselves.

For a moment, looking at the beauty all around her, Marie-Laure was tempted to believe his offer. These lovely gardens filled with heavy-scented tropical blossoms, the emerald lawns, the rolling ocean view. All she had to do was say the word, and half of this could be hers. But when she glanced at Brad, she caught a strange expression on his face, a distance and coldness that sent warning prickles up her spine.

"Come, let's eat," he said, with a quick smile. His expression was neutral again, and she told herself that she was just being silly, that she had just imagined that icy look.

~ *36* ~

*M*ahoney arrived at the Villa Mimosa early the next morning. They were sitting on the terrace, sipping lemonade, looking out over the sloping lawns, at the towering cedars and the needle cypresses pointing into the clear blue sky, out to the tranquil view of the Mediterranean whose color had once made Johnny Leconte redefine the word "azure."

Scott and Julie had been found frightened but unharmed, locked in the trunk of Brad's car, though Mahoney had no doubt he would have killed them, too. Brad would have wanted no witnesses.

Bea—or Marie-Laure, as they must now learn to call her—had her head wrapped once more in bandages, and she said wryly she was beginning to like the shaved-head look. She was badly cut and bruised, but it was nothing compared with the relief in her heart, now that she knew who she was and the fear was finally gone.

She was just glad she didn't have the stiff white plastic collar that Poochie had to wear to stop him from scratching the row of stitches on the back of his own poor shaved head. He was lying happily at her feet, sated with as much steak as a dog

could eat. And Nick was holding her hand as she told them the story of what happened to her that day at Diamond Head and how Brad had caught up with her at the San Francisco airport.

"It's all over now," Phyl said comfortingly as they watched the children racing joyously across the lawn to the pool. "You have to learn to forget, to get on with your life."

Marie-Laure smiled at her affectionately. "It's thanks to all of you I'm still alive. And I intend to stay that way." She glanced around at her home, at her children, her man, her friends. "After all," she said, "I've got a lot to live for."

Phyl leaned back against the cushions. Her eyes were still swollen from the tears she had shed, and she looked pale and exhausted.

"You could use a touch of that red lipstick," Mahoney said with a grin, pulling a chair companionably next to her and pouring himself a glass of lemonade.

She glared at him, but he thought it was a weak glare, none of her usual flashing-blue-eyed stuff.

"The U.S. cavalry to the rescue," she said sarcastically. "Just a bit too late."

"Yeah. Even the Concorde wasn't fast enough. And they haven't yet found a way to beam us over, like Captain Kirk. But the FBI and Interpol have those magic computers that keep us all in touch. So the cavalry did get there in time after all." He threw her a serious glance and added softly, "Thank God."

"But how did you find out it was Brad?"

"Two and two. I should have caught it earlier, when I heard Hawaii mentioned. A private plane piloted by Brad Kane came in from Hawaii that night." He shrugged. "I should have known."

"No man is infallible," Phyl said gently, not wanting him to feel guilty.

"And no woman," he replied, meeting her eyes. "Maybe you should remember that."

He held her eyes for a long moment. She knew he meant what had happened to her baby, to Marie-Laure, to Brad. She

could not be all things to all people anymore. She was not perfect. She just had to be Phyl Forster, a woman doing the best job she could. And getting on with her own life.

Mahoney leaned over and whispered in her ear, "Guess what?"

She leaned back and looked at him. "What?"

"I've made a reservation tonight at the Moulin de Mougins. Remember, I promised one day I'd take you there— see if their chicken is as good as mine?"

She put her head back and laughed, and then she kissed him. It was a happy kiss. "Mr. Long Shot," she said, remembering.

His eyes crinkled at the corners as he gave her that wide, mocking grin.

"That's me," he agreed, taking her hand and kissing her back.

She nibbled at a salad, and Brad did not seem to be hungry. He sat silently, drinking his whiskey, watching her.

Black clouds appeared over the sea, blocking out the sun, and a sudden strong wind whipped the waves into dark, foam-speckled mountains. She shivered, looking nervously at him in the deepening stormy dusk, wondering why he was so quiet. "Brad, I think I should leave in the morning," she said quickly. "You have been a wonderful host. Thank you for showing me the Kanoi Ranch and Kalani and for your generous offer. But I cannot accept. I just don't want any part of it."

He looked at her expressionlessly. Still, he said nothing, and Marie-Laure felt those warning prickles again. She thought apprehensively that even though Brad was looking at her, he didn't seem to be seeing her.

She got up and walked nervously to the edge of the gazebo. She leaned against the rail, looking out at the ocean, wishing she could think of something to say to break his strange silence. She turned to speak to him, to apologize again for her sudden departure. And then she saw the shotgun, lying on the chair behind him. It was a handsome weapon with a polished wooden stock ornamented with silver.

"That's a beautiful gun," she said, surprised she hadn't noticed it before. "But what do you shoot here?"

"*Predators,*" he said viciously. "Sit down, Marie-Laure Leconte."

There was a sudden whiff of danger in the air, as tangible as the aroma of the whiskey. She froze, staring at him.

"*I said, sit down.*"

There was an edge to his voice that made her obey. Her knees buckled, and she sank into the chair opposite him. "I'm sorry I can't stay any longer," she said, frightened, "but it's better this way. My father was right. I should not have come—"

"Be quiet," he snapped impatiently, "and listen to me, you silly girl." Her brown eyes widened with shock. "Of course you are right," he said in a remote voice. "You should not have come here. And your father should not have come here.

Archer Kane should have killed him at the Villa Mimosa when he killed his mother. It would have been the best thing for all of us." He smiled coldly as he took another gulp of his drink. "And it would have saved me a lot of trouble."

"What do you mean?" Marie-Laure pushed back her chair. She got to her feet and edged nervously away from him. The Doberman gave a low growl and it glowered menacingly.

"You were stupid and silly to think I would give you even the smallest fraction of the Kanoi Ranch. You have seen it. You know that it belongs to the Kane family. That it was our hard work, our intelligence, our dedication, *our superiority* that made this place. All Marie-Antoinette Leconte and her son contributed was money. Not another goddamn thing. They didn't build this house; they didn't create Kalani; they didn't plant the avenue of banyans and build that little ranch house and the medical facility and the church and the houses for the workers. They did nothing, Marie-Laure."

He fell silent again, and she looked appeasingly at him. "I know that, Brad," she said quickly. "You have done wonders—"

"Jack was right," he said, as though she had never spoken. "He said he should have killed the Monkey that night on the island when they had the fight. He should have stuck that knife into his heart and been done with it. He regretted it all his life. He said to me, 'I know in my bones he is still out there somewhere, like a coiled rattlesnake waiting to strike. He will try to take that fortune from us one day, son. He will want to take everything the Kane family has worked for all these years: our sweat and toil, our land, our heritage. *Our name.* Make no mistake, he will come to claim his fortune, and when he does, we must be ready to act. Quickly and without mercy.'"

Marie-Laure drew a sharp frightened breath as Brad slammed down the empty glass. He stood up, towering over her.

"My father is dead," she cried. "He never wanted anything to do with Kalani and the Kanoi Ranch. He never

wanted to come back here. He didn't want anything from the Kane family."

"But *you* are not dead, Marie-Laure. And one day *you* will get to thinking about things. About this rich ranch and this beautiful house and Kalani and all that money. And you will go to a smart attorney with your story and your claim. You'll want more than half then, Marie-Laure. You will want it all. And you see, I cannot let that happen."

"You're crazy," she cried, stepping backward away from him. "I told you I don't want anything from you. I don't want the Leconte name ever to be associated with the Kanes. My father was right about you. You live above the law; you have no morals; your grandfather killed his wife to get his hands on her money, and he would have killed Johnny, too, when he was eighteen. I should never have come here. I should not have listened to you. I should have trusted my father."

Purple lightning zigzagged suddenly across the midnight dark sky. "It's too late now," Brad said. He leaned against the rail with his arms folded, watching her under hooded lids.

"I was going to leave tomorrow," she said, edging toward the steps. "But I think it's better if I go now."

His cold, bitter laugh followed her as she hurried down the steps, freezing the blood in her veins. She started to run. She heard Brad shout a command, and she glanced over her shoulder. "Kill," he cried again. And then she saw the Doberman, a fleet black arrow in the stormy darkness, racing toward her. She screamed and flung up her arms as the powerful dog launched itself at her. She felt a searing pain as its jaws clamped down on her arm. Then she heard Wong shout.

"Down, Makana," he yelled at the dog, and ran toward her. "Drop it. Down, you bastard dog."

The dog let go on command, and Wong flung himself between her and the animal.

"Kill," Brad yelled again, running toward them through the dark and rain with the shotgun in his hands.

The Doberman grabbed the old Chinese man by the throat and sank its teeth deep into him.

"Oh, God, oh, God," Marie-Laure screamed. The old man was on the ground, and the dog was tearing his face to pieces. There was blood everywhere, spurting from the big artery in his neck. A shot rang out, and the dog lifted its bloody mouth from the old man. It stared for a moment at her, then gave a thin, unearthly wail. Its burning red-brown eyes glazed over, its legs crumpled, and it slid in slow motion to the ground, beside Wong's body.

Fear lent wings to Marie-Laure's feet, and she took off down the slippery path, waiting for the shot that she knew would send her into eternity, too. Nothing happened, and she glanced back over her shoulder. Brad was standing in the pouring rain over the two bodies. She saw him throw the shotgun aside and kneel beside them. "Oh, God," she heard his anguished cry, "look what they have done now." He raised his head to the sky, howling his agony.

She fled down the path toward the house. She had to get out of here as fast as she could . . . she would go to the police . . . tell them her story . . . tell them he was a madman. . . . Even as she thought it, she knew it would not work. They would look at Brad Kane, the gentleman rancher who owned a good part of the islands, whose family had lived here for generations. And they would look at her, a hysterical young woman with some wild story about an attack, and she knew whose side they would take.

She started running down the drive to the gates; then she remembered that her money and her credit cards were in her room. She dithered helplessly; she could not get far without them.

She looked back toward the house and saw the servants running, heard their cries of distress and guessed she had a few minutes' grace. She ran to her room, grabbed her pocketbook, and fled back through the gardens down to the gates. The guard had heard the shot. He had run to see what the trouble was, leaving the gates unguarded. She pressed the electronic device that opened them and slid through. Then she

began to run down the hill, jogging steadily in the rain, her heart thudding in her throat.

It seemed ages before she saw a gas station, and she began to slow down. She checked her watch. She had been running for twenty minutes. He wouldn't dare come after her in a public place, she thought, fumbling in her bag for a coin.

She went to the pay phone and called a cab. Then she went into the washroom and cleaned herself up. Her arm was bleeding, and she washed it, then took off her T-shirt and wrapped it around the wound. She put on a light sweater to hold the improvised bandage in place. She rinsed her face with cold water and combed her wet hair and then went back outside to wait for the cab.

Her throat was parched from running, and she got a Coke from the machine and sipped it, still trembling inside. She thought of Brad's grieving face as he looked down at Wong and his wild, agonized howl. And she remembered the dying dog, its eyes glazing over, sliding in slow motion to the ground. She knew that Wong had saved her life, and because of him, Brad would not be coming after her. Not yet.

The cab circled into the court, and she ran toward it. She climbed in thankfully and leaned back against the cushions.

The next United flight left in two hours. Two hours! It stretched in front of her like eternity. She bought a ticket and hurried from the counter, hiding herself in the crowd, watching, waiting. But there was still no sign of Brad Kane when at last her flight was called.

She breathed a sigh of relief when she finally boarded the plane and took her seat. Now she was safe.

And then she arrived in San Francisco. And Brad was there, waiting for her.

Now, sitting on the terrace of her family's beautiful old farm in Provence, Bea wondered how she could have ever thought she would be safe again. Brad Kane was obsessed with the Lecontes. He was crazy. She had not realized how fast he would act. And how silently. She had not known that he was in

the Gulfstream and on his way to San Francisco before she had even boarded her United flight. She could not have known that he was a man who could buy anything he wanted and that he would know where to go to get what he needed—the syringe with the fast-acting anesthetic that would safely put her out for hours, for instance—so he could kill her and make it look like an accident. And then the Kanoi Ranch would finally be only his.

She felt his presence before she saw him. There had been no sound; he was just suddenly there, a deeper shadow against the blackness. She saw the glow of his cigarette as he put it to his lips.

"So, Marie-Laure," he said in that quiet, flat tone, "we meet again."

Poochie bristled and lurched to his feet. He growled and showed his teeth warningly.

Brad laughed. "I hope you haven't brought that mutt here to defend you. Somehow I don't think he's the right breed."

"Where are the children?" Bea asked quickly. She was amazed that her voice sounded so calm. Now that she was seeing her killer face-to-face, she felt a hatred so intense it shocked her. But she had to keep a veneer of calm if she was to win. She had to know he had kept his word and they were all right.

"I kept my promise," he said. "They are in a taxi en route to the Villa Mimosa."

She peered warily into the dark, tracking his hand with the cigarette. "How do I know that's true?"

He shrugged indifferently. "I guess you will just have to trust me, Marie-Laure."

She saw him crush out the cigarette, and then he walked toward her. She put her hand in her pocket, gripping the sharp little kitchen knife. The sweat of fear stuck her hair to her head, and she trembled with hate for him and for Jack and Archer. They had gotten away with their crimes, but she wasn't

going to allow Brad to get away with his. Not again. She would kill him first. She sobbed as she realized what she was thinking. Brad Kane was turning her into a killer, a murderer. No better than all the Kanes.

Then she saw the gun in his hand. Poochie gave another deeper growl. She could see his bared fangs gleaming, and she gripped his collar more tightly.

"We are going for a short ride, Marie-Laure," Brad said, ignoring the dog. "A little sight-seeing. Pity it's so dark, but then you must know these roads like the back of your hand." He took her arm and marched her to her car. He held the door open and indicated with the gun for her to get into the driver's seat. Poochie got in next to her, whining, not understanding.

Brad climbed into the back and said, "Okay, start driving. Make a left at the T junction. You remember, where it begins to climb steeply."

Marie-Laure sensed the gun leveled at her head. She started the car and did as he said. Of course, she knew the place he meant. It was a lookout point where she had spent many a lazy afternoon, scanning the peaceful valley hundreds of feet below, watching the cars crawling like ants up the steep roads to the beautiful *village perché* on the opposite side; listening to the summer sounds of the birds and the crickets; feeling the sun-warmed rocks beneath her as she lay there, admiring the poppy fields spread like a red carpet that changed with the months to acres of lavender or sunflowers, and vines ripening under the hot sun, readying for the fall harvest. The lookout point was an even more precipitous drop than Mitchell's Ravine.

Her hands shook as she drove slowly up the hill, casting around wildly for a way to escape. She still had the knife, but it was no match for his gun. Goddammit, she told herself savagely, she wasn't drugged this time; she would fight for her life. . . . She was not just going to let him push her over the edge again. . . . He would have to shoot her first. . . .

It suddenly occurred to her that Brad could have shot her

just now on the terrace, if he had wanted to. She had been a
sitting duck. He could have saved himself all this trouble. But
he had not. He didn't want to shoot her. That's why he'd had
the Doberman attack her and why he had pushed her over
Mitchell's Ravine. Because he didn't want it to look like murder. He still wanted it to look like an accident.

She stopped the car at the top of the road. "Drive to the
edge," he commanded. She did as he said, then switched off
the engine, waiting. Brad did not make a move, did not say a
word. The silence was deafening. She imagined the gun pointing at her head, but now she was sure he did not want to use it.
The familiar night sounds began to penetrate her consciousness: the croak of tree frogs; the scurrying of nocturnal animals; the startled whir of disturbed birds. Somewhere, in the
valley far below, she saw a car's headlights. She watched hopefully as they flickered, then disappeared. And then nothing.
She was alone with Brad Kane.

She heard Poochie whine as Brad got out of the car. In the
glimmering darkness she could just make out the outline of the
gun, pointed at her.

"Why are you doing this?" she screamed, suddenly needing to understand. "I told you I don't want the ranch. I don't
want the money. I don't want anything you've got—"

"You still don't see it, do you?" he said. "All his life Jack
was waiting for the Monkey to come back and steal his land, to
take his birthright from him. I'm only protecting my interests,
keeping Kanoi for the Kanes. I cannot allow you or any future
Lecontes to jeopardize that. It is, my dear Marie-Laure, time
to redress the balance of things.

"I think this is the best way," he said, and she could see he
was smiling at her. "We have to make sure this time, don't
we?"

He opened the car door. He reached in and released the
hand brake, started the engine, and put it in gear. Brad held
her back with one arm as he reached for the accelerator. With
a terrified scream Marie-Laure suddenly wrenched herself
free. She hurled herself out the other door and Poochie leaped

out after her, barking frantically. She lay stunned on the rough stony grass as the car lurched toward the precipice. It teetered for a few seconds on the edge, then slid over gently. She heard the terrible shattering of glass and the great rending of steel as it bounced from rock to rock down the steep slope—and then the huge explosion as it burst into flames. She would have been in that inferno if Brad had had his way.

Fear brought her to her feet, but Brad grabbed her from behind. He locked his arms around her and forced her toward the edge of the precipice. She screamed, endless throat-tearing screams, digging in her heels, clinging to the thorny branches in their path, scrabbling for a foothold on the loose stones. She had to get the knife, it was her only chance. She had to kill him before he could kill her. She heard Poochie's wild snarl and saw his black silhouette against the red glow of the inferno as the big dog hurled himself at her attacker, taking Brad by surprise and knocking both of them to the ground.

Marie-Laure rolled away and scrambled quickly to her feet. She saw Brad put the gun to the dog's side, and she kicked it out of his hand. She reached down to grab it, but he was too quick for her. He snatched it, then smashed it savagely down on the dog's head. Poochie gave a high-pitched yelp and fell back. Marie-Laure cried out with fear and anger as Brad grabbed her foot and dragged her once more toward the edge.

She kicked out at him and rolled away, but he was on top of her in a second. Then he was banging her head against the stones. The pain was intense, and she knew it was never going to stop. She was slipping away into unconsciousness, and she fought it. She couldn't let him win; she *would not*. . . . Somewhere in the back of her brain, over the noise of her own screams, she became aware of a new sound. Then suddenly there were lights and other people.

Brad was up on his feet in a minute, pulling her with him, holding her in front of him as a shield. Groggily she made out the half circle of gendarmes. Their guns were aimed at them, and dimly she heard Nick's voice shouting to her to "hold on."

And then she slid backward down the familiar black tunnel into unconsciousness.

"Brad," Phyl called softly. "Brad, it's me."

He peered into the lights, puzzled. "Rebecca," he said in a harsh whisper. "What are you doing here? I thought you were waiting for me in San Francisco. We were going to Kalani. Remember?"

Phyl's numb heart felt as though it were no longer part of her body as she looked at him. This was not the charming lover she had known. It was not the urbane man of the world, the rich, handsome rancher, who had it all. She was looking at a stranger.

Taking a deep breath, she walked into the circle of light created by the cars' headlights. Brad was still holding Bea's limp body, and she could not tell if she was dead or alive.

"Let her go, Brad," she said softly, close to him.

His pale eyes searched hers as he said, "I had to do it. You know that, don't you? You, of all people, must understand."

"I do, Brad. I understand. But I think I know a better way."

She was shaking with terror. All it would take was one quick thrust and Bea would be over the edge.

Brad looked at the surrounding gendarmes. He seemed suddenly to come to reality. "It's too late now, isn't it?" he asked, looking at her searchingly.

She nodded, unable to speak. He was changing in front of her eyes, from the cold-blooded, mad hunter with his prey back to the easy, charming man she had known.

"And too late for us," he added softly. "If I hurt you, I'm sorry, Phyl. You were the only woman I might have loved."

He pushed Marie-Laure toward her. Then he put the gun to his head. His wild, mad eyes met Phyl's for a split second. "You traitor, Rebecca," he said viciously as he pulled the trigger.

Her own screams echoed in her ears as Brad's handsome blond head exploded into a thousand bloody fragments and he spun over the edge into the abyss.

~ 36 ~

Mahoney arrived at the Villa Mimosa early the next morning. They were sitting on the terrace, sipping lemonade, looking out over the sloping lawns, at the towering cedars and the needle cypresses pointing into the clear blue sky, out to the tranquil view of the Mediterranean whose color had once made Johnny Leconte redefine the word "azure."

Scott and Julie had been found frightened but unharmed, locked in the trunk of Brad's car, though Mahoney had no doubt he would have killed them, too. Brad would have wanted no witnesses.

Bea—or Marie-Laure, as they must now learn to call her— had her head wrapped once more in bandages, and she said wryly she was beginning to like the shaved-head look. She was badly cut and bruised, but it was nothing compared with the relief in her heart, now that she knew who she was and the fear was finally gone.

She was just glad she didn't have the stiff white plastic collar that Poochie had to wear to stop him from scratching the row of stitches on the back of his own poor shaved head. He was lying happily at her feet, sated with as much steak as a dog

could eat. And Nick was holding her hand as she told them the story of what happened to her that day at Diamond Head and how Brad had caught up with her at the San Francisco airport.

"It's all over now," Phyl said comfortingly as they watched the children racing joyously across the lawn to the pool. "You have to learn to forget, to get on with your life."

Marie-Laure smiled at her affectionately. "It's thanks to all of you I'm still alive. And I intend to stay that way." She glanced around at her home, at her children, her man, her friends. "After all," she said, "I've got a lot to live for."

Phyl leaned back against the cushions. Her eyes were still swollen from the tears she had shed, and she looked pale and exhausted.

"You could use a touch of that red lipstick," Mahoney said with a grin, pulling a chair companionably next to her and pouring himself a glass of lemonade.

She glared at him, but he thought it was a weak glare, none of her usual flashing-blue-eyed stuff.

"The U.S. cavalry to the rescue," she said sarcastically. "Just a bit too late."

"Yeah. Even the Concorde wasn't fast enough. And they haven't yet found a way to beam us over, like Captain Kirk. But the FBI and Interpol have those magic computers that keep us all in touch. So the cavalry did get there in time after all." He threw her a serious glance and added softly, "Thank God."

"But how did you find out it was Brad?"

"Two and two. I should have caught it earlier, when I heard Hawaii mentioned. A private plane piloted by Brad Kane came in from Hawaii that night." He shrugged. "I should have known."

"No man is infallible," Phyl said gently, not wanting him to feel guilty.

"And no woman," he replied, meeting her eyes. "Maybe you should remember that."

He held her eyes for a long moment. She knew he meant what had happened to her baby, to Marie-Laure, to Brad. She